Information, Knowledge ~~and Economic~~ Life

Information, Knowledge, and Economic Life

An Introduction to the Sociology of Markets

Alex Preda
University of Edinburgh

OXFORD
UNIVERSITY PRESS

OXFORD
UNIVERSITY PRESS

Great Clarendon Street,
Oxford OX2 6DP

Oxford University Press is a department of the University of Oxford.
It furthers the University's objective of excellence in research, scholarship,
and education by publishing worldwide in

Oxford New York

Auckland Cape Town Dar es Salaam Hong Kong Karachi
Kuala Lumpur Madrid Melbourne Mexico City Nairobi
New Delhi Shanghai Taipei Toronto

With offices in

Argentina Austria Brazil Chile Czech Republic France Greece
Guatemala Hungary Italy Japan Poland Portugal Singapore
South Korea Switzerland Thailand Turkey Ukraine Vietnam

Oxford is a registered trade mark of Oxford University Press
in the UK and in certain other countries

Published in the United States
by Oxford University Press Inc., New York

© Alex Preda 2009

The moral rights of the author have been asserted
Database right Oxford University Press (maker)

First published 2009

British Library Cataloguing in Publication Data

Data available

Library of Congress Cataloging in Publication Data

Library of Congress Control Number: 2009931631

Typeset by SPI Publisher Services, Pondicherry, India
Printed in Great Britain
on acid-free paper by
MPG Books Group, Bodmin and King's Lynn

ISBN 978–0–19–955694–6 (Hbk.)
       978–0–19–955695–3 (Pbk.)

1 3 5 7 9 10 8 6 4 2

CONTENTS

◻ PREFACE

In late February 2009, Paul Krugman, the *New York Times* columnist and Nobel Prize laureate for economics, published an op-ed piece which opened by agreeing with Alan Greenspan (characterized as a 'staunch defender of free markets'), that major (failing) US banks had to be nationalized (Krugman 2009). What had already happened in Britain and in Continental Europe without comparable excitement was now seen as the ultimate means of preventing a worsening of the crisis, with incalculable consequences. While Paul Krugman was quick to state that nationalization is only temporary and that banks will be returned to private ownership as soon as possible, readers' comments, published in the newspaper's electronic edition, seized the occasion for raising a perhaps more fundamental question about the need for a 'new capitalism' which will reposition the relationship between markets and citizens.

It is impossible to address the crucial issue of a repositioning without acknowledging markets as modern forms of social life, and without understanding how they work. Without such an understanding, it is impossible to investigate how their connections to citizenship, the civil sphere, or family life—to enumerate only a few aspects—are set up. What is more, the call for repositioning the relationship between markets and citizens, a call coming from the latter, implies an understanding of markets going well beyond issues of resource allocation. This call, and the underlying assumptions, opens yet another opportunity for economic sociology not only to contribute to public debates, but also to reaffirm its position within the dialogue of social science disciplines. Admittedly, the investigation of markets as forms of social life is only one subfield of economic sociology; nevertheless, it is one which has made considerable progress over the past quarter century or so, one which has known important cross-fertilizations with other sociological fields, and one which has generated several robust research programmes.

When markets become the source of heightened instability—not only economic, but social as well—it is time, perhaps, to have a closer look at the conceptual and empirical achievements of the sociology of markets, to examine various research programmes, and to identify areas for future investigations. This book offers readers an introduction to the main concepts, issues, and research programmes developed on both sides of the Atlantic over the last quarter century, while identifying and discussing their theoretical roots in classical sociology. However, it is not my aim here to write an intellectual history of the sociology of markets. Neither is it my aim to simply discuss alternative schools of thought, or North American v. Continental European sociologies of markets, or the sociology of markets v. economic theories of markets. I also do not draw a strict line between the classic sociological treatment of markets and contemporary developments; rather, classical and contemporary perspectives are discussed together, along the lines provided by the major themes of each chapter.

The path I follow here is to address the sociology of markets on several conceptual levels, with respect to one key notion: that of information. On each of these levels, incorporated in separate chapters, I examine how different research programmes have brought about specific understandings of the notion of market information and, related to this, have drawn specific conclusions with respect to the character of market transactions, their positioning in social life, and the relationship to other social institutions. The reasons for choosing a sociological notion of information as the central concept around which the chapters of this book are structured, are given by the near unanimous (sociological as well as economic) view of transactions as the key analytical unit in the study of markets, together with the conceptualizations of transactions as based on information. As I argue in more detail in the following pages, placing a sociological notion of information at the core of an analytical investigation of various research programmes in the sociology of markets provides a unitary frame in which different conceptualizations, relationships among key concepts, various understandings of the same concept, as well as avenues of future research can be better identified and discussed. This approach also offers the possibility of identifying the positions taken by different research programmes with respect to each other, the degrees to which they overlap or diverge. Last but not least, taking a sociological concept of information as the ordering principle of this investigation provides a good conversational opportunity with economics which, too, takes the notion of information as the keystone of the conceptual architecture of markets. Nevertheless, choosing information as the conceptual lens which directs this investigation necessarily implies a selection: such a lens orients the observer's gaze upon specific issues, approaches, and topics, while others move towards the edges of the observational field.

This being said, I should warn readers that I do not provide here a broad discussion of the concept of information, its origins, and its various developments in the natural and social sciences. I work with a sociological concept of information, which is set up in the introduction of this book. Neither do I follow here the strategy of a sociological critique of economic models of markets, in the sense of showing their limitations, all the empirical details they overlook, etc. In the present context, I do not believe in the intellectual value of such a strategy. While I discuss the origins, development, and role of the economic concept of information, I do it in the chapter dealing with forms of economic expertise in relationship to markets. In other words, I regard economic models of markets as a *sui generis* form of expertise, to be investigated with the tools of the sociology of scientific knowledge.

After having warned readers about what cannot be found in this book, it is time to say what is in it. The introduction, *Markets, Information, and Social Action*, develops a sociological concept of information, in relationship to the notions of social action, knowledge, trust, and uncertainty. The theoretical background here is provided, among others, by Karl Marx's, Max Weber's, and Georg Simmel's conceptualizations of the links between knowledge, trust, and competitive transactions, as well as by Alfred Schütz's and Harold Garfinkel's analyses of social action and trust, respectively. Based on Erving Goffman's and Harold Garfinkel's investigations of social action and information, I suggest a sociological notion of information as irreducible to routines; information is more appropriately seen, I argue, as the production and handling of uncertainties in transactional interactions. This notion of information is also supported by a metaphor developed in the introduction, and echoed in each chapter of this book: that of playing a game of soccer, in which competing players generate for each other surprises and unexpected moves, which have to be dealt with in interactions during the play.

While I am using this metaphor as a tool for guiding readers through the topics discussed here, this is not the only reason for invoking soccer. More importantly, step by step throughout the book, the metaphor indicates how sociology can develop a genuine approach to markets while keeping open the dialogue with economics. The concept of (strategic) game underlies the economic conceptualization of markets and information is undershood in close relationship to issues of strategic behaviour and signalling in games. Paralleling this approach, the sociological investigation of competitive transactions—i.e. of market games—cannot do without playing close attention to what participants in such games concretely do while playing them within specific socico-material settings. This is why throughout the book I use the expression 'a play of a game', which I borrow from Erving Goffman (1972, p. 33). With that, I want to draw attention to the significance and multi-layered character of the concrete actions and institutions which shape the features and outcomes of market games. Moreover, I want to point out that plays of market game should not be studied in isolation from other competitive games modern societies are infused with.

The metaphor of the play of a game of soccer provides the five domains of investigation which are followed throughout the chapters of this book: the play's flow and interactions, the teams, the comments upon the play, its materiality, and its situatedness in civic life. A number of interrelated themes are repeated throughout the chapters, in a manner analogous with that of leitmotivs in music: transactions, cognition in markets, valuation, and market boundaries. These themes are examined anew, from a different angle, in the chapters of this book. Additionally, each chapter introduces and discusses a number of specific themes, such as the social structural underpinnings of market transactions, or the relationship between markets, on the one hand, and firms, on the other. Each chapter underlines theoretical arguments with concrete examples from both published and ongoing empirical research.

Chapter 1 examines what is going on among the players of the game during transactions. It takes the interaction order as the fundamental order of markets, and investigates transactions from the viewpoint of the inter-action forms which shape them. I discuss here among others the issue of transaction boundaries, in relationship to their legitimacy, and show—based on empirical case studies—how these boundaries are constituted in interaction. Another theme of this chapter is that of price discovery; while this latter occupies a major place in the arsenal of economic theory, there have been preciously few studies of how prices are discovered within interactions. Drawing on these studies, I argue that prices should be seen as interaction-based achievements, in relationship to procedural features deployed by market actors. The third theme examined here is that of the relationships between emotions and cognition in market transactions. While the former have been very often seen as irrational and as impeding upon the calculations undertaken by market actors, I argue—again, based on concrete examples from recent research—that in market transactions the relationship between emotions and cognition is not that simple. Emo-tions appear rather as an essential element in the cognitive procedures of market actors. A fourth theme discussed here is valuation: drawing on the work of Erving Goffman, I examine valuation procedures unfolding in market transactions, and the relationship between such procedures, on the one hand, and the competitive character of transactions, on the other. A fifth theme of the chapter, drawing on all the above mentioned, is how information is produced in market interactions. I show that information is irreducible to uncertainty-processing routines: the latter provide only the background against which informational surprises are produced and handled as intrinsic to transactions sequences.

After having dealt with sequences of the play, Chapter 2 focuses on the teams playing the game. I examine in this chapter the social structural underpinnings of market transactions, distinguishing among networks, status groups, and communities, and investigating how proponents of each approach deal with the issue of information in transactions. Perhaps not surprisingly, information plays here a prominent role, although its understanding differs from that of interaction-oriented approaches. Dis-cussing the now classic notion of embeddedness, its critiques, as well as alternative developments, I investigate how more ambitious structural approaches (notably Harrison White's, but also Joel Podolny's and Ronald Burt's) take markets as the starting point for a general theory of social relations. I take up again the themes of valuation and boundaries, respectively, albeit from a different angle, discussing how social structural approaches have understood these issues, with consequences different from the interactionist perspective. Another central issue of this chapter is that of authority: based mainly on Max Weber, I discuss how various forms of group-specific authority (with a special focus on charismatic authority) intervene in market transactions.

Chapter 3 deals with the comments made before, during, and after the play by specialized commentators. In the same way in which we can hardly imagine a soccer match without the comments of sports journalists and pundits, it would be hard to imagine markets without the expert comments which are an intrinsic part of playing the game. The approach followed in this chapter comes partly from the sociology of the professions, partly from the sociology of scientific knowledge, and partly from economic sociology. I examine here, among others, the historical developments which led to the notion of information playing the key role in economic models of markets. Based on historical as well as ethnographic research, I investigate the various forms of expertise which play a role in markets, from statistics and economic models to chart analysis, from risk to credit analysis. The examination and discussion of the performativity thesis cannot be left out here: hence, readers will find a more detailed discussion of the work of Donald MacKenzie and Michel Callon, among others, as well as of the criticism thereof. As in the previous chapters, the themes of jurisdiction, cognition, and valuation play a prominent role here, albeit they are illuminated from a different angle.

Chapter 4 deals with another aspect of the soccer metaphor: its material underpinnings. More recently, and in relationship to forms of economic expertise and to the growing technologization of transactions, the issue of these underpinnings has drawn the attention of scholars. I start by examining various conceptualizations of technology in relation to markets, of which jurisdiction, standardization, and agency are perhaps the most important. Money is treated in a section of this chapter as a particular transaction-relevant technology. One of the central themes here is the relationship between technology, cognition, and transaction-relevant data. I discuss, among others, the notions developed in Karin Knorr Cetina's more recent work, and examine how they support a specific research programme in transaction-relevant cognition. Based on recent empirical work, I also discuss the relationship between technology, data, and market liquidity, a link initially highlighted in the work of Bruce Carruthers and Arthur Stinchcombe.

Chapter 5 deals with the relationship between market transactions, on the one hand, and social institutions, on the other. In terms of the metaphor which introduces the book, the chapter deals with the stadium which stages the game of soccer. In the same way in which a stadium is located in the city—that is, in civic life—markets cannot be understood independently of their links to social institutions. A major institution of economic life is the firm, and the chapter opens by examining the relationship between firms and markets, relationships which often have been understood in terms of opposition. States and supranational regulatory bodies are additional types of institutions examined here in their relationship to markets. Next to jurisdictional and regulatory issues, the theme of valuation—understood as the rationalization and justification of market transactions and institutions—is investigated in more detail, with reference to the economy of conventions approach, but also to newer developments in cultural sociology.

The conclusion brings together the themes constituting the leitmotivs of the five chapters, and examines them in relationship to the various research programmes discussed throughout the book, with the aim of identifying the various understandings of key notions in the sociology of markets, understandings which lead to different research programmes. A second aim here is that of identifying the interfaces between these programmes, together with topics central for future research. The strategy I follow is neither to plead for a unitary sociology of markets, structured around a dominant definition, nor to simply acknowledge diversity. Rather, the focus here is to show how different understandings of the same key concepts, which lead to different research agendas, allow at the same time for particular interfaces where promising research topics crystallize. These interfaces are also the loci where various sub-disciplines meet: economic sociology, the sociology of scientific knowledge and technology, the sociology of culture, the political sociology, and sociological theory, to name but a few. Additionally, I discuss a series of topics which deserve more attention in the sociology of markets, and tentatively explore the ways in which these could be addressed in future research.

By the end of the book, I could have hopefully persuaded readers not only about the relevance of the sociology of markets within the disciplinary field, but also about its potential for empirical research. It is time now to draw the curtain on this prologue and prepare the stage for the introductory act: the first scene is set, appropriately enough, in front of a bank.

⎕ ACKNOWLEDGEMENTS

This book couldn't have taken shape without the constant support and interest of David Musson, my editor at Oxford University Press. During the writing process, David Musson and Matthew Derbyshire have helped me clarify aspects of the book, checked upon the manuscript's progress, and sustained a dialogue which has helped me move forward.

Several people have read and commented upon various chapters of the book, formulating suggestions and criticism without which this book would be in a much poorer state. If it's still in a poor state, it goes without saying that it is my sole responsibility. It has become now almost a tradition for me to submit manuscripts to the collective scrutiny of the research seminar on the sociology of finance and information led by Karin Knorr Cetina at the University of Konstanz in Germany. These meetings, taking place shortly before the winter holiday season and taking up to half a day, have been wonderful occasions not only for having great intellectual debates with very good friends, but also to argue my positions against the precise, detailed, and straightforward critical comments made by the seminar's members. Some of them have read more than one chapter, or have read them twice, and I stand in their debt for the interest and effort they have put into this enterprise.

As so often, my gratitude goes to Karin Knorr Cetina for taking time to read and comment upon chapters of this book, for her insights and willingness to engage in rigorous discussions. Stefan Laube, Werner Reichmann, Barbara Grimpe, Vanessa Dirksen, Leon Wansleben, Jessica Haas, and Katja Lesche have also provided very useful suggestions and criticism.

At the University of Edinburgh, Donald MacKenzie has also read and commented upon several chapters, and I am indebted to him for the interest he has shown for this project from its inception, for his good advice and continuing support, and for his readiness to read drafts of the manuscript. Juan Pablo Pardo-Guerra and Friedrich Eierdanz have also formulated very helpful suggestions concerning some chapters, and I have greatly benefited from working with them as students.

In saying this, I cannot fail to mention that this book has benefitted in many ways from the wonderful research projects undertaken over the years by post- and undergraduate students at the universities of Konstanz and Edinburgh, projects which have helped me understand better how markets work. Special thanks go here to Barbara Grimpe, Stefan Laube, Juan Pablo

Pardo-Guerra, Lucia Siu, Sandra Kleipa, and Cecilie Roeren from whose work I have learnt so much.

Last but not least, I am greatly indebted to Roxana and Dante for supporting and encouraging me through all the phases of this book, and for putting up with me in a time when there was little room left for anything else but writing.

LIST OF FIGURES AND TABLES

Figures

Tables

Introduction
Markets, Information, and Social Action

Markets Matter

One cloudy day in March, 2008, I overheard a conversation between two students on the campus where I work, as we all were queuing in front of a cash machine. One of the students, tightly clutching a geography handbook, asked the other whether she had heard about the attack on the bank we were queuing in front of. And no, it wasn't a terrorist attack: it was a speculative attack. Apparently, the day before, financial traders had launched a coordinated attack on the share price of that bank, one of the biggest in the country. Within less than 30 minutes, the price went down 17 per cent (Kollewe 2008). A couple of days before, Bear Stearns, the fifth largest US investment bank, had been bought by JP Morgan for $2 per share, down from over $120 only six months earlier. During those days, the prime spot on the front page of newspapers and on TV news channels was taken by worldwide markets still falling, in spite of the Federal Reserve having injected hundreds of billions of dollars. Worries about job losses, mortgage payments, and tighter credit were getting louder. Politicians and central bank governors were quoted as for or against intervention. Some were in favour of central banks intervening by cutting down interest rates, or by selling currency reserves. Others argued that, ultimately, markets cannot be influenced.

About six months later, the situation became worse. One of the biggest US banks, Wachovia, was being saved from bankruptcy in a government-supported acquisition by Citibank. In exchange, the Federal Deposit and Insurance Corporation (FDIC) was absorbing Wachovia's $42 billion losses (Dash and Sorkin 2008). Yet, a few days later, the situation had dramatically changed: Wells Fargo, another US bank had stepped in and made a competitive acquisition offer which was ultimately approved by Wachovia's board. Suddenly, there was competition (however short lived) for acquiring failing banks, and competition brought about surprises. It created new, unexpected situations.

While the market for failing financial institutions did not last long (with the offer far outstripping demand), these episodes reveal how competitive exchanges create surprises. In the above case, a key surprise was the share price offered by Wells Fargo. If we were to adopt a standard formulation, the price was a signal which 'guide(d) the allocation of resources' (Mankiw 1997, p. 83). In this perspective, markets appear as akin to gigantic telephone switchboards, collecting and distributing signals, which will then flow into decisions about resources. The power, significance, and impact of markets are provided precisely by them functioning as switchboards, collecting and distributing signals. (We shall later see that this definition becomes more complicated than we might expect.)

However, we should ask first: what exactly is meant by signals here? If markets are information processors, as standard wisdom teaches us, what is this information? Is it the hand signs commodities traders make to each other in the pits of the Chicago markets? Is it billboard panels we drive by without looking, or TV adverts many of us simply ignore? Or is it the carefully orchestrated absence of price displays in luxury boutiques? What does it mean to have information in the market? Does it mean knowing a price? Knowing other people? Knowing trading rules? And, generally, how do people know information in the market? Does this mean knowing somebody who might know something? Does it mean watching prices on a screen? And, how do all these activities shape markets?

Information, Uncertainty, and Competitive Actions

Once we start looking more closely at what information[1] means, things which seemed to be simple suddenly become complicated. For now, at least, one thing is sure: we cannot make much progress in understanding markets without first examining what is meant by market information, how this is produced, circulated, and used, and how all these processes involve the knowledge and actions of participating actors. A good way of rolling out this examination is by providing first an empirical example from the world of competitions: since markets are broadly seen as systems of competitive transactions, let us see first how competitions work.

We seem to live in a world full of them: think of all the contests, championships, talent shows, and challenges present in almost every domain of life, across the board from the arts to science, education, or leisure. Yet, perhaps the purest forms of competition, competitions for competition's sake, can be found in the world of sport. Take plays[2] of the soccer game, for instance. Here, we have both explicit and tacit rules stating which action routines are allowed where on the playing field, establishing the size and shape of this field, the duration of the play, the number of players and of adjudicating actors in the field, the artefacts allowed, and the like. Such rules have (limited) variability and negotiability: an informal match on the recreation ground will not necessarily follow all FIFA's (the International Federation of Association Football) formal rules. We also have the material settings within which the game can be played: built stadiums, but also parks where goalposts are marked with schoolchildren's backpacks. Material assemblages can mark complex, internal divisions among the specialized sections of a stadium, as well as recognizable boundaries to the outside world.

In a professional match, the key positions of public, players, referees, sports commentators, or coaches are not easily interchangeable (with the exception of substituted players who become spectators, or substitute players being sent on the field).[3] Such a match can be seen as a chain of transactions—of actions and responses to actions—which cannot be forecast in their unfolding. While expectations about specific sequences of action/counteraction can be formed, we cannot foresee such sequences before the play has started. The impossibility of forecasting from the start moves in a play of soccer, to reduce the play to a chain of routines obeying expectations makes the chain of actions a specific play of the game. In this play, surprises arise continuously: deceptive moves, unexpected positioning of players, or turns of action which were not foreseeable by participants. It is such surprises which make a match so absorbing.

While a play of soccer certainly implies routines, it is by no means reducible to them. Plays of soccer also imply rules, organizations such as clubs, institutions such as national leagues, but soccer itself is not reducible to any of these elements. We may know by heart all FIFA regulations, for instance, but based on this we cannot foresee the outcome of any match. This is not to say that regulations do not put constraints on the play: it is to say that such constraints do not determine the outcome of any one play.[4] And, while there are many resources to be allocated in the world of soccer (money being perhaps the most important), the game is also about things such as prestige, fairness, cunning, or endurance. Players are judged in relationship to such attributes, according to what they do during the play. All in all, then, soccer (and not only) can be seen as a set of fairly complex competitive exchanges which, while operating under material and institutional constraints, continuously involving the use of routines, is geared towards generating surprises, unforeseen actions, and uncertainties. Not incidentally, this is what the public likes most: a sport without surprises is often judged as dull and disappointing.

Now, let us make things a bit more complicated and remove the stricter distinctions between observers and players. Observers go on the field and play, come back, observe for a little while, go back and play, and so on. The public[5] has a specific pool of knowledge, and is at the stadium by virtue of this knowledge, which allows members not only to observe the game, but to play it as well. The public constitutes not only the observers of specific transactions undertaken during the game, but also a pool of players. Playing the game changes the knowledge of the public. We would need to imagine here a soccer stadium where the public watches the game played by some players. This observation is not only direct, but also involves mediated representation of what is happening on the playing field. A good example from real life is an observer looking at players through the lens of a video camera. Then, some players come to the benches and others go into play. Those on the benches make observations and comment upon them, shout to the players, tell their own stories from the field, and so on. The players who are back on the benches start describing their own experiences in the play, while others go back on the field and play, and so on. (Some observers can specialize in making authoritative judgements upon the play.) The fact that the public both plays the game and observes it, is susceptible of continuously generating informational surprises: observers will not only comment on actions, but also on new players, or on new sequences of the play. This imprints a continuous dynamic on the public's knowledge, which will be in flux due to the surprises and unexpected elements occurring during the play, plus the interpretations of the observers, augmented by the players' accounts, etc.

The situation gets more complicated if we imagine that at a nearby stadium a game of American football takes place, in the same arrangement where observers and players shift positions all the time. Assuming the American football match is broadcast at the soccer stadium, the soccer crowd will make observations on the football public as well (including observers and players) and vice versa. These observations will be significant for what happens on each other's stadium, and for the ways in which each other's players' actions will be judged, etc. While usually in soccer and football games the assumption is that the ball remains unchanged during the play, we can imagine a situation where changes in the ball (elasticity, curvature, and the like) during the game are measured and factored in. This produces additional informational surprises, which affect the dynamics of knowledge in each stadium, as well as between stadiums (assuming that the wear and tear of soccer and football balls is comparatively investigated while playing the game). In such a situation, the investigation of material changes in the ball would become part of the play itself. The overall picture is that of interconnected competitive games unfolding on the grounds of continuously producing uncertainties (aka informational surprises). While the outcome of a soccer match would be a specific score, this would by far not be the only outcome. In soccer, the outcome is not only the specific score, but also a specific social appreciation (or valuation) of players, valuation made on social attributes broader than the number of goals scored in the play of the game. (In soccer, for instance, this valuation can be made on attributes such as speed, agility, or fair play.)

This analogy illustrates and anticipates at the same time the main argument of this book: that markets as systems of competitive transactions require the continuous production and handling of surprises, or uncertainties.[6] Instead of regarding market information as routines reducing uncertainties, I argue that in markets information means surprises, to which players react. These surprises, however, are produced in an ordered and orderly fashion: in the same way in which a soccer match takes place in a stadium, is regulated by the sport's institutions, and draws upon routines, market competitions produce surprises in ways which are bounded by institutions, material arrangements, and routines. Nevertheless, as in soccer, it is the surprise which drives action forward.

In soccer, competitions are laminated[7]: they include several layers of meaning concerning what the competition is about. Players compete not only to score goals and for money, but also for assessment on attributes such as speed, agility, fairness, cunning, and the like. These layers of competition unfold simultan-eously and are interdependent. In markets as interconnected competitive plays, we encounter the same phenomenon: competitions have many layers, not all of which pertain to the allocation of existing resources, but also to valuation on social attributes. In soccer, we can have situations where a league match takes place in a stadium, while on an adjacent field amateurs kick the ball around; two different versions of the same game, yet with different kinds of surprises and valuation outcomes. In markets, we can encounter similar situations, where different versions of the same games are spatially and temporally adja-cent. This points to the fact that we have not only several kinds of market games, but also different kinds of plays within the same game. Therefore, the strategy followed here is not that of investigating whether various plays of competitive games follow one and the same template (be it that of homo oeconomicus or of 'the market'). The strategy is to investigate the elements involved in these competitions, taking the production of surprises as the focal point.

Having established the above analogy as the base for this investigation, I will now move forward, taking readers through an examination of the links between transactions, knowledge, and trust. In the same way in which moves and passes on the soccer field imply skills and knowledge, market transactions imply these too. And, in the same way in which a soccer match implies expectations and trust on the part of the players, as well as of the public, market transactions, too, imply trust and shared expectations. In the follow-ing, I investigate the connections between knowledge and trust, starting from arguments originating in classic sociology. Afterwards, I will discuss a socio-logical notion of information, positioning it against this background. For the most part of the discussion, the analogy with the play of soccer will stay in the wings, though I will bring it to the fore again, in the last two sections of this introduction.

Knowledge in Market Transactions

An appropriate starting point for this examination is the notion that market transactions are anchored in knowledge. Adam Smith's famous observation about the invisible hand that coordinates the actions of various market actors without the intervention of any central overseer expresses the idea that, in striving to realize their individual economic interests, actors will interact with each other, exchanging news and observations, and drawing the appropriate conclusions with respect to their plans and actions (Smith [1776] 1991, p. 351). In addition to the differentiation in knowledge implied by the division of labour, social interactions (in the marketplace, but not only) appear as self-regulating coordinating devices, which circulate news, stories, or gossip.

After Smith, political economy made room for the idea that market transactions circulate news and stories around, and that this circulation influences the ways in which market players perceive the prices of goods and react to them. Nevertheless, news and stories are not the only kind of knowledge implied by transactions. For Karl Marx ([1872] 2002, pp. 70, 84), for instance, commodities are embodiments of human labour; as such, they not only incorporate knowledge and skills used in producing them, but also convey knowledge related to their use. The circulation of commodities through society also means the circulation of knowledge, in the form of tacit skills (related, for instance, to the use of a particular commodity), as well as in the form of explicit knowledge. In addition to this practical knowledge and skills (which can be made explicit only in part), political economy highlighted the importance of formalized knowledge: the French econometricians and physiocrats, for instance, saw visual representations and descriptions of economic processes as tools of taxation policies, among others, and as a kind of knowledge indispensable to the state (Schumpeter [1954] 1994, p. 232). At the same time, being an entrepreneur engaged in market exchanges requires specific organizational skills (expressed by John Stuart Mill, for instance, as 'superintendence' or 'control') and knowledge of manufacturing and marketing, among others.

When buying and using a device such as an MP3 player, for instance, we acquire certain tacit skills related to the use of the device: these skills can be tactile among others (e.g. precision in moving our fingers). At the same time, we may search for and circulate stories related to the technical performance of the device, data related to this performance, stories about the manufacturer, and the like. In fact, many commodities we buy come packaged with not only data about technical performance or chemical composition, but also instructions for use, data and stories about the manufacturer, instructions for possible complaints, and many more. Thus, economic transactions trigger the social circulation and dissemination of various layers of knowledge and skills.

Marketplace transactions reproduce and circulate such elements of (tacit) knowledge, together with explicit knowledge, such as the calculation of salaries, of the costs incurred by the reproduction of labour power, and so on.

Sharing and circulating knowledge and skills, however, does not impede upon the competitive character of market transactions. Karl Marx ([1872] 2002, p. 516) considered that capitalist accumulation cannot be achieved without increased productivity as a competitive factor. This productivity, while knowledge-based (i.e. realized through technology and skill improvement) increases the competition-related uncertainties which workers face. In his turn, Max Weber defined markets as struggles, and monetary prices as products of struggles (Weber [1921] 1972, p. 58; see also Simmel [1908, p. 247]; Swedberg 2003, p. 119; François 2008, pp. 238–9). For Weber ([1921] 1972, p. 382), haggling is the specific manifestation of markets. Following Werner Sombart, Max Weber ([1921] 1972, p. 383) considers that the market is the only form of socialization which is not grounded in 'personal fraternization' and hence susceptible in principle to broadly valid ethical constraints. In his analysis of financial markets, Weber ([1921] 1972, p. 382) considers that the procedural trust underlying oral transactions triggers a process of 'community-building through money use' (*Vergemeinschaftung kraft Geldgebrauchs*). Community is built in this case not only on the grounds of shared, tacit rules of behaviour, in the absence of any explicit, written rules which should regulate transactions, but also on the grounds of using the same artefacts and techniques. Nevertheless, in transactions prices are means of struggle among market actors. Weber ([1921] 1972, p. 58) uses here the words *Kampfmittel* and *Kampfpreis* (means of struggle and struggle prices, respectively), seeing market transactions as competitions or struggles determined by interests and power.

Georg Simmel (1908, pp. 282–3) saw competitive market transactions as just one subtype of a more general social phenomenon—the struggle. As a basic form of social interactions, struggles do not exclude, but often go hand in hand with cooperation. Competitive struggles are ubiquitous in modern societies; market competitions are characterized through the formal character of the antagonism among competitors (we do not want to vanquish them once and for all), by orientation to valuation, and by boundaries (competition among comparable rivals).

The idea of the market itself, understood as a system of competitive exchanges, requires that participants have knowledge and skills which they put to use not only in competition (Schumpeter [1954] 1994, pp. 554–6), but also to create links between economic and political institutions, for instance. Taking knowledge as the platform on which market transactions take place implies that in a majority of situations market-relevant forms of knowledge are taken for granted by players: they remain unquestioned and are trusted as appropriate for the specific situations in which they are used.

Trust in Transactions

Let us re-examine the problem from the perspective of the world of effective action (Schütz 2003, pp. 61, 66), to which economic transactions belong. This world is characterized by problems and doubts different from the ones specific to the world of contemplation, for instance. In order for action to take place, one has to suspend doubts, based on the assumption that other actors as well will share the expectation about the unproblematic character of the situation in which action unfolds (Luhmann 1990, p. 43). These mutual expectations provide the grounds for routines in everyday life, routines which, in their turn, constitute to a very large extent the basis of our doings. These routines also apply to the categories and classifications which orient actions, without requesting, for instance, that transaction participants reach complete (tacit) agreement about them beforehand. Rather, shared routines become visible as actions unfold. This, however, leaves room for uncertainties, and for unexpected turns of action.

There are situations in which such shared expectations do not work very well, situations in which doubts can arise. These can be situations in which we enter transactions with a new partner, in a new context, or about a new product. Moreover, there are situations in which we might try to anticipate the outcome of transactions, or the future actions of transactions partners. In all situations where routines are partially or entirely insufficient as grounds for our doings, uncertainties arise. These uncertainties can take the form of ambiguities: is the new partner reliable or not? Is the product of an acceptable quality or not? Is it legitimate to ask for a warranty? Uncertainties, however, can take the form of a lack of specificity as well: who is this new merchant? What does the new product do?

Since, as argued above, economic transactions are part of the world of effective action, the way of dealing with doubts (aka the suspension or insufficiency of routines) would neither be to contemplate or fantasize about who the new merchant in town might be, nor to generally reflect about the merchants' position in society. The way of dealing with such a suspension or insufficiency would be to use other routines to compensate for this insufficiency, or, if this proves unsatisfactory, to find new ways to compensate for them. Such routines can be: contacting acquaintances and friends and asking them about the new merchant, or doing an Internet search. And if this proves unsatisfactory, then we could actively seek people who have dealt with this new merchant in the past, contact them, and ask them about that person's past behaviour. We would then be able to receive stories, data, or names, for instance, and based on all this, we could form a judgement. If we are already members of an economic organization, this task would prove easier than in isolation: we would have colleagues to ask, or contacts in other organizations; we could go to business conventions or to lunches as places where we could gather stories, data, and the like. Of course, in the process of collecting these stories, names, or data, we would be confronted with the same problem of trustworthiness, which we would be able to solve based on routines—that is, on entrenched mutual expectations.

Trusting somebody like a transaction partner, trusting the legal system to recognize and protect the transaction you are just about to enter, or trusting that the goods you are about to buy have a certain quality, all this implies acting upon specific expectations about the institutions, people, and objects directly and indirectly implicated in economic transactions. These expectations are that all the elements on which transactions, their outcomes, and their consequences depend, are unproblematic. These elements are taken for granted and not made into something doubtful.

The more general trust-relevant arguments coming from classic sociology are twofold: first, Max Weber's argument that religious precepts (namely those of Protestantism) provide the normative basis of capitalist accumulation, and that these precepts have constraining force (Weber [1920] 1988, p. 33).[8] Capitalist production (and markets by implication) is then defined by a self-sustaining ethic, with religious roots and universalistic claims. Adherence to this ethic requires acknowledging debts and obligations towards transaction partners; the general acknowledgment of these debts and obligations creates trust. I trust my transaction partners, for instance, because I acknowledge them as adhering to the same normative views to which I, as a businessperson, adhere, views which regulate our relationships. In this perspective, then, reciprocal, personal trust is grounded in acknowledged adherence to a normative set of principles.[9] Market exchanges are shaped by an ethics of competition, yet one which submits to the above-mentioned principles. That religion-based ethical principles can still be influential in shaping market transactions is shown, among others, by the fact that stock exchange transactions in Islamic countries (such as Malaysia) have been influenced by social movements which seek to impose ethical principles of investing derived from religious precepts (see Pitluck [2008]).

However, there is more to trust than commitment to norms. Weber ([1921] 1972, pp. 201, 205) saw transactions in quasi-closed economies (of the kind we might encounter in traditional village communities) as characterized by inward trust and outward distrust: in other words, while in such an economy members would trust each other (because of longstanding family ties, reciprocal obligations, the conformist pressure of the community, or because their status and honour are at stake), they would enter transactions with strangers on the basis of distrust and would try to con them as well, in a (from the perspective of the community) perfectly legitimate fashion. While a mountain hut, for instance, would be sold to the neighbouring farmer at a fair price, sanctioned by the community, and on the basis of acknowledged property deeds, the same hut would be sold to an outsider looking for a holiday home at a much higher price and, sometimes, even without regular property deeds, so that it can be claimed back later.

Capitalist market transactions, where money is the major (if not the only) medium of social relations[10] (as opposed to family and tribal obligations, among others) erode distinctions between inside and outside transactions. It does so mainly because, to a large extent, it can substitute personal trust (as given by family and community ties, obligations, and controls) with impersonal trust. Additionally, market transactions increase reciprocal obligations and interdependencies in highly individualized societies: since everybody can enter transactions with everybody, the only condition being availability of money, market actors become increasingly dependent on each other, a process which is not restricted to present economic transactions, but includes past ones as well.[11] But if in traditional, closed economies of production (such as that of rural communities) stories were trusted because they came from trusted people, who in their turn were trusted because they were part of reciprocal bonds and obligations intrinsic to the community as such, how can stories and data be trusted in an impersonal economy where capital is the mediator of all social relationships? How can one trust stories and data furnished by complete strangers? We have to keep in mind here that without such trust durable transactions would not be possible; what is more, the reproduction and expansion of market transactions would not be possible. I may be conned once, but, after having learnt a lesson or two the hard way, I will simply refuse to enter transactions with people whom I don't know, or who do not come from my village, or from my extended family. If everybody does this, there will no market transactions at all.

The alternative would be to see ethics and trust as grounded in emotional commitments. The economic life of modern, complex societies is highly differentiated, meaning, among others, that economic actors have to specialize and exchange their products with other actors. These exchanges imply relationships of trust, which cannot be entirely reduced to the legal formalization of contracts. In fact, this very differentiation and specialization which characterizes modern economic life implies an increased degree of solidarity, akin to a living organism whose parts perform specialized functions (Durkheim [1893] 1984, p. 80). This organic solidarity (Durkheim [1893] 1984, p. 85) grounds relationships of trust, which ultimately rest on a common emotional bond visible among others in religious rituals (Durkheim [1915] 1965, p. 465; Collins 2004, p. 49). In its most basic form, solidarity can be specified here as a mutual orientation of social actors, orientation grounded in common practical actions, providing participants in a social situation, for all practical purposes, with a shared view of the world.

Mutual, implicit trust becomes the non-contractual base of every economic contract; a mutual orientation of actors (rooted in common rituals) is absolutely necessary for the existence of society as a whole (Durkheim [1915] 1965, p. 475; [1893] 1984, p. 158). Without mutual bonds, no interaction could take place. Since market transactions are nothing but social inter-actions, they must be anchored in a mutual orientation. I trust my transactions partners even when they do not come from the same family or village, simply because we share a set of basic assumptions and expectations about us as social actors. At a very basic level, I trust my transaction partners to treat me as a social being, and they trust me to do the same. This makes untrust-worthiness an exception, and not the rule. Therefore, the general attitude in market transactions would be that of trust (tested by moments and episodes of breaching this trust, or of distrust), even in situations where transaction partners do not know each other.

Trust appears then as moral commitment (with two distinct varieties: ethical norms, or mutual orientation), as mutual acknowledgment and adjustment of interests, or as a combination thereof (Cook, Hardin, and Levi 2005, p. 5; Fligstein and Dauter 2007, p. 108; Fourcade 2007, p. 1021; Fourcade and Healy 2007, p. 281). For instance, adherence to ethical prin-ciples does not preclude mutual adjustment of interest; quite the contrary, the latter may be derived from the former. Trust does not exclude objectified forms, such as trust in legal systems and institutions (economic and political), or trust in technological data processing. We could see then trust as a form of social routines, related to persons, artefacts, or institutions, routines which enable transactions. But we can also see trust as anchored in a mutual orientation which must be made visible within interactions, as basic assump-tions related to the ways in which market actors deal with each other.

Trust and Impersonal Knowledge

This indicates that in relationship to market transactions, trust can be under-stood in different ways, as personal knowledge of people, as skills in dealing with artefacts, but also as based on norms, or as mutual orientation. We can distinguish among forms of trust related to various kinds of knowledge; some of these kinds concern procedures, while others concern people. Some concern objects, while others concern norms of social life. Overall, these forms can be classified as personal or impersonal trust, with several subtypes. Since personal trust has been discussed in the previous sections, I will focus here mainly on impersonal forms of trust.

Impersonal trust has procedural aspects, consisting among others in fol-lowing the rules and prescriptions (some of which are explicit and some of which are not) for defining, identifying, initiating, conducting, closing, accounting for, and recalling transactions. Among forms of impersonal trust, we can distinguish at least interactional, calculative, and institutional trust (in practice, though, they mingle all the time).

Interactional trust refers to the mutually shared procedures and orientations which allow transaction participants to initiate, unfold, and complete action sequences.

Calculative trust builds upon Max Weber's argument ([1920] 1988, pp. 10–12) that the distinctive feature of Western-style market capitalism is calculation, understood as tools and technologies with the help of which economic processes and market exchanges are redefined as efficient. Tools and technologies imply procedures for projecting, conducting, evaluating, and adapting economic processes (including here market transactions), procedures which are trusted as such by market participants. Procedural formalization creates specific reciprocal expectations for each step of the transaction process. When buying a house, for instance, we follow a specific procedure (initiating a search, finding a solicitor, etc.), which we often might see as a hassle and an expense of time and money, but this formalized procedure provides us with specific, step-by-step expectations, increases the reliability of the transaction and therefore the trust we put in it. Procedural formalization also allows encoding economic transactions in legal terms, establishing thus formal rights and obligations for transaction partners. This encoding contributes to stabilizing reciprocal expectations. The standardized character of formalized data makes it recognizable and transferable across various contexts (Stinchcombe 2001, pp. 51–3). Think here of how a supermarket receipt is part and parcel of a formalized procedure of shopping. Such a receipt constitutes not only a memory of what has been bought, providing standardized information: data about the commodities which have been bought, their quantity, and their prices. It is also a legal document, enabling specific actions when breach of trust is discovered after the transaction, or when the buyer has changed her mind. In many cases, a shopping receipt will state the right of the buyer to return products within a specific time window, irrespective of any irregularities in the quality of that specific commodity.

Additionally, the ways in which data circulate can be procedurally formalized: we trust descriptions and prescriptions, among others, because they come to us following specific procedures and in specific forms. Think here of the user instructions or the data we find on products: we trust them because they come in specific, standardized, recognizable form and through specific procedures.

Trust can also be based on our assumption that the artefacts, technologies, and other material arrangements supporting market transactions will work in reliable, foreseeable, and consistent ways across various settings and contexts, for all actors and actions relying on them. We expect automated teller machines, for instance, to work in similar ways and with similar procedures time and again, for all users, independent of location and time of the day.

In such cases, we place our trust in the artefacts and machines themselves, in close connection to the trust in specific procedures of using them, without knowing much (if at all) about the engineers who have designed them, or about the technological detail of their functioning. Forms of calculative trust in contemporary market transactions, for instance, are closely related to our expectation that the artefacts and material arrangements supporting calculative procedures will work in reliable, constant, and consistent ways across various contexts.

What is more, forms of calculative trust are incorporated in artefacts and thus objectified: we expect cash registers in supermarkets not only to work in the same way, time and again, but also to incorporate (and thus automate) specific calculative procedures, with respect to adding items, the deduction of price reductions, and the like. Such calculative procedures are performed with minimal intervention from human actors: it suffices to scan a shopping item on the register, and recognition and calculation procedures will be automatically performed. Thus, the melding together of calculative trust and artefacts opens up the possibility of automating economic transactions: that is, of devising specific, well-defined instructions for completing calculative tasks starting from the initiation of a transaction and terminating in its completion and recording. Automated checkout counters, as we see them in some supermarkets, are an example of a partial automation of economic transactions.[12]

A further form of trust emerges when the rules and procedures we submit to (and expect other market actors to submit to as well) are not directly and immediately tied to a particular market transaction (or type thereof), but related to more general forms of social organization relevant for the transaction in question. This form can be called institutional trust. In the above example of the shopping receipt, this works as a legal document by stating (or pointing to) the rights and obligations of transaction partners, within a legal system that goes beyond the boundaries of a specific transaction. In case of dissatisfaction with a product I have bought, for instance, I can use the receipt for formulating economic claims (a refund). This requires a set of specific procedures for dealing with such claims, as well as a set of legal procedures (for complaining about the quality of a good I bought, for instance). In such cases, I put my trust in the procedures that define economic entities (the firm that sold or manufactured the good), as well as legal (the courts of law) and political ones (e.g. supervisory and regulatory bodies).

A consequence of institutional trust is that economic transactions are anchored in the expectation of sets of procedures that cannot be limited to strictly economic ones[13]. That is, actors put trust in these procedures on the expectation that, should a specific, immediate set of procedures fail, other sets of larger significance will intervene (breach of trust in a transaction can lead to legal action).[14]

Interactions and Transactions

Having investigated the forms of trust, or routines which constitute the background against which market transactions unfold, we can proceed now to the notion of information and examine it from the perspective of action itself. Going back to the introductory analogy, the picture we get up to this point is that of a soccer stadium where players, spectators, and referees play the game against the background of specific expectations concerning their reciprocal roles during the game (defender, middlefielder, referee, etc.), the routines they are going to use (passes, dribbles, shots, and so on), the ontological stability of the ball during the game (it will not suddenly turn into a tennis ball), or the stability of the field (it doesn't suddenly turn into a tennis court), among others.

Yet, these expectations (which enable the conduct of playing routines during the game), together with the awareness of the stadium, of rules, of the clubs, of football organizations, etc. constitute the background to the play of the game, but not the play itself. The outcome of this latter will be shaped while the match unfolds, with and within each of its sequences. Similarly, in market competitions, the element of playing the game is irreducible to trust as routines, although it is shaped against the background provided by them.

What are these elements of the play in market transactions?

1. First, there are verbal exchanges about states of the world. These exchanges are often seen in economic sociology as a 'sea of discourse' in which market actors swim (White 2000, p. 118). They can take place in various settings—formal or informal—and provide market participants with several distinct things: observations of the world, characterizations of elements of the world (or judgements), and stories which rationalize such observations and characterizations. Observations, characterization, and rationalizing stories are relevant for transactions. An example: we observe in everyday life gas prices going up—a drive by the gas station suffices for this. This observation may be shared with and confirmed by others we know. Actually, it is the sharing, the confirmation, and the whole discussion around 'have you seen the prices?' which makes this into an observation. Casual talk at the water cooler concerns itself very often exactly with sharing observations for the purposes of (dis)confirmation. Yet, as such, an observation needs an explanation in order to be made intelligible. The question 'why are gas prices going up?' needs to be answered, by using shared narrative repertoires which we regard as plausible and which we can connect to broader life experiences and observations. Saying that an alien spaceship has sucked out the Earth's oil deposits is not part of such a repertoire. Saying that the war in Iraq has made prices go up by creating more demand, and

opportunities for speculation, and insecurity at the same time, is part of the repertoire.

Verbal (and non-verbal) exchanges imply procedural knowledge which cannot be made entirely explicit. The procedural knowledge used, for instance, in evaluating a newspaper story about a car manufacturer is not fully specifiable. Routines used for legitimating narrative repertoires are impossible to explain in full. Moreover, this procedural knowledge makes use of specific situational resources: a story told at the water cooler can take different turns and be judged differently according to the storyteller's reputation, context of the narrative, participants, and the like. This means that the procedures involved in verbal exchanges cannot be specified independent of the situation in which they are used. Their full formalization could work only if we conceive of cognitive procedures as discrete mental states that are switched on in specific situations (then we could develop an algorithm for matching states of the world with mental states, and situations with procedures, respectively). But since procedures cannot be separated from situational interactions, such a matching is not possible (see also Coulter [1995, 1999]).

2. Verbal and non-verbal exchanges from which representations of states of the world are inferred and assessments of such states are made. Such exchanges do not address observations—they are not utterances of the kind 'look, prices are going up!' They are themselves the object of observations and rationalizations. For instance, when stock exchanges still had trading floors, traders could observe each other, infer, and assess states of the world from such observations. This situation is analogous with that of two soccer players observing each other's actions during a sequence of the play, and drawing from this inferences about what a third player is doing, or about the state of the play. (Needless to say, the state of the play will not be the same for everyone.) A trader observing his neighbour shouting 'twenty five', or making a hand sign to that effect, will rationalize this as being related to a specific state of the world ('there are sellers at twenty five in the market'), and will justify his own actions with respect to it. The boundary between (1) and (2) is of course a fluid one, in the sense that verbal exchanges about states of the world can lead market participants to infer different representations about such states. A participant at the annual convention of, say, the dentistry equipment manufacturers' associations, will not only talk to other participants about their products, technological performance, sales, and the like, but will also observe other participants talking among themselves. They will infer representations of the state of the world from such observations: about possible alliances and collaborations, about whether the published sales figures are trustworthy, about the performance of rival products, and the like.

Observing two competitors talk at a trade fair, a drop in sales, or the disappearance from supermarket shelves of a specific product sends the observer to changes in the state of the world. Such observations can be consequential: they can trigger more observations, analysis, interpretation, as well as specific decisions. (For instance, finding out that the two former competitors plan now a common line of products will affect the decisions of the observer.) The observer, then, is neither disinterested nor passive, but part of the effective world of market exchanges: observation is investigative, and in this respect different from contemplative forms. It is akin to the investigative observation of a scientist who, say, while seeing an intriguing cell formation under the microscope, decides to perform further experiments in order to understand it better.

Observation can be direct (i.e. face-to-face) or indirect. I can directly observe two competitors talking at a trade fair, or I can read a story about the two competitors having had talks. Stories, reports, news, and the like can act as observational instruments for market actors: such stories are lenses through which the world, and by monitoring them market actors situate and evaluate their actions within the broader world. One advantage of indirect observation is that it contributes to the uncertain coordination of dispersed actions (Thévenot 1993, p. 276) by orienting the attention of dispersed actors to the same event or class of events. While a private conversation at a trade fair cannot be directly observed by many, a story about the conversation can be circulated to and read by many dispersed market actors, orienting their attention to this particular change in the state of the world. This is even more so when the story is a scoop about secret talks, backroom deals, and the like. Sometimes, such stories are purposive revelations made by the deal partners, meant to focus observation upon them: a 'secret deal' attracts a lot more attention than just a deal. In this sense, in economic life, stories are akin to observational instruments.

Observing two competitors talking to each other at a trade fair requires interpretive skills, recollection of past episodes about the relationships between competitors, knowledge about the product lines, and so on. Similarly, reading and evaluating a newspaper story requires not only simply reading skills, but also a certain knowledge about the uses of metaphors, backhanded compliments, or ambiguities as rhetorical instruments, together with knowledge about the reporter's reputation, his track record, and the like. This situational knowledge is not amenable to formalization and is only partly discursive. It is not generalizable or easily transferable from one person to the next.

3. The handling of various artefacts, through which representations of states of the world, inferences about such states, and justification of the own actions with respect to them are generated. Company reports, balance sheets, price lists, price tags, product descriptions, but also buildings, shelves, or the product themselves can be among these artefacts. Some investors, for

instance, decide to buy the shares of specific companies after spending hours of observation at the supermarket, looking at how the products of the said companies are placed on shelves, whether they are bought or not, or testing them in their own families. The same goes for consumers, who do not necessarily want to invest in shares when visiting a supermarket. When shopping in a supermarket, consumers make observations (about the environment and about products as well), infer representations of the states of the world from them, and justify their actions accordingly. Not to mention the fact that the use of the products themselves contributes to such representations, to judgements, and the justification of further actions.

4. The manipulation of, and contact to technologies and devices which represent states of the world or help build such representations. Screens displaying prices and volumes of financial securities being traded, or an ongoing flow of images associated with political, economic, and sometimes even personal narratives belong to this category. (News of Amy Winehouse being arrested for the umpteenth time, for instance, can lead to inferences about her musical output, from here to inferences about the financial future of her label, and then to the evolution of the share price of the respective media corporation.) Within this broader category we can distinguish at least between two kinds of technologies: those of visualized narratives, on the one hand (think TV evening news), and those which produce data flows, on the other. More and more of the latter are actually technologies of intervention as well: they allow not only the direct perception of states of the world from abstract, narrative-less data, but also intervention in the relevant states of the world, from within the given frame. In other words, intervention does not require a separate device or technology, but takes place on the same screen on which the data flows (this will be discussed in detail later).

Information and Transactions

These elements of market transactions can be grouped in the following general classes: verbal and non-verbal interactions (see also Goffman [1970, p. 5]), and the handling of material elements (artefacts and technologies) present in interactions. Interactions are endowed with at least two key properties: they are sequentially constituted and polythetic (Schütz 2003, p. 485).[15] Being sequential, it is impossible to determine at any given step in the chain whether the next steps will (fully) correspond to the repertoire of routines available to participants. Being polythetic, action sequences require judgement (Schütz 2003, p. 496): that is, definitions and clarifications showing that (at least up to that point), common grounds and orientations are taken as valid by the participants to action. Situational definitions need not be mutually exclusive, but can overlap, leading to laminations: that is, to inter-related definitional layers, which not only provide participants with resources for action, but which can also constitute surprises. In this perspective, we are confronted with two interrelated elements: (*a*) the uncertainties or surprises unavoidably generated in action sequences, and (*b*) the judgements which allow progression to the next step in the action. Information can be seen as the processing of surprises in interaction, against the (relatively stable) background of common expectations provided by routines.

Information is judged and lived, and is 'something not recalled but re-created out of the resources of the available order of possibilities of experience, available sensory materials, actions, etc.' (Garfinkel 2008, p. 158). Information, then, is not synonymous with routines (i.e. with certainties): information is the (joint) work implied by dealing with surprises.[16] Routines (and the trust which goes with them) constitute the background against which information is produced in action. Being socially distributed, routines create partitions among domains in which competitive transactions take place. The generation of transaction-relevant information is then constrained by the social domains of knowledge specific to certain sets of routines. In other words, informational surprises are created not for 'the public', but for specific publics defined by specific knowledge domains, publics which constitute both the observers and the pool of potential participants to competitive exchanges. A new, fuel-efficient model unveiled at a car show is an informational surprise[17] in the first place for the public from which observers and participants to transactions in specific categories of objects are drawn.[18]

If we connect this with the classic sociological argument that, at the bottom, market transactions are basic forms of social competition, it follows that such competitions have a sequential character and are polythetic as well. Being sequential, they cannot be reduced to following routines, but provide opportunities for surprises and unexpected elements, which in their turn can become competition-relevant resources. This also means that players can (and will) generate surprises as intrinsic to the competition they are engaged in. (Surprises can be constituted not only by saying or doing something, but also by silence or by the absence of expected reactions.) At the same time, if we understand market transactions as polythetic, then competitions will include several definitional layers. A competition can be not only about money, but also about who is more persistent, or quick, or persuasive. We are reminded here of the soccer metaphor, where the players' competition is not only about scoring goals, but also about their specific gameworthiness. This also means that in market transactions, laminated layers of competitions will unfold in the same play, depending on how players create and make use of surprises as a relevant resource.

The opposite of information would be ignorance: in its extreme form, ignorance is given by the surprises which cannot be processed in action (see Garfinkel [2008, p. 162]). Harold Garfinkel (2008, p. 157) illustrates this with the example of *Kriegsspiel*: a game of chess where the two opponents cannot see each other's pieces and moves. Players are told by a referee (who can see both chess boards) when they have won or lost a piece. Moves are made 'in the light of one's thoughts about the others' thoughts about oneself' (Goffman 1970, p. 101)—that is, by trying to infer the possible directions from where surprises might come. Information, argues Garfinkel, is irreducible to any single element of the whole interaction setting: players must use all the resources at hand in order to make judgements upon continuously arising surprises, judgements which will enable them to build step by step a representation of the states of the world, and advance thus in their actions.

Continuing the analogy with the play of a soccer game, which opened the discussion, we can see markets as (structured) competitive exchanges, taking place in stadiums (i.e. in front of specific publics, and within the framework of specific constraints), and geared towards the production and handling of informational surprises as tools and resources for achieving specific valuation outcomes. In a soccer match, surprises are produced all the time: unexpected moves, deceptions, limited reciprocal observations of the consequences of other players' actions, and the like. (In a play of soccer where members of the public can become players in the field, the potential for surprises is much greater.) This informational character emerges from the play's sequential and polythetic character: it makes the result uncertain until the end of the match. If they were entirely foreseeable on the ground of routines, plays of games would be rather dull.

Information and the Social Ordering of Knowledge

The above arguments mean that information is part and parcel of what constitutes the market order, and not something external with respect to this order (Boehm 1994, p. 162); that the production and handling of market information cannot take place outside social interactions; that in these interactions market actors use forms of situational knowledge in order to handle informational surprises. At the bottom, markets are not competitions 'in the wild': they are made possible by social arrangements which order heterogeneous forms of knowledge, creating partitions across various publics, partitions within which surprises are produced (see also Boehm [1994, p. 172]). The ordering of knowledge, however, should be understood as dynamic, not as static: the informational surprises produced in transactions influence it.

If we accept that markets are social competitions anchored in the ordering of heterogeneous forms of knowledge—as argued above—then the multi-layered processing of surprises is intrinsic to this ordering. It is undertaken by specific groups of actors who would then achieve control over interpretations, as well as over processing procedures. Groups of analysts, for instance, have not only different interpretations of stories and data, but also different procedures for producing such interpretations, as well as professional and organizational arrangements which legitimate their control over interpretations. Analysts also have their own status hierarchies, formal and informal rankings, and social competitions with prizes, judgements on the 'analyst of the year', and the like. If competing groups control different, alternative procedures of interpretation, then they become an additional source of informational surprises. In terms of the play of the soccer game, commentators at the stadium are not distinct from the play, but part of it.

The above arguments open up the possibility of a sociology of markets that is not limited to investigating the social factors influencing the allocation of goods. If we understand markets as information-generating competitions, anchored in the social ordering of heterogeneous forms of knowledge, then a sociology of markets will have to investigate not only how information intervenes in competitive exchanges, but also how the latter are set within specific knowledge frameworks. In this perspective, the sociology of markets has at its core the fundamental concepts of information and knowledge, yet will investigate transactions unfolding within heterogeneous forms of knowledge (some fixed on artefacts, some related to groups of actors). It provides a specification of information-generating competitions as a key component of dynamic and complex societies, without limiting itself to a functionalist answer (i.e. the distribution of scarce resources).[19]

This is not to say that markets are unproblematic, or that they are the best (or the sole) arrangement for everything. Quite the contrary: a sociology of markets will have to highlight the tensions inherent in transactions, the links (and the conflicts as well) with other forms of social competition and/or cooperation, the role of controlling social groups (e.g. political institutions), as well as the moral and social implications of expanding market transactions.

A sociology that understands markets as informational competitions taking place within specific knowledge frameworks will have to investigate at least the following:

1. The forms and types of interactions through which competitions are achieved, and how information is produced within competitive interactions. This amounts to paying serious attention to the micro-analytics of transactions, understood as interactional achievements. If we accept transactions as the basic analytical unit of the sociology of markets, then we need to pay close attention to interactions as the fundamental form in which

transactions and relationships can be grasped (see also Goffman [1971, p. 194]). A micro-analytics of competitive transactions investigates how these activities create surprises and endow them with specific properties, in relationship to the cognitive activities of participants. This does not mean that emotions are left out of the picture. Quite the contrary: such an investigation will not work on the premise of an opposition between cognition and emotions, but will focus on their interplay within concrete transactional situations. Moreover, the focus on transactions as interactions will pay attention to the background of routines and mutual understandings deployed by participants, investigating how they make possible the production of informational surprises. This implies an extension of the sociological research programme from the examination of uncertainty-processing routines (see Beckert [1996]) to the examination of how uncertainties are produced against the background of routines. Also, a micro-analytics of competitive transactions pays close attention to the valuation processes at work here. In the same way in which competitions on the soccer field are about social valuations (along attributes such as speed, endurance, or cunning), competitive transactions are about social valuations as well—about what Erving Goffman (1970, p. 96) calls gameworthiness. The task here is to investigate how such valuations intervene in the constitution of prices, and how they affect the outcome of transactions.

2. A sociology of markets centred on information investigates how the social distribution of knowledge sets up parameters within which information-based competitions take place, and how these parameters affect information. Social distribution of knowledge includes here forms of social knowledge related to the status, situations, and relationships of participants. To come back to the soccer metaphor, we need to investigate here the social parameters of the playing teams and their publics, parameters expressed in network, group, and organizational features, among others. We need to investigate how these publics are constituted along social attributes, how 'admission tickets' or procedures are set in place for letting participants in the stadium where the game is played, and how such entrance tickets are intrinsic to playing the game. And, in the same way in which a stadium has boundaries—material, spatial, temporal, and social—we would need to investigate how the boundaries of competitive transactions are constituted, and the role they play with respect to the legitimacy of such games.

3. A sociology of markets pays close attention to the 'commenting public' which is part of the game's play—that is, to how authoritative judgements and opinions are fed into and influence the game itself, shaping its informational features.

4. An information-centred sociology of markets pays close attention to the material tools and artefacts used in playing competitive exchange games. It

investigates the technologies used in producing, storing, processing, and distributing informational surprises, such as price data. It also investigates technologies used by the 'commenting public' playing the game, such as news and analyses.

5. Finally, a sociology of markets investigates the impact of rules upon competitive games, and of the bodies which set them up, watch upon, and intervene in the game. Such rules constrain the ways in which information is generated within competitive exchanges, as well as how these exchanges relate to society at large. To invoke again the soccer metaphor: the match and its stadiums are not set in the middle of nowhere, but are part of the city—that is, of the polis, understood as social and political communities with established institutions. In the same way in which soccer matches resonate within and are consequential for the city, plays of competitive games resonate within the polis. In the same way in which soccer matches are overseen by boards and associations (of clubs, leagues, city councils, etc.), plays of competitive games are relevant for and involve boards (or organizations) from outside the game itself. We would need then to investigate the relationships between social and political institutions, on the one hand, and informational competitions, on the other, examine how rules, regulations, and interventions shape the game, how they constrain or enable the ways in which information is produced.

The following chapters are an attempt to examine competitive informational transactions along these lines, summarizing, presenting, and discussing research done during the past decades in the field of economic sociology. In the preceding paragraphs, I have argued that the basic analytical unit of the sociology of markets, the transaction, cannot be separated from the interaction order. In the same way in which a soccer match cannot take place but in interaction sequences, these latter are intrinsic to market transactions. It is time, then, to descend upon the places where transactions are played: in the following chapter, I will take readers not only to well-equipped stadiums, but also onto some green fields, not to mention a couple of streets where traders kick the ball—in their own way, of course.

☐ NOTES

1. The plasticity of the notion of information in everyday language is quite convenient: when we say that we have received information, there is information waiting for us, we are going to send information, or this and that is valuable information (or not), we mean a variety of interactions and practical handlings of artefacts, ranging all the way from face-to-face verbal exchanges to looking at flickering numbers on a computer screen, or peering down through a microscope. Information, however, can be seen as a non-human process as well: for instance,

as a measure of physical organization or as the reproduction of selection processes (Capurro and Hjørland 2003, pp. 344, 360–4). In this case, information has an eminently material character, consisting in exchanges and interactions at various levels of the organization of matter. When seeing information as a social process, we need to distinguish between the meanings of the term, on the one hand, and the concrete actions implied by each of these meanings, on the other. At the same time, we need to keep in mind that information as a human process has a material character as well, since it cannot be separated from the production, handling, and use of artefacts.

At the level of social processes, information can be seen at least as: (*a*) patterns of communication, broadly understood; (*b*) forms of control and feedback; (*c*) the probability of a message being transmitted through a channel; (*d*) the content of a cognitive state; (*e*) the meaning of specific linguistic forms (Bogdan 1994; Capurro and Hjørland 2003, p. 356). Information appears thus as a resource, a commodity, as perception of patterns, and as a constitutive force in society.

From the general and imperfect enumeration above, it appears that information can mean different things to various social science disciplines, and that such a level of generality will not bring us much further in understanding the relationship between market exchanges and information. Even if we narrow down the investigation to sociology, we can see that the meaning of the term momentarily stays very general: the 'information society' is characterized by the infrastructure supporting 'informational services' (Lash 2002; Webster 2002, p. 73)—in other words, by changes in the economic composition of developed societies, changes favouring specific classes of industries (the service sector, specialized in data processing and analysis, as well as parts of the entertainment sector). In other, more specific interpretations, information is seen as communication among people who do not know each other and who have little basis for mutual understanding (Porter 1994, p. 217). Especially dispersed people, who have little direct contact with each other, if any, will need technologies of large scale trust in order to be able to communicate with each other (Porter 1994, p. 220). This leads to the creation of information as standardized objects with the help of which people communicate. This would mean that information can be anything related to such technologies of trust, not just numbers. It would also mean that something like gossip among friends would be excluded from the category of information, which would be counterintuitive.

2. Following Erving Goffman (1972, pp. 33, 61), I distinguish here between a game (a set of rules prescribing and constraining action routines), a play of a game (the concrete event of applying such routines in a sequence of actions), and gaming encounters (the specific sequences involved in playing a game of X).

3. We can of course encounter less formal plays where members of the public can be drawn into the play, but such possibilities are still limited, among others because the play has to be made witnessable.

4. In special circumstances, the win of a match can be awarded by decree to one team, but this is an exception rather than the rule and usually understood as punishment.

5. The public is not understood here as the fiction of the 'general public'. In the same way in which the public on a soccer stadium is overwhelmingly made up of fans of soccer—people with a specific knowledge, attachments, and preferences, etc.—the public of competitive transactions can be restricted according to profession, income, education, or gender, among others.

6. The notion of uncertainty is understood here not as a general theoretical reflection (of the kind 'where is the world going?'), but as action sequences which do not fit situational expectations, requiring responses from participating actors. In a soccer match, for instance, a dummy pass is meant to deceive the opponent by running counter to his expectations: it constitutes a surprise to which the opponent's actions adapt ad hoc, even if this implies drawing upon a pool of existing routines, analogies with past situations, and the like.

7. I borrow here the concept of lamination from Erving Goffman (1974, pp. 82, 156–7), understood as the unfolding of various layers of meaning within one and the same activity, layers achieved through transformations of 're-keyings'. Re-keyings are redefinitions of an ongoing activity, understood by participating actors as taking the said activity in a different direction. In a soccer match, for instance, when two players compete for the ball, this can be understood by participants as a trial of skill or as a means of averting a potential goal.

8. In *The Protestant Ethic and the Spirit of Capitalism*, Weber ([1920] 1988, pp. 190–3) argues that the ethic of capitalist accumulation is grounded in a specific theology, which increases the uncertainty of redemption, and thus sets hope as the fundamental driving capitalists to accumulate capital and use it in a rational fashion. Because redemption becomes an uncertainty, capitalists strive to lead a righteous life, based on frugality, continuous accumulation, and economic calculation. They hope thus that their souls will be redeemed. In this perspective, capitalist economic transactions are ultimately driven by a specific form of religious ethics.

9. Max Weber, for instance, states that capitalist market transactions have an objective character, in the sense that they are not conditioned by group or tribe membership; the same criteria would apply to transactions between members of the group, on the one hand, and between a member and a non-member, on the other. These criteria are those of profitability, and are determined by the universalist ethics of capitalist calculation (Weber [1922] 1972, p. 49). This doesn't necessarily mean cooperation: for Weber, capitalist market exchanges are characterized by conflict and compromise of interests, which determine prices.

10. Georg Simmel, writing after Marx, saw money as the objectified form of social relationships in the capitalist society. Money is important not only because it affords us to buy commodities, but first and foremost because in a highly individualized, atomized, and differentiated society, it provides us with the means of entering into social relationships of various duration and stability (Simmel [1901] 1989, pp. 394–5).

11. Weber sees this increased interdependency as being triggered primarily by the expansion of financial markets: in the process of buying and selling financial securities, a web of tributary relationships is created (Weber [1894] 1924, p. 274). This increases reciprocal dependency and thus contributes to holding together a highly individualized and atomized society.

12. The automation is partial because, among others, the buyer side still relies on human ad hoc decision. An automated grocery shopping system could be imagined as software which automatically detects and evaluates the contents of the fridge and then, based on the owner's past preferences, scans online supermarket offers and buys accordingly. Such a system would require a combination of calculative, objectified, and institutional trust.

13. One consequence of this would be to question the usual distinction we make between economic institutions, on the one hand, and other types of institutions on the other, a distinction that has caused much discussion in economic sociology. Max Weber, for instance, saw the stock exchange not only as an economic institution, but as a political one as well (Weber [1894] 1924, p. 316). As such, economic institutions contain elements of

political power as well, are oriented to political interests and subject to political influences. This argument was repeated later, in a modified form, by Karl Polanyi (1945). It should not be confused with the idea of structural embeddedness (Granovetter 1985), according to which economic transactions are embedded in networks of relationships. It has been sometimes expressed, however, as the political embeddedness of economic transactions (e.g. Zukin and DiMaggio [1990]).

14. This does not mean, however, that illegitimate (or even illegal) transactions cannot link in with legitimate ones and parasitize their resources. An example in this sense is provided by illegitimate services (e.g. sex for money) being offered in the backrooms of legitimate businesses. I discuss such situations in Chapters 1 and 2.

15. The sequential character of actions means that they are not revealed in their entirety at once, but unfold step by step: buying bread requires putting on a coat, getting out of the door, walking to the bakery, etc. The polythetic character of action means that, because they are sequential, action parts can be subsumed to various definitions. Getting out of the door can be part of going to buy bread, or of going to see a neighbour.

16. There are close parallels between Garfinkel's position, on the one hand, and Martin Heidegger's argument ([1926] 2001, p. 75), on the other. Heidegger sees the breakdown of routines (for instance, when a tool does not work) as revealing the self's attitude of care to the world. This revelation generates surprises, not the routines as such. I am grateful to Karin Knorr Cetina for pointing out this similarity.

17. Strictly speaking, informational surprises are constituted within webs of interactions which include handling an array of artefacts such as images of the car, as well as storytelling, rhetorical strategies, and much more.

18. A new car model cannot be an informational surprise for somebody who does not drive and does not invest in financial securities, though talk about the model, or images of it can be used to create surprises, say, at a dinner party. This shows that market information can be transformed and transplanted outside economic exchanges, based, as argued above, on the polythetic character of information.

19. Arguments coming from economic anthropology had made clear the limitations of a functionalist approach according to which markets are simply arrangements for the distribution of scarce material resources. First, scarcity and abundance are a matter of collective perceptions (see Sahlins [1972] for a critique of the notion of abundance), and therefore cannot be separated from group interactions. What is scarce and what is not, what is a resource and what is not are distinctions emerging in a group's activities. Second, resources themselves have a dynamic character, changing with the activities of a group, and not being limited to material artefacts.

1 Information and the Interaction Order of Markets

The Salizada San Moisè, one of Venice's most elegant streets, is also one of the places where African peddlers align in a row every day, displaying their merchandise on blue plastic sacks rolled out on the pavement (the sacks also serve for transporting their wares). They do this right in front of the über-elegant fashion stores which line both sides of the street. While the peddlers' merchandise selection is rather limited (mostly handbags, sunglasses, sometimes watches as well), it is also an exact copy of some of the handbags and sunglasses sold inside the stores bearing the names of well-known designer houses. The items sold inside have price tags starting at about one thousand euros for a modest handbag, and very quickly working their way up into the rarefied zone of several thousands. (You have to look hard to discover the prices on minuscule lists in the shop windows.) The same handbag model sold by the peddlers will go for maybe about fifty euros—and even less, if one bargains harder.

And this happens all the time: passers-by stop, take a closer look, engage with the sellers, examine the handbags, and then start bargaining, trying to drive the price down, while the African seller, miming exasperation, finally agrees to sell, say, a 'Gucci' for forty euros or so. Now and then, through an apparently well functioning early warning system, the peddlers get wind that policemen are approaching; they quickly stuff their handbags in the plastic sacks and run away laughing. After the patrol has passed, they come back and unroll their merchandise displays on the pavement again. Passers-by observe the whole ritual of being chased by the police with the same kind of amused interest shown in observing the change of the guard at Buckingham Palace. During this time, all the elegant shops stay empty. Only rarely does anyone venture inside; in fact, if you peek through the window, you can hardly see any shop assistants inside, although the store is open for business. To a stranger, these shops appear as elegant, rarefied environments meant rather to be looked at from a distance instead of places where clothing, footwear, and bags are sold.

We shouldn't think that such a situation, where cheap replicates are sold side by side with very expensive originals, can be encountered only in Southern

Europe, or that it is part of specific capitalist 'cultures'. Such situations are more common than one may think: we need to go no further than a shopping mall where very expensive jewellery stores coexist with discounters (sometimes adjacent to the expensive boutiques) selling indistinguishable, yet incomparably cheaper versions of rings, necklaces, and bracelets (Underhill 2004, p. 118). At first sight, such a situation may seem strange: how can empty, very expensive stores spatially and temporally coexist with sellers offering visually (near-) identical copies of their merchandise at much lower prices? In terms of the soccer play, how can a premier league match be contiguous with amateurs kicking the ball in the street? Why do not the cheaper sellers drive out the more expensive ones? How does information (about price, quality, and sellers) work in these transactions? Why is price information hidden or not revealed from the start, or not made prominent, and why isn't it the object of negotiation in luxury stores?

Answering these questions (and more) requires paying attention to how market transactions unfold as social interactions, and how the elements constitutive of these interactions shape the outcomes and the features of markets. In the end, all market transactions are interaction forms, no matter whether they involve haggling for a handbag with a peddler, signing a mortgage loan for buying a house, or buying music by clicking a button on the computer screen. It is so because conducting economic transactions cannot be done without the participants' reciprocal orientation towards each other, and towards the object being transacted. Moreover, economic transactions belong to the world of effective action (Schütz and Luckmann 2003, p. 30), which is inter-subjective. I do not conduct transactions in the world of my dreams (though I can dream of being a currency trader, or a salesman), but in the effective world. Without an orientation to others and to transaction objects, we cannot act in this world. (And, it should be added here, even in the dream world I would need to imagine transaction partners, customers, etc.) This orientation to others, without which we cannot conceive any transaction, implies that the interaction order is not just an external frame in which transactions are embedded for reasons of, say, practicality. Neither are interactions simply external constraints or resources for transactions. Interactions are constitutive of transactions: the particular sequences in which interactions unfold shape the reciprocal expect-ations and understandings of participants, their perceptions and definitions of the process and, with that, the outcomes of transactions. In other words, economic transactions are situational, and not just situated actions.

If transactions were just situated, but not situational, their main features, sequential character, and outcomes would be constrained or enabled by the resources of the situation, but not shaped by it. That is, it would be ultimately irrelevant to these features whether a transaction takes place by phone, face to face, or over the Internet, whether it involves just fleeting interactions or more sustained ones, or whether we see or do not see the transaction partners.

Intuitively, we would say that this is not so: interaction forms matter with respect to transactions. It is not the same whether we buy something from an Internet retailer or in a shop, in a face-to-face interaction. (This may also help explain why certain commodities do not sell well over the Internet.)

Moreover, some economic transactions could never take place exclusively on the Internet: to give but one example, the collapse of major investment banks such as Lehman Brothers or Merrill Lynch in the crisis of 2008–9 raised the issue of finding buyers willing to take control of and rescue these banks. This, in turn, involved days of meetings and negotiations among CEOs of major banks from North America and Western Europe, representatives of the Federal Reserve Bank of New York and of the US Treasury, among others. A solution (i.e. Bank of America buying Merrill Lynch and Lehman Brothers filing for bankruptcy) was found in these protracted chains of concrete interactions, over the phone and also face to face. It cannot be said that the economic transaction (i.e. Bank of America buying Merrill Lynch) was only constrained by these interactions. Before the telephones started ringing on a Saturday morning at 6 a.m., there was no transaction in sight. The transaction took shape within the interactions. It is therefore mistaken to think that interactions are just an external frame embedding transactions, or that interactions matter only with respect to how we shop. Examples such as the above show that they matter much more. This being said, we need to spell a theoretical argument linking interactions with transactions. While the investigation of market transactions as interactions can shed light on a host of relevant issues, for reasons of space and also of topical continuity I focus in this chapter on examining a restricted number of these issues. They are given as follows:

1. How are the boundaries of transactions shaped in interactions? This is relevant not only because—in terms of the metaphor used here—plays of soccer have to be connected to the outside world, but also because, due to the polythetic character of market transactions, common definitions of what is going on have to be achieved in the situation. Such definitions imply setting up or acknowledging boundaries—that is, not only distinctions among, but also possible connections across domains of action.

2. How do interaction features shape transaction-relevant information? This is relevant for understanding how surprises are created in transactions, and how they contribute to the constitution of transactional boundaries.

3. How do interaction features shape the actors' decisions? In economics, as well as in economic sociology, issues like pricing and decision-making in transactions have long been given a prominent role. Yet, what does it mean to discover a price? What does it mean to make a decision to buy or not? Issues like decisions and discoveries cannot be seen as separated from the interaction contexts where they occur. Before starting with the issue of boundaries, however, a short discussion of the types of market interactions is necessary.

Market Interactions and Situations: Encounters, Engagements, and Platform Performances

Traditionally, the interaction order has been seen as dealing with face-to-face situations, in which two or more actors engage in verbal and non-verbal exchanges. Indeed, the study of verbal communications seems to bear strong similarities with economic exchanges: conversations imply partners transacting in an orderly fashion, taking turns at speaking and at listening, occasionally in front of an audience (see also Sacks, Schegloff, and Jefferson [1974]). Conversely, many economic transactions are shaped as conversational interactions (think of buyers at shop counters, at a manned supermarket checkout, and also of brokers on the floors of traditional stock exchanges). In face-to-face situations, participants have a joint focus of attention and respond to each other's situated actions (Goffman 1983, p. 3). However, we do not need physical co-presence in order to develop a joint focus of attention and respond to the partner's actions (see Knorr Cetina [2009]): if a salesman calls me on the phone to confirm the shipment of the goods I have ordered (or to tell me that they are unavailable), joint focus and reciprocal responses will develop in the absence of any physical co-presence.

The situation of Internet-based transactions, however, is trickier. Here, in many cases, we lack the physical element of voice as supporting co-presence, among others because transactions need to be conducted within seconds or within fractions of a second (online financial markets are a case in point). In other cases (e.g. online retailers), the elements of individual co-presence have been eliminated altogether or replaced by other features. When buying a plane ticket over the Internet, for instance, there is apparently no co-presence involved; when buying a laptop computer, or a book, however, there are user comments and reader's reviews, as well as pictures intervening in the conduct of the transaction.

Following Karin Knorr Cetina (2009, p. 63), then, we can distinguish between two kinds of situations which shape economic transactions: natural and synthetic situations. In natural situations, elements of physical co-presence (body, voice) structure the joint focus of transaction participants. When buying a handbag from a peddler, the transaction is structured as a specific conversational interaction, involving bodily elements, material artefacts, and talk. Peddlers use their body (posture, hand movements, eye contact) in order to draw attention to their goods and make passers-by stop. On their part, passers-by use their bodies to signal disinterest or readiness to engage in a possible transaction (for instance, avoiding eye contact can signal unwillingness to engage). In synthetic situations, appresentational technologies enable the coordination of transaction participants.[1] For instance, when buying a plane ticket over the Internet the interface addresses me in an increasingly individualized way and guides me through the sequences of the transaction. During this process, the airline company is visualized as a transaction partner, and requests to perform further steps are formulated as conversational turns (e.g. please type in your credit card details, please choose your seat, etc.).

Along with these two types of situations, we can distinguish at least the following interaction types as grounding transactions: encounters, engagements, and dramatizations, or what Goffman (1983, p. 7) calls platform performances. An encounter is a temporally and spatially bounded transaction, characterized by an uncertain outcome and by the socially sanctioned display of socially relevant attributes (see also Preda [2009a]), a display which is relevant with respect to the outcome of the exchange. A peddler's success with selling a handbag will depend, among others, on his display of socially relevant attributes: charm, humour, ability to approach people, to respond to the passers-by's displays of interest, among others. On the buyer's side, the same displays influence the outcome of the play, although the attributes themselves may vary: toughness, mimed indifference, simulated dissatisfaction, and the like. These displays prove to each of the actors, and, taken together, to the public, the gameworthiness (Goffman 1970, p. 96) of the participants—that is, that the participants have what it takes to play the game. Displays are a key element of the valuation processes taking place in transactions, valuations which cannot be reduced to settling on a price for the handbag. In many instances, settling on a price for a 'Gucci' or a 'Valentino' is the outcome of such displays of gameworthiness.

Displays of gameworthiness can change the ways in which the participants' other social attributes, such as gender, are judged upon. Thus, the trading floors of financial exchanges used to be regarded as a male world in which, for the purposes of transactions, only one gender role was acknowledged by participants—the male one. Yet, ethnographic research reveals that different gender categories are used by traders, and that they are judged differently, in relationship to and depending upon gameworthiness. A female trader can be perceived as a great player, commanding respect as a woman (Levin 2001, p. 121), while a male trader, perceived as less gameworthy, can attract scorn and be characterized as a lesser man.

Displays can be competitive or cooperative: in a street encounter with a peddler, or in an encounter with a shop assistant, the displays of social attributes tend to be cooperative: the seller will react to the buyer's displays in a cooperative fashion (e.g. praising the choice, complimenting the buyer, and the like). In other situations, displays tend to be competitive: that is, the seller and the buyer can competitively display attributes like knowledgeability. Or, the buyer and seller can competitively display different attributes, countering friendliness with faked disinterest, for instance. Think here of buying consumer electronics, where the seller's display of knowledgeability, in competition with the buyer, can be a positive factor for closing the sale.

Market encounters are not limited to situations like those on Venice's main drag or in the bazaar. Market encounters can also take place in synthetic situations where the transaction is technologically formed. Take day trading in online anonymous markets: here, players transact without knowing each other and without having the possibility of any physical (visual or audio) contact. Yet, individualized encounters appear to be necessary in order for the transaction to take place (see Preda [2009a]).

While encounters are spatially and temporally well defined, non-iterative (we don't buy handbags twice in a row on the same day), with problematic outcomes, and grounded in displays of social attributes (competitive or not), market engagements are characterized by the following: first, their spatial and temporal boundaries are not necessarily well defined. Engagements can replicate themselves in various locales and do not always have a foreseeable end. Whereas in many encounters the outcome can be seen as having a binary structure (I will buy this handbag or not), in engagements the uncertainties related to the outcome can be more complex. Engagements can involve more than two players at a time; while during an encounter the number of participants usually does not vary and competitive interjections can be punished (e.g. another peddler intervening by offering a cheaper or nicer handbag), engagements can have variable numbers of heterogeneous actors. In engagements, as well as in encounters, the displays of socially relevant attributes can be decisive. Probably an adequate instance of economic engagements is buying and selling big economic entities, like Merrill Lynch or the Bank of Scotland.

Activities like selling an investment bank, an oil rig, an advertising campaign, a new shoe fashion, or an architectural plan for an office building involve chains of transactional engagements. Not only them: selling a car, or a highly priced piece of jewellery, or an expensive fashion item imply interlinked engagements too. Seller and buyer engage in protracted interactions, exchange pleasantries, and sometimes even private stories; tests are done; participants take their time, and helpers can be drafted in. Chains of transactional engagements can involve multilayered communicational activities (conversations, e-mails, phone calls) which are not regularly present in encounters. In such cases, groups engage in talks over longer periods of time, without necessarily having a preset end. Locales can change, and actors can be added or removed from such engagements. While the boundaries of encounters to their social environment can be clearly delimited, market engagements can overlap with other social activities, adding more layers to their laminations. For instance, a peddling encounter will start and end there in the street. A boardroom negotiation can begin in the office and be extended so as to overlap with a dinner, with playing golf, or with drinks at the pub.

Displays of socially relevant attributes are as relevant as in encounters (e.g. capability to persuade other players, to charm them, to fend off undesirable alternatives, to become aggressive when deemed necessary, etc.). Activity and situational overlaps multiply the aspects factored into competitive displays of gameworthiness, and can even lead to different competitions on gameworthiness becoming laminated on each other, influencing thus the outcome of transactions in unforeseen ways. For instance, a negotiation in the boardroom can include displays along the lines of toughness, or flexibility, or charm. When such a negotiation continues in the evening at the pub, further situation-specific competitions can be laminated upon it, such as drinking contests or dexterity in a game of darts.

A third type of market interactions is provided by dramatizations, or platform performances. In such cases, dramaturgical actions (partly with a ritual character) are performed in front of a public, which also provides potential transaction partners. Such dramatizations are probably one of the oldest forms of conducting market transactions. Examples here are street sellers who make public demonstrations of their merchandise, exhibitors at trade fairs, stalls at town markets, or TV shopping shows. Dramatizations are carefully bounded in time and space and can have an iterative character. While scripted, they also involve improvisational elements. In transactional encounters, a private interaction can be set in a public space, but maintains some distance from the audience: selling you this handbag is just between you and me, although we are on the street. There can be onlookers, and some of them may want to buy a handbag as well, but distance to the public is maintained. On the trading floor, clerks may watch, but do not intervene in transactions. In setting up a product demonstration-cum-sale in a supermarket, in the street, or at a trade fair, the public is expected to engage, because it includes potential, yet unknown transactions partners. The uncertainty of the transaction is not only if the partners will buy or not, but also who these partners will be. Synthetic situations have their platform performances as well: think here of product demonstrations on TV shopping channels, or of telethons (raising donations via TV shows). Forms of virtual expertise, such as online reviews and endorsements, can be part of these dramatizations as well.

This being said, it does not mean that in practice the above forms of transactional interactions are clear cut: engagements, for instance, can include platform performances (the presentation of a new advertising campaign in the boardroom) or encounters, in the same way in which dramatizations can include both encounter moments and engagements (the peddler trying to hook passers-by or inviting a member of the public on the stage to try the product). Encounters, engagements, and dramatizations include various combinations of artefacts, bodily movements, and verbal exchanges as the building blocks of transactions. The issue, though, is how these building blocks produce something called information, and how this latter influences the outcomes of transactions. Before addressing this, however, we need to deal with the issue of how the play of the game is distinguished from what is going on around—that is, with transaction boundaries.

Boundaries and Market Interactions

Boundaries are usually understood as distinctions or classifications (Lamont and Molnár 2002), schemes which order the social world and differentiate domains of activity, not dissimilar to the borderlines demarcating countries (the sociological notion of boundary stems from the idea of borders). At the same time, boundaries can comprise not only an element of inclusion or exclusion (the inside or outside factor), but also one of communication and cooperation as well: groups with different interests can work around a project or object incorporating several relevant distinctions for the group in question (see Star and Griesemer [1989]). To give but one example, the takeover of Merrill Lynch by the Bank of America in September 2008 involved, among others, teams of accountants (trying to identify Merrill Lynch's liabilities), bankers (trying to persuade other bankers to commit themselves to this transaction), regulators (trying to assess the impact of the deal on the economy), and lawyers (trying to work out the legal formula for the take-over). All these teams, with different trainings, skills, perspectives, and the like, communicated and cooperated around the 'Merrill Lynch problem', highlighting it along various distinctions (legal, political, financial, and the like).

At least the following kinds of boundaries can be distinguished with respect to market transactions: spatial, temporal, legal, and social boundaries. While spatial and temporal boundaries concern the place and time of transactions, legal boundaries concern their legal definitions and status, the rights and obligations incurred by transactions, and the formal mechanisms for reinforcing these rights and obligations. Social boundaries concern at least issues of participation to transactions (which groups or persons are entitled to participate or not), as well as the definition of specific transactions (for instance, as family or group activities, as serving specific functions, or as having a certain character).

Boundaries are relevant, among others, for the legitimacy of economic transactions: that is, for how these transactions relate to other social institutions and to society at large. Legitimacy and legality of economic transactions do not overlap: for example, peddling on the main drag in Venice is obviously regarded by passers-by as legitimated (otherwise they wouldn't buy the handbags), but not as legal (otherwise peddlers wouldn't be chased by the police). Where does this legitimacy come from and why does it matter? There are many kinds of economic transactions, and not all of them are legitimate or legal. The problem is that, in defining markets, one is confronted with the issue of legitimacy and, therefore, with that of boundaries as well. Can we talk of markets in narcotic substances, artefacts, or living beings (human and non-human) irrespective of their legitimacy? Can we non-metaphorically say that there is a market in, for instance, tiger penises or sex slaves (and if yes, why don't we see trading indexes published in places such as the *Financial Times* or the *Wall Street Journal*)? This would amount to say that markets amount to a more or less confusing collection of transactions, be they in back alleys or on the high street. Intuitively, many people are rather disinclined to take this view. Beyond intuition, however, we have to look at how transactions are played on specific fields and at certain times, with regard to specific publics, and how the existence of specific stadiums with their own observational arrangements shapes competitive exchanges.

Take space and time boundaries: the fact that transactions are bounded in time and space, and that these limits are visible for participants, endows transactions with distinctiveness and connectivity at the same time. In other words, by being able to tell when buying a handbag from a peddler has started and when it has ended, and where it took place, we are able not only to distinguish it from other social activities, but also to connect 'buying a handbag' with 'strolling on the boulevard'. We are also able to distinguish 'buying a handbag from a peddler' from 'buying a handbag from the Gucci store' on the same street. Not only that, but space and time boundaries let us separate and recognize elements of a transaction as economic or not.

An example of how boundaries work is provided by the research of Michèle de La Pradelle (1996), who has examined the working of a town market in southern France. Town markets have both spatial and temporal boundaries, partly legally codified and partly not. They can take place only on certain days of the week, between specific hours, and on specific streets. The displays of merchandise are spatially differentiated: better clothes are presented separately from cheaper ones, for instance. Making some goods more visible than others allows the sellers to deploy specific sales strategies, where the prices asked stand in direct relationship to the visibility of the merchandise. Even the (tacit) permission or interdiction to touch the goods tells something about their price and quality. All these distinctions (and many more) build up 'sales assemblages', which are effective in the interaction with buyers (de La Pradelle 1996, pp. 108, 110).[2]

Take here also the classic distinction between transactions for money, on the one hand, and gift exchange, on the other. This is a classic topic in the sociology and anthropology of economic life (see Mauss [1950] 1999, pp. 161–4). As the argument goes, economic transactions, when completed, do not imply any further reciprocal obligations. Gift exchanges imply a whole series of social obligations which are not legally codifiable, contribute to maintaining social ties, and have to do with honour (e.g. you have to return the gift, but not immediately and not the same object). In practice, however, there are situations when such distinctions are not clear cut at all: take the street selling of homeless newspapers, which is presented as an economic activity meant to support homeless sellers. Some buyers do not take back the change, or buy the newspaper and discard it without reading anything. How to distinguish here the gift from the economic transaction? And how to distinguish between situations when a gift might take place (the change can be kept) from the situation when no gift giving takes place? How to show gratitude for the gift as different from the grateful acknowledgment of the sale? It turns out that participants in such encounters can enact these distinctions in an orderly fashion (Llewellyn and Burrow 2008, pp. 574–6), and that this enactment is conditioned in part by the spatial and temporal boundaries of the transactions.[3] That is, transaction-relevant distinctions (with respect to price, to the status of change money) are neither given, nor mental constructs, nor intrinsic to the social structure (homeless seller v. passer-by), but enacted in the interaction-qua-transaction. The spatially and temporally bounded character of the interaction plays a crucial role with respect to such practised distinctions.

An example of social boundaries—this time related to mutual obligations—comes from the investigations of Karin Knorr Cetina and Urs Bruegger (2002): currency traders transacting online acknowledge and are expected to honour mutual obligations to sell and buy currency from each other, when one of them needs (i.e. is constrained) to conduct a specific transaction. Failure to do so is sanctioned. Mutual obligations, as well as their sanctioning, are not independent of the features of the conversation (conducted with the help of an online messaging system) which constitutes the transaction. Since the conversational system is a rapid one, requests for transactions have to be acknowledged as such and honoured within a very short interval. Failure to acknowledge a request leads to definitional interventions, which make the situation explicit. Failure to honour the request after a definitional intervention leads to sanctions, namely, exclusion from the conversational system. In this case, moral reciprocal obligations do not come from a formal code of conduct or from the institutional features of the system, but emerge as intrinsic to conversational transactions and as determined by their spatially and temporally bounded character. Sanctions (i.e. exclusion), too, are shaped by the bounded character of the transactions.

This highlights the role of social boundaries in legitimating financial transactions: they establish who will and who will not be entitled to enter a transaction. Social boundaries can be tied to criteria of wealth, religion, social or ethnic origin, or to professional memberships. They can be not only inscribed on the bodies of participants (including their skills), but also in their knowledge or in the artefacts they operate with. Institutional traders, for instance, wear not only distinctive garments and badges (Zaloom 2006, p. 61), but also possess specific bodily skills which allow them to transact with each other on the trading floor. They also have access to computer systems and interfaces to which day traders do not (although day traders trade in real time too). Historically seen, stock exchange brokers have very early formed status groups[4] who controlled access to financial transactions based on control of space, time, and socio-economic criteria (see also Preda [2005]).

We need not, however, go to the trading floor to find examples of how status boundaries work: back to our introductory example, the expensive fashion boutiques found in Venice and elsewhere control access not by imposing any explicit restrictions, but by setting up spatial boundaries in such a way as to let only certain people in. In fact, anthropological research indicates that high-end stores are designed in such a way as to keep customers out (Underhill 2004, p. 113), not in, while admitting only specific social categories, without ever saying it so explicitly.[5] For instance, in shopping malls most stores have open-spaced entrances which blur the boundary between hallway and store. High-end jewellery boutiques situated in malls, however, have clearly marked walls and doors (sometimes clad in expensive marble, contrasting with the glass walls of other stores), which work not only as a security measure, but also as a deterrent for undesired passers-by. The spatial arrangement of expensive fashion boutiques, too, is designed in such a way as to make only certain categories of customers feel at ease: the rarefied displays, the conspicuous absence of any sales attendants (who are there, but behave 'discreetly'), and the intended invisibility of price tags concur as control mechanisms for access. More recent ethnographic observations in such stores (Roeren 2008) suggest that they are purposively operated so as to create private spaces for customers (there are almost never several customers at once), where, for instance, the duty of the sales assistant is to always defer to the customer's opinion.

The boundaries which set up the ways of access to legitimate transactions also offer the possibility of attaching illegitimate ones to them: the park where a hotdog stand does legitimate business during the day can become the stage for dealing in illicit substances at night. The backroom of a legitimate barber-shop can become the place where illicit sexual services are bought and sold. Because the backstage (see Goffman [1959, p. 106]) of a legitimate business is not situated outside its boundaries, but it's not visible to the public either, it offers opportunities for illegitimate transactions, tolerated not only as an additional source of income, but also as a social arrangement accommodating reciprocal interests. In a similar manner, hustlers can be tolerated in front of legitimate shops because they can help chase shoplifters, circulate stories, and influence pedestrian behaviour (Venkatesh 2006, p. 198). Yet, the boundaries have to be respected: the park becomes a trading place for illicit substances only at night and only in certain areas; sexual favours are sold only in the backroom. Trespassing boundaries can lead to community interventions and to conflicts (see also Gambetta [1993, p. 199]). A neighbourhood can mobilize against gangs selling drugs in the public park during daylight, or can negotiate spatial and temporal limits for such activities; the backroom of a barbershop can be used for paid sexual encounters, but only under certain circumstances; hustlers can be allowed to solicit in front of certain shops, but only under certain conditions (Venkatesh 2006, pp. 153, 157, 203). Vending books on the sidewalk is not only a matter of regulation, but also a technology through which commercial activities situated in a legal limbo can be transformed, transferred into the domain of lawful transactions, and thus controlled. By allowing the selling of printed matter on the sidewalk, the New York City Council instituted a technology of controlling commercial activities undertaken by homeless people, transforming these into licit economic activities, restricted to specific city areas and to specific times (Duneier 1999, pp. 136–7).

Informational Surprises and the Interaction Order of Economic Transactions

Let us now return to the issue of information and knowledge, and address the second question formulated in the opening of this chapter, namely, the production of information in market transactions. When passing by a fashion boutique, when looking at the handbags displayed by a peddler on the pavement, or entering the boardroom at the start of acquisitions negotiations, we judge upon our perceptions according to past experiences. We take what we see as 'signals' that this is 'business as usual' and that our actions will be grounded in the orderliness of everyday life. Note here that this everyday life can be that of a corporate manager, used to boardrooms, or that of a tourist who had bought handbags from peddlers before. What we take as 'signals'—that is, the cries of a peddler, the marble-clad doorway of a fashion boutique, or the tailored suits of my negotiation partners—are judged and acted upon within the frame of ordinariness, or what Harvey Sacks calls 'doing being ordinary': 'seeing the usual in a scene…permits all kinds of routine ways of dealing with it' (Sacks 1995, p. 221). When some people enter a boutique door, they are seeing the usual in that action, while other people will not. When going into the boardroom, some people will do their usual routine. Those for whom entering boardrooms is not a routine will not usually go in there either. Seen in this perspective, boundaries work less as signals which alter beliefs or convey information (Spence 1974, p. 1), but as part of routines or as routine-enhancing arrangements. (It is rather improbable that looking at a door or a window will just suddenly alter beliefs.) Moreover, it is difficult to argue that boundaries would work as informational signals because they refer to significant 'unobservables' (Spence 1974, p. 107): from the perspective of participants, boundaries as routines refer to very observable activities.

What becomes informational is then not the boundary as such, but boundary breaching: crises which disrupt routines, generate uncertainties, and require non-routine interventions from the participants. In other words, information is triggered by those operations which effect transformations upon the relationships between transaction partners, including here the objects of transaction (Rawls 2008*b*, p. 79). A homeless person entering a fashion boutique, an unknown face in the boardroom, a blink on the trading screen, or an offer to pay in produce instead of in euros for a handbag are disruptions of various magnitudes, which impact upon the participants' relationships, even if for a short period. The production of relevant cues for further actions is triggered by such disruptions, which require cognitive processing.[6] An example of informational surprises as boundary breaches is the following: during the crisis events of August–October 2008, the German government publicly announced (on a Sunday) that it will fully guarantee savings deposits. This announcement angered the UK Treasury, for which it came as a surprise (apparently without any indication of it coming), because they feared that money would then migrate from partly guaranteed UK deposits to fully guaranteed German deposits. This surprise was represented as a breach of boundaries, in the sense that it ran counter to former agreements and it jeopardized a European response to the crisis (Wintour 2008). While the surprise can be seen differently (and with different consequences) from various perspectives (savers, bankers, governments), it constitutes information. Concerned groups and participants have to react to it. It creates a situation of uncertainty where a reaction is needed.

Generating uncertainties (aka disruptions of routines) cannot be separated from the practical actions of the transaction partners. They have first to be acknowledged as such—that is, as uncertainties—in a mutually intelligible manner by those involved in economic transactions. 'Mutually intelligible manner' means here that players use situational resources in order to interactively define what is going on as disruption, as something new and unexpected. It rests on the assumptions that: transaction partners assign the same kind of relevance to the interaction; appearance and intention of the interaction overlap; the transaction is recognizable as an instantiation of a larger category of actions; the relevance of the transaction will remain relatively constant throughout the interaction; and these characteristics of the transaction will not change if participants exchange positions (see also Garfinkel [1963, pp. 214–15]).

In other words, trust (as a background for disruptions) has a procedural dimension which is directly related to the properties exhibited by the interaction. Relevant properties here are given as follows: recognizability of the transaction as goods-for-money, recognizability of the intention to complete the transaction, and recognizability of the transaction as an instance of a broader category of transactions (i.e. economic as opposed to, say, family gifts). These properties cannot be fully identified prior to the transaction: they are intrinsic to the sequential character of economic interactions. At the same time, they can be relevant, in the sense that uncertainties can be produced in relationship to them at any sequence in the transaction. It is in this process that information emerges as practical operations of establishing, acknowledging, and glossing[7] upon disruptions of routine activities. These practical operations, however, involve the cognitive responses of participants: they involve observations (look at that!), classifications (what is this?), definitions (this is event A), and recollections (is this like what we have seen in situation B?), among others.

For instance, a transaction cannot be recognized from the start as goods-for-money; this becomes clear only further in the interaction. Think here of the confusion between family chores as an obligation, on the one hand, and paying a younger family member for such chores, on the other. One can ask a younger family member to mow the lawn as an obligation, or one can offer money for this activity. The character of mowing the lawn (obligation or transaction) is established first in the interaction and depends on procedural trust. The potentially informational character of the latter is relevant in the sense that (*a*) it can influence the completion and the outcome of the transaction; (*b*) it allows economic actors to engage in transactions where institutional features of trust are absent; and (*c*) it is ethically binding, in the sense that actors engaging in a transaction are obliged to stick to its sequential organization.[8] This does not mean that one and the same activity cannot be defined in different ways within different interactions involving exactly the same participants. One day, mowing the lawn can be requested as a family obligation, and the next day it can be defined as paid work by exactly the same participants, who should be able to account for this change when challenged to do so.

Seen in this perspective, there is no conflict between procedural trust and information. Procedural trust actually supports, rather than inhibits the production of information in transactions. I can engage in a bargaining sequence with a yet-to-be-determined result (the informational surprise) exactly on the basis of this procedural trust. At the same time, procedural trust itself can be a source of informational surprises. For instance, when procedural incongruence becomes evident in the sequences of a transaction, this latter can be interrupted. Procedural incongruence can also lead to re-footing (see also Goffman [1981, p. 128]) economic transactions as something different (for instance, as gift giving, or as kinship-related duties).

This explains why and how market transactions can take place between total strangers, in situations where institutional features of trust are absent. The handbag peddlers on Venice's fashion drag (and elsewhere) are a case in point here. While there is no legal or institutional guarantee for such transactions (no sales receipt, no warranty certificate, no registration of the peddler with the Italian chamber of commerce, etc.), passers-by continue to buy handbags from them. They do so because initiating a transaction implies entering a series of ethical obligations irreducible to an abstract, universal normative system, namely, the obligation to proceed to the next step of the transaction in a mutually intelligible fashion. It is this obligation which provides participants with their basic source of trust, and its violations constitute as many informational occasions. A procedural breach can act as an indication that appearance and intention do not overlap, and may lead participants to break the transaction sequence or revise their expectations. From this perspective, economic transactions always imply a 'division of moral labor' (Goffman 1970, p. 131): they cannot work without reciprocal commitments contained in the mutually shared definition of their action. Because of this division of labour, repairs, shifts, and re-footings are always possible: for instance, when redefining household chores not as a family obligation, but as paid work, or vice versa. It is from here that economic transactions get their connectivity—that is, their capacity to link in with non-economic social interactions, such as family life, for instance.

This is also why con artists invest so much in maintaining procedural trust, and go to great lengths in achieving the overlap between appearance and intention, while providing for the possibility of detection (see also Garfinkel [1967, p. 137]). In the recent case of a con woman who swindled £400,000 worth of antiques and jewellery from Parisian dealers, the woman 'appeared to be convincing—they were persuaded that she was their usual type of affluent customer' (Weaver 2008). She had jewellery delivered on train platforms at railway stations, avoiding thus address identification. According to reports, even when her cheques bounced, the dealers insisted in sending invoices, on the assumption that she will pay. It appears that in such cases procedural trust—the con woman looking and acting as 'the usual type' of rich customer—plays a seminal role in trying to deny informational surprises. The jewellers took bounced cheques as 'mistakes', 'temporary difficulties', and the like, and continued requesting that she fulfils the moral obligations implied by the transaction. Or take another recent, though much more cunning con artist: 'the talented Mr. Madoff' (Creswell and Thomas 2009). According to reports, Bernard Madoff, who operated a Ponzi scheme (disguised as a money management firm) for over 40 years, causing $65 billion in losses to his clients, took great care to present himself as an 'elder statesman', a crusader for the small investor, cultivating Washington regulators and preaching prudence.

Information in Transactions and in Experiments

We can also think of market transactions by analogy with a scientific lab where discoveries are made: in the lab, discoveries are made starting with information—that is, with disruptions of routine observations. Seeing the same data again and again is not informative in itself, except when it is taken as a disruption of the measuring instruments (and in this case produces process-relevant information). Seeing data disruptions is the starting point for producing information; this 'seeing', however, is a cognitive operation which cannot be separated from interactions. The discovery of a new pulsar, for instance, is the stabilization of a cultural object 'extracted from a succession of observational runs with the optical and electronic equipment' (Lynch 1992, pp. 248–9). In this sense, scientific cultures are ensembles of conditions that 'allow the generation of unprecedented events' (Rheinberger 1997, p. 140).

Moreover, scientific laboratories are structured in such a way as to generate uncertainties in a systematic, controlled fashion: participants in a scientific experiment, for instance, do not expect any kind of uncertainties, but only specific classes, the boundaries of which are carefully maintained. We should not forget here that a primary task in a scientific experiment is to keep 'impurities' (i.e. random uncertainties) out. The spatial and temporal boundaries of scientific experiments, for instance, are set in such a manner as to filter impurities out. This does not mean, of course, that impurities cannot seep in and challenge the results of the experiment; nevertheless, by orienting themselves towards certain classes of uncertainties, participants in a lab experiment already perform cognitive operations (such as classifications) which limit the production of information. While scientific assemblages are specifically and purposively geared towards the production of uncertainties (and hence of information), the same cannot always be said about market assemblages. Yet, uncertainties emerge all the time in market transactions, in a fashion not dissimilar to that of the lab. These uncertainties create information, which in its turn cannot be separated from the cognitive activities of the participants.

Perhaps a better comparison here would be that among scientific discovery, ritual gift exchanges,[9] and market transactions. Scientific laboratories are arrangements geared towards producing disruptions, and hence information. Ritual gift exchange can be situated at the opposite end of the spectrum: it is anchored in carefully orchestrated routines (e.g. Bourdieu 1980, p. 172) and geared towards keeping surprises (i.e. information) at bay. Infringement of routines is socially sanctioned (through loss of honour, or social stigmatization, among others). Market exchanges are situated somewhere in the middle: while not specifically geared towards the production of uncertainties as an aim in itself, they are not specifically geared towards keeping uncertainties at bay either, in the way ritual gift exchange is.

Compared with the scientific experiment (see Figure 1.1), the boundaries of ritual exchanges (time, place, setting, participating actors, and audiences) are also carefully set. However, ritual gift exchanges cannot keep all impurities (for instance, accidents) out. What ritual exchanges do is process even random uncertainties in a ritual fashion: an unforeseen event, like the gift giver tripping over during a gift-giving sequence will be seen as a bad omen, as a menace to the social ties among the participants, as the fury of insulted gods, etc. Market exchanges do not keep random uncertainties (or unwanted information) out in the way scientific experiments do. Nor do they process these uncertainties in a fashion similar to that of ritual exchanges, by ascribing them to the domain of the sacred, for instance (although there can be plenty of ritual in market transactions too). Because they do not have recourse to such solutions, market transactions always are confronted with the problem of distinguishing between relevant classes of uncertainties, on the one hand, and irrelevant uncertainties, on the other (what economic theory calls noise—see, for instance, Shleifer 2000, p. 12). These distinctions, however, cannot take place outside the interaction sequences which produce information. Lacking the preparatory cognitive operations of the scientific experiment, as well as the reductive possibilities of ritual exchanges (not everything

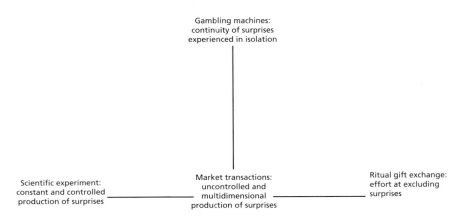

Figure 1.1 The production of informational surprises

can be reduced to the will of gods, or spirits), market transactions would be then faced with more informational challenges: using the resources of the situation, and in the interaction, they would have to establish the types of informational surprises and their consequentiality. Maybe not all poorly clad women entering a fashion boutique will be curious tourists; some may be eccentric heiresses, and need to be treated as such. But this cannot be entirely deduced from attire; this can be established only in interaction. Moreover, the mere act of somebody entering such a boutique without looking like a fashionable person can constitute an informational surprise for the sales staff; this is part of the interaction and will be dealt with in further interaction sequences. The surprise, then, is not preset with respect to the interaction chain, but intrinsic to it. If the sales staff are used to the eccentric billionaire coming to shop in flip flops, this will be no surprise to them—it is one of their routines.

It follows from the above that the notion of information as generated by uncertainties should not be understood as restricted only to large-scale uncertainties—that is, to so-called 'events which shake the world'. On a world scale, informational uncertainties can be quite small. On a situational scale, however, they can be quite big. Nor should it be understood that, once information is cognitively processed (i.e. in further interaction steps) and routines crystallize, no new information can be generated. Since interaction steps unfold sequentially, processing informational surprises at one step does not preclude that further surprises will be generated within the sequence. For instance, it may come as a surprise that the dishevelled person in front of the sales clerk in the high-end boutique is actually a billionaire, but this does not preclude a further surprise such as the loss of the wallet (and the incapacity to pay). Therefore, the order in which informational surprises are generated, their number and quality are not preset with respect to the interaction order. This highlights the fact that, by definition, information will be imperfect (see also Rawls [2008b, p. 69]): there can always be outcomes transactions partners do not know about (Oh, I forgot my wallet home!). Imperfect information then is not a matter of the actors' limited cognitive capabilities, of limited access to sources, of biased interpretation of signals, or of actors withholding information from each other (see also Akerlof [2002, p. 413]). Informational asymmetries are intrinsic to the interaction order of economic transactions.

Price Discoveries in Market Interactions

Continuing the investigation of the second question from this chapter's opening, it is now time to turn to a couple of concrete examples in order to see how informational surprises work. At the same time, some of these examples already introduce and deal with the third of the opening's questions, namely, price discoveries and decisions. A distinction introduced earlier was that among transactional encounters, engagements, and platform perform-ances. We can find examples of transactional encounters in natural as well as in synthetic situations. In natural situations, street sales come immediately to mind. In synthetic situations, online anonymous transactions such as those of day traders are an appropriate example.

In street sales of homeless newspapers (see Llewellyn and Burrow [2008, pp. 573, 575]), for instance, the price of the newspaper is set in such a way as to restrict the chances of the buyer having exact change. This leaves two possibilities: the seller handing back the change, or the buyer telling the seller to keep it. If the change is given back, it is part of an economic transaction. If the buyer tells the seller to keep the change, it will be a gift exchange (not a tip, since there is no service involved) and has to be acknowledged as such. However, this is not known before the corresponding step in the interaction sequence. The act of taking the change back (as in an economic transaction) or leaving it with the seller (as in a gift exchange), respectively, has to be first established and acknowledged as such in the interaction. Such a transaction (buying a homeless newspaper) can have a dual character (economic and symbolic), yet this can never be established in advance, but only in the unfolding of the interaction, and marked by conversational sequences, together with body language. Such conversational sequences (i.e. telling the seller to keep the change) in their turn have to be constructed and acknow-ledged as informational surprises—which they also are. While such informa-tional surprises can also be ritually staged (the seller has a specific bodily and conversational repertoire with which s/he acknowledges the gift), it is never-theless a surprise, since it cannot be established a priori. Therefore, the character of an apparently very simple transaction emerges first on the basis of information—that is, of an uncertainty created and processed in the interaction.

Market transactions can present very similar informational characteristics, this time not in relationship to the character of the transaction, but in relationship with the process of price discovery—that is, of establishing the moment and the conditions under which the transaction will take place. A transaction is always a chain of interaction sequences—it can begin with the customer examining the merchandise, or stopping by, or just glancing in passing at the wares (as it happens with our Venetian handbag sellers), and end with goodbyes after the money has been counted or change has been given back. Yet, at the start of this chain it is never clear whether the transaction will actually take place and if yes, how (a potential customer may walk away or buy something unexpected). Here comes price discovery in play, something which has long preoccupied economists. Price discovery means attaining a price level at which the transaction will take place (which, in more general terms, means that supply meets demand). In interaction terms, this means attaining a turn in the conversation where one of the partners asks the other to finish the transaction sequence, and this request is accepted. In other words, one of the transaction partners asks the other to *anticipate* the end of the transaction, and the other agrees to this anticipation. In bargaining, this works by producing price-relevant informational surprises (they can also be related to the quantity or to the quality of the product, or to the persons involved). In some transactions, price discovery cannot even be a discovery of prices. In upmarket art galleries, potential buyers are not expected to look at price lists or to enquire about prices, on the principle that 'if you ask how much the painting is, then you cannot afford it' (Coslor 2009). Nevertheless, price discoveries in the sense of anticipating sequence completion are encountered in these environments as well.

A study of bargaining in Chinese street markets, for instance (Orr 2007, pp. 80–1), shows that the prices uttered by the sellers do not work as a signal or information for the buyer, but only as a cue for initiating the conversational production of 'price surprises', which work as real information. A response to a question like 'how much are the earrings?' is taken as a starting point for a sequence in which a 'price surprise' is generated (e.g. $45 instead of $80); this surprise, in its turn, works as the point from where the closure of the transaction can be anticipated. Since the closure of the transaction cannot be anticipated at the start of the interaction, information appears here as a relevant point in the sequence, starting from which uncertainties can be processed.

This is not dissimilar from the ways in which manufacturers of industrial goods price their products. While there are price lists, they serve only as an orienting tool in negotiating prices—that is, for formulating concrete offers to specific customers. These offers are established in managerial meetings, where sales representatives, accountants, and pricing analysts, among others, try to evaluate the relevance of their competitors and the possibilities of gaining new orders (i.e. taking business away from competitors) based on a 'special price'. At the same time, perceptions of status and prestige play a role in debating whether to lower the price or not (Zbaracki and Bergen 2009, p. 18).

In synthetic encounters such as online trading, participants are anonymous with respect to each other and cannot engage in conversational exchanges. Here, traders sitting in front of their screens must scan the data displays looking for uncertainties which can generate surprises (see Preda [2009*a*]). Trading screens appear as arrangements of blinking cells; price and quantity data change several times per second. The blinking in itself cannot be informational here. They may constitute signals in the sense of Harold Garfinkel's 'sensory stimuli which are by definition meaningless' (Rawls 2008*b*, p. 67), but not as attributes conveying information. Information is constituted by observational surprises—that is, by unexpected displays on the screens. Unexpected means here not only that some new data may appear to which traders can relate their positions, but also that some data may be too persistent on the screen. In order to make sense of this, traders often engage verbally with their unseen counterparts in the manner called by Erving Goffman response cries—that is, vocalizations which align traders to the events unfolding on the screen (Goffman 1981, p. 100). Such vocalizations can express surprises in emotional form (more about which in the next section); they can acknowledge the offer of an unseen partner as right or they can reject it. Price data becomes information from the point where it is related to an uncertainty (What's this? What does this guy want?), requiring cognitive processing (observations, classifications, comparisons, calculations) which may lead to action. This cognitive processing, in its turn, cannot be separated from interactions with the screen, such as vocalizations and (sometimes) conversations with unseen, unknown traders.

A similar mode of generating surprises in online trading is reported from the world of professional traders as well (Siu 2008, pp. 117–18). In China, professional futures traders organize 'gang battles': they rent rooms in hotels and equip them with computer terminals, trading from there. A key aspect of the battle (aka cornering the market for a specific group of futures contracts) is to confuse opponents about the traders' identity and actions, and to create permanent on-screen surprises.

If we are to compare face to face with synthetic market encounters, a first distinction would be that in face-to-face transactions the possibilities for informational surprises seem to be fewer. Such transactions can and do produce surprises but, like in a controlled experiment, noise is kept at bay by an array of social routines. For instance, we expect sellers in shops to be minimally trained and to play specific institutional roles in the same way in which we expect handbag sellers on Venetian streets to be ready to bargain. We expect shops to have a certain degree of material stability—walls stay in place, decoration and merchandise will not suddenly and radically change while we are shopping. By contrast, in synthetic transactions noise cannot be easily kept at bay by social routines. Some kinds of synthetic transactions tend to minimize the amount of noise they let in: buying a book or a plane ticket on the Internet is not subject to many informational surprises. This, however, is not always the case: Internet search engines which compare goods are geared towards such surprises. For instance, flight comparison sites work with changing prices, and the true price cannot be seen before initiating the transaction. Other sites offer goods at 'surprise prices', which can be seen only from the point when the transaction has been initiated. eBay works as an informational marketplace, in the sense that it is geared towards the constant generation of informational surprises (see also Smith [2007]).

Synthetic situations such as online trading are highly informational: they are geared towards constantly generating surprises. Consequently, we can distinguish here among different degrees of transaction informationality, according to the amount of uncertainty generated during the transaction: the higher this amount, the more informational the transaction will be. The informational character of a transaction has consequences for the kinds of social relationships it is anchored in—this will be discussed in more detail in the following sections.

Turning now to transactional engagements, we can highlight here, based on empirical studies, how informational surprises are generated in high-end fashion boutiques, and in online currency transactions, respectively. In high-end fashion boutiques, clients know they are not supposed to pay any attention to the price labels (which are not made visible). Ethnographic observations suggest that clients rarely enquire about the price and prefer to check the label discreetly, when they think sales clerks are not looking (Roeren 2008, p. 34). Any attempts on the part of customers to bargain about the price will be frowned upon by sales clerks; clients can be sent away with words like 'we are not a bazaar here'. Boundary-wise, however, fashion boutiques work as private spaces in the midst of public environments. The sales clerks are expected to treat clients as if the latter were moving within their own private space (be unobtrusive but ready to help at any time, carry clothes and handbags around for customers, always accept that the customer is right, etc.). Interactional ambiguity related to the dual character of boutiques (as private spaces v. public environments) plays a significant role with respect to concluding transactions, in the sense that, if customers were treated as being in a public environment, they would walk away. Treating customers as being in a private space, however, generates informational surprises: there are situations where, for instance, customers walk out of the dressing room and into the store naked, going to displays in order to pick up new items (Roeren 2008, p. 23). Sales clerks have to deal with such a surprise in an appropriate manner—that is, by keeping the ambiguity between public and private (i.e. telling the customer that this shouldn't be done while keeping the private character of the space). In this situation, the customers' behaviour generates information which can be critical with respect to completing the transaction.

Another, perhaps even more relevant aspect here is how to generate informational surprises in conversations with clients so as to anticipate the closure of the transaction. Not all visitors of high-end fashion boutiques will buy an item; at the same time, boutiques can survive only if at least some visitors buy. Sales clerks cannot ask directly: a question like 'are you going to buy this?' would be permissible in a normal store, but is out of question in a high-end boutique. Neither can sales clerks follow customers through the store, since the logic of the entire space is that of privacy. Clerks, however, use conversational exchanges initiated by customers to anticipate transaction closures: in these exchanges, informational surprises can be generated by both sides. For instance, while the client is trying an item in the fitting room, sales clerks would go round through the store and gather items which might go with the one the customer is trying, then present the items to the customer while she is in the fitting room. These informational surprises work as starting points for conversations in which occasions for anticipating transactional closure are generated. Moreover, informational surprises in this case multiply the possibilities for transactional closure (the new items represent new transaction possibilities). In their turn, customers generate informational surprises by telling sales clerks about what other fashion items they've got at home, so that the clerks can, by using this cue, participate in conversations where they try to anticipate transactional closure. In this case, price discovery does not take place by producing surprises about this data, but about the parties involved in the transaction. Whereas in encounters this rarely takes place (due, among others, to their limited duration), in engagements surprises about partners seem to play a much more important role.

Labour markets include situations similar to those of high-end boutiques, in the sense that not price, but personal surprises are the item to start with. The most important thing for head-hunters is to build up portfolios of names—individuals who can be persuaded to leave their companies and take jobs with the competition (see Finlay and Coverdill [2002, pp. 96–7]). Some companies do not want to give away the names of their employees. In other instances, it is difficult to find out concrete names because of the sheer size and complexity of the organizations being head-hunted. Head-hunters have developed ruses and strategies to get personal names,[10] for instance, by cold calling the targeted company and pretending to be a firm who wants to put an order requiring specific skills from a specific department in the targeted company.

Another instance, although in the reverse, can be found in synthetic situations such as online currency trading. In their ethnography of foreign exchange markets, Karin Knorr Cetina and Urs Bruegger (2002, pp. 927–8) highlight the fact that currency traders engage with each other based not only on swapping stories and reciprocally drawing attention to events (which can be seen as gift exchange), but also on the expectation that, when asked, traders will honour an unspoken obligation to sell or buy from each other specific amounts of currency at set prices. If this unspoken commitment is not honoured, the culprits will be excluded from a trader's circle of partners. The ability to honour a trading request even in adverse circumstances (i.e. which may entail losses for the challenged trader) can also be seen as a feature of gameworthiness, one which entitles traders to be part of the playing team. Thus, traders are caught between pursuing self-interest (increasing their profitable trades) and accepting less profitable trades (or even losses) when challenged on their gameworthiness. Currency trading, thus, has both ritual and instrumental features. The first are required by maintaining reciprocal obligations, generated by the play of the game, while the latter are required by making a profit. Yet, profits cannot be made without maintaining game-worthiness; traders are sometimes put in situations where these obligations have to be readjusted. The readjustment is triggered by informational surprises, such as when a trader refuses to honour a request to trade. Price discovery, in this case, depends on relational readjustments, which cannot be foreseen, but have to be discovered while initiating a transaction. While the solicited price may be set (the trader making the request needs to sell at that price), it will not be realized until a willing trader is found. In this case, price discovery depends on information about the counterpart, information which is not obtainable in advance (I cannot know whether trader A will accept my request until I ask him). As in the case of high-end boutiques, in honour requests the transaction depends on relational information produced during the transaction itself:

1. OK tks anything in 3 M DEM
2. # Sorry ntg there friend
3. srry???????? ever heard from
4. reciprocity ????????
5. ? if u won't quote I will cancel previous deal
6. # Mom
7. # Really sorry but ntg in DEM for the mom so noth. done in CHF frnds
8. consider this relations as finished Bibib
9. # Interrupt #
10. # End # (Knorr Cetina and Bruegger 2002, pp. 927–8).

The above excerpt illustrates the transactional features discussed in this section: the request for an anticipation of closure (line 1), followed by negation, and then by surprise (line 3), redefinition of the transaction as a moral obligation (line 4), and then a challenge on gameworthiness (line 5). After a second denied request for anticipation of closure, effort, and repeated negation (revealing the trader's inability to prove himself gameworthy), the business relationship is defined as a non-relationship. Note here that relationships are neither taken as granted nor as something independent of the interaction: they need to be tagged as such by fulfilling requests for closure. Traders send reciprocal reminders about the fragility of their relationships, and about their dependence on requests and challenges.

Market transactions as dramatic performances presuppose an audience in front of which information is generated and price discovery is performed. Auctions are here perhaps the classic example: price discovery is performed in front of an (closed) audience, and the witnessability of the process is a key condition of its validity. Witnessability, however, superposes on anonymity: even if bidders in the room are seen, their identity is not announced. Bidders can also remain anonymous, bidding over telephone or sending an agent to the auction floor. Even in such cases, the witnessability of the bids remains crucial. This means that, at any given time, there must be an audience witnessing the price discovery process, which consists of sequences in which players take turns at announcing their bids. The witnessability of the social interaction itself is intrinsic to the price discovery process (Heath and Luff 2007), and cannot be maintained without producing informational surprises which draw the public's attention to the changes produced in price data. Witnessable informational surprises, in their turn, require a specialized role: an auctioneer who coordinates bid sequences and makes them visible to the audience, through bodily movements as well as through verbal announcements. This is why a major task of the auctioneer is to keep a 'two at a time' order throughout the auctioning sequences. At no point are more than two bids made witnessable to the audience: an immediately past bid, and a response (the information) to this past turn. The witnessability of these surprises must include their origin—that is, the participants uttering the bids. Auctioneers solve this problem either by pointing to the bid's origin, or by announcing the bidder's invisible presence (on the phone or through an agent—see Heath and Luff 2007, p. 70). The price discovery process here—that is, the price at which, say, a work of art will be sold—depends on producing informational surprises, namely, data increments which cannot be known in advance. While the starting point of price sequences is provided by estimates made by experts and included in auction catalogues, such estimates—doubtlessly important—cannot determine the price discovery process—that is, neither the magnitude, nor the sequence of increments, nor where the sequence will end.

TV sales, in their turn, can be staged differently: performers showing the properties of the product in question can take turns at being the audience for each other, while jointly performing at the same time for the TV public. During this, decreasing quantities available from that product are inserted on the screen, showing an ever restricted availability. The sellers' performance is geared towards informational surprises (did we ever know that the frying pan was capable of doing A and B?), while availability constitutes in itself an additional surprise.

All in all, across the forms of transactions-qua-interactions discussed here (see also Table 1.1), we can distinguish between at least two modalities in which price discovery takes place:

1. A self-referential modality, in which price data itself act as informational surprises. This is the modality of the auction, of online anonymous trading, and of street markets. It also appears to be the modality of pricing industrial goods in managerial meetings.

2. A second modality, in which price data cannot constitute a surprise. Here, informational surprises about participants and availability appear to be

consequential with respect to price discovery. It is the modality of shop engagements and of TV shows. Of course, there are also hybrid forms such as the 'hard sell' (Clark and Pinch 1995), where transactions are staged in front of a live audience, and sellers continuously produce surprises about the price (they will lower it), availability (very limited quantities will be always available), and participants (recruiting members of the audience as co-performers, eliciting personal information, and the like).

When talking about information as surprises, we cannot ignore the role played by emotions in generating them. I will now turn to examining the link between emotions, action, and market transactions. With that, I continue examining the third question of the opening, about how decisions are made in transactions.

Information, Market Interactions, and Emotions

While the impact of emotions in economic life has been debated for decades, their role and place in transactions is less than clear; neither is it entirely clear what is meant by emotions. If we understand them as attachment or desire, then we go back to issues like beliefs and values, which create structures of emotional attachment. In this perspective, then, emotions are intrinsic to our orientation to the world, including objects of economic exchanges and transaction partners. This lies at the core of Simmel's argument that money (which as a medium of exchange is apparently completely objectified and detached from the self) makes possible the crystallization of subjectivity and individuality

Table 1.1 Market interactions and informational surprises

	Face-to-face situations	Synthetic situations
Encounters	Definition-related surprises (market v. gift exchange) Price surprises	Stability-related surprises Price surprises
	Spatially and temporally well defined	
Engagements	Partner-related surprises Status-related surprises Price surprises Witnessability (public or private)	Relational surprises Status-related surprises
	Less well-defined boundaries Can overlap with other social activities	
Platform performances	Witnessability (public) Price surprises Availability surprises	Witnessability (public) Availability
	Dramaturgical actions in front of public; can have an iterative character	

(Simmel [1901] 1989, pp. 607–8). This means that money, exactly because of its objectivity (which Simmel compares with that of the intellect) allows the orientation of the self to the outer world; it is a medium through which the will is 'filled in' with content (I want that). Thus, any economic transaction would have, in Simmel's words, not only an intellectual (i.e. calculative) component, but also an emotional one (because the self attaches itself to the world through transactions).

This argument can be seen as resonating with Max Weber's more general argument that capitalism has not only a calculative component, provided by relentless rationalization, but also a charismatic component, given by capitalist figures, as well as by certain types of transactions (Weber [1921] 1972, p. 378). For instance, figures of grand capitalists, as well as activities like financial speculation, exert a special fascination with the public and have a clear emotional appeal. In his turn, Thorstein Veblen ([1899] 1994) has shown how certain patterns of consumption, displayed in public, create not only lifestyles (including an emotional component), but also contribute thus to social stratification. This has been highlighted by a large number of consumption studies (for an overview, see Zelizer 2005b), which show how consuming economic goods creates and reproduces a variety of social relationships (e.g. family ties, friendships, community relations).

However, in order to see how emotions intervene in market transactions in a more specific way we need a more precise definition than simple attachment. Here, things become really complicated. Emotions have been sometimes associated with lack of rational judgement, with impulse, affects, and cognitive biases in decision-making during transactions (e.g. Lo and Repin 2002; Peterson 2007; Ricciardi 2008, p. 104). In relationship to financial markets, for instance, emotions are often reduced to fear and greed, without paying much attention to how something like, say, greed, can be made mutually intelligible in transactions. Sometimes, in organizational research, emotions are seen as boredom, pride, anger, or love (Flam 2002, p. 101). The additional issue of trust complicates the matter here (why should we accept to transact with somebody we recognize as greedy), as does the issue of extreme forms of behaviour (e.g. financial panics). At the other end of the spectrum, we encounter sociological positions on emotions which see them as 'trust, confidence, optimism, and their opposites of distrust and pessimism' (Pixley 2004, p. 44), or as interests (Pixley 2002, p. 73).

Against the background of this very broad spectrum of human attitudes and interactions, it has been pointed out that emotions are physical, not psychological states, and as such to be distinguished from trust and risk, which are matters of perception (Berezin 2005, pp. 110–11). Since market transactions (be they face to face or synthetic) require the bodily engagement of participants, we can examine how emotions intervene here and to what effects (including their role in price discovery processes). The argument goes like this: while emotions are neurophysiological changes experienced by participants in economic transactions, the individual experience of such changes needs to be cognitively processed and made mutually intelligible in the interaction. Without cognitive processing, mere physiological changes cannot be made sense of (am I having a heart attack or am I excited because I won the game?). This processing requires acts, categories, operations, and definitions which are mutually intelligible and can be used by participants in the situation to coordinate their actions and to establish common points of attention. They can be used, among others, to underscore the surprise character of something happening in front of participants—that is, to draw attention to information being produced. Moreover, since emotions themselves are not foreseeable, they constitute informational surprises, working thus as preannouncements of uncertainties. With that, emotions can provide a starting point for further cognitive operations, in which transaction participants cooperate in projecting further actions which process the surprise.

Seen in this perspective, there is no clear cut distinction between cognition and emotion in market transactions, in the sense that the latter cannot be seen as the antithesis of the former (see also Strack and Deutsch [2004]). What happens is rather that at least in certain situations emotions and cognitive activities build an interactional ensemble of practical operations, which shape the constitution of information. An example in this sense is provided by Stefan Laube (2008a), who examines the interactions of brokers on a European stock exchange. Brokers trading in one large room in front of the screens utter imprecations, shout words like 'in plus!', 'in minus!', or vocalize on a regular basis, without these being addressed to any particular person. Swear words or vocalizations like 'hoooi!' and 'oooh!' clearly signify arousal, and this arousal itself constitutes an informational surprise for the other brokers present in the room. By processing this uncertainty (why oooh?) brokers prefigure new informational surprises, and prepare thus the ground on which these will be dealt with. In this sense, emotions constitute meta-information—that is, information about the information to be produced.

In some situations, adjacent brokers concur in uttering 'alert cries' meant to draw the attention of the entire audience to the changes happening on the screen. In such cases, the conversational rules of turn taking (Sacks, Schegloff, and Jefferson 1974) are not followed: brokers utter cries in unison, reciprocally confirming the information. This is indicative of a collective awareness (see also Heath et al. [2002]) to the production of information about market transitions (for instance, to sudden drops in prices). In such cases, price discovery is produced collaboratively: for instance, by using tonality and voice modulations in their alert cries, brokers indicate when the price is going up or down.

This, however, is not all. In situations when securities prices fall, traders need to sell in order to avoid taking even bigger losses, since they do not know whether and when the price of a specific security will go up again. But selling is not that easy, especially when a security has been held for a longer time. In such situations, traders use insults, cries, and curses as tools for defining and conducting their selling. Utterances like 'f**k!', 'ooh', 'it hurts', 'I'm so sick' are intrinsic to the traders' decisions to sell a specific security (Laube 2008b, pp. 39–40). They are not irrational moments of arousal, but thoroughly rational response cries and glosses, which define the traders' bodily anchoring in and physiological experience of the market in a given situation, orienting them towards specific actions. A loss will be experienced as physiological pain, and the traders' response cries to such experiences are part of the ways in which they define the situation, acting accordingly. Experiences of pain can be justified post hoc as thoroughly rational, in the sense that they orient traders away from even bigger losses.

Thus, emotions on the trading floor do not appear as irrational outbursts which impede cognitive functions and rational decision-making, but rather as interactional accomplishments (see also Wilkinson and Kitzinger [2006]) which enable cognitive operations, as well as the projection of further courses of action. The discovery of prices does not appear as taking place according to a pre-set plan, but rather as specific sequences in interaction chains, sequences produced in the collaborative work of brokers.

We can compare here the role of emotions on the trading floor with emotions in gambling interactions. Gambling machines, for instance, are designed in such a way as to multiply the stakes of a bet: nickel games will be multiplied in ways unforeseeable by the player (Schull 2005, p. 69). Additionally, players do not know the outcome of any particular game. Seen in this way, gamblers are confronted with at least two kinds of informational surprises: one given by the stakes they have in any particular game, and the other by the outcome of the game. But since gambling machines are also designed in a way which insulates players from the environment and encourages them to play several rounds, the emotions shown by players are related to issues of attachment and of motoric coordination with the machine. For instance, players can be pleased or excited if they get the feeling of abandonment to the rhythms of the machine (Schull 2005, pp. 77–8). The informational outcomes (winning or losing) do not count as much as the material coordination with the gambling machine (Schull 2006, p. 234). Since the machine announces, as well as defines the informational surprise (win or loss, and how much), and since players are aware that outcomes depend on a randomizing programme, they do not relate to other, seen or unseen partners, in the way in which they would do in a transaction. While in machine-supported gambling experiences emotions seem to support the players' isolation and engagement in an alternative world, in financial transactions emotions serve to stabilize cognitive operations and make them mutually intelligible.

This has important consequences for understanding the ways in which phenomena like volatility are produced in financial markets: the interactional resources of price discovery may have a general character, but the combination of these resources is situation specific. Moreover, since price discovery as an interactional achievement is not plannable or foreseeable, it follows that market players will discover prices (by generating informational surprises) at different moments in the interaction. Consequently, they will react to these discoveries at different moments, generating thus further surprises for other actors, and therefore further price movements. Imagining a number of situations on trading floors where groups of traders trade at once, no matter how similar these floors may be, traders will make discoveries at different moments in their respective interaction chains. Their reactions to these discoveries will be perceived as surprises on other trading floors, triggering reactions, which in their turn will be seen as surprises, and so on. This helps us understand how price volatility emerges as an interactional phenomenon, even when the arrangements for trading are very similar, when traders have access to the same kind of data and the same technologies, or when they share the same 'interpretive frames'. Since trading is an eminently situational phenomenon, organized sequentially and depending on the production of informational surprises, volatility is an inherent effect of this arrangement.

This also helps us better understand the difference between financial markets and other kinds of markets, which are not characterized by price volatility to the same extent. I have argued in the previous paragraphs that some markets are more informational than others, depending on the number and the kind of surprises they are geared to generate. Financial markets are probably the most informational, in the sense that their interaction arrangements are geared towards continuously generating surprises. This dovetails with seeing markets as scopic systems and as trading in information (Korr Cetina 2005, p. 42), which would not be possible if information were reduced to signals and to uncertainty reduction.

While interactions are the basic format of market transactions, the interaction forms discussed in the previous sections have various length and durability. While an encounter with a street peddler takes only a couple of minutes, a boardroom negotiation will go for hours and perhaps continue over dinner. While buyers of fake handbags change all the time, participants in the negotiations to buy a bank, for instance, can remain the same over weeks and months. This interactional length and durability points towards the emergence of anchored relationships from interactions—that is, of iterable formats involving the same participants who acknowledge a 'framework of mutual knowing, which retains, organizes, and applies the experience the ends have of one another' (Goffman 1971, p. 189). The next chapter examines the links between market transactions, on the one hand, and various kinds of anchored relationships, on the other.

☐ NOTES

1. Appresentation is a concept initially formulated by the German philosopher Edmund Husserl (1995, p. 112) and designates the fusion of perception and representation. Computer technologies have an appresentational character: for instance, when using instant messaging I do not see my conversation partner, but nevertheless perceive her as co-present, due to the fact that she reacts to my conversational turns.

2. This situation bears certain resemblance with the social organization of the Moroccan bazaar, as examined by Clifford Geertz (Geertz, Geertz, and Rosen 1979). The spatial differentiation of the bazaar (with different alleys for spice, clothing, footwear, and so on) appears, among others, as a means for the circulation of gossip, the reciprocal observations of traders, and for adjustments among them.

3. A similar situation is analyzed by Peter Bearman (2005, p. 173) with respect to the Christmas tip received by doormen in New York City. The tip can be defined as a gift, but also as lump payment for the services performed by the payee for the payer over the year. The ways in which this definition is achieved depends upon the situational features of the interaction.

4. The notion of status groups, analyzed among others by Max Weber, designates groups based on a common 'appreciation of honour' (Weber [1921] 1972, p. 179): that is, groups which occupy a specific social position by virtue of their control of membership and of presenting to the world an image based on prestige and honourability. Status groups can be associated with specific professions, but not always; for instance, while medics and lawyers are status groups, so are society ladies, who lack any definite profession. Oftentimes, status groups control a domain of social activity. Among their characteristics are rituals of prestige and honourability, often conducted in public (Collins 2004, pp. 115, 269–70).

5. The spatial and temporal formats of auction houses can work in a similar manner. While upscale auction houses are closed, ticketed affairs, where only knowledgeable people (or their representatives) take part, more popular auction places have a spatial format open to the street, and auctions take place at regular intervals. There are, however, social mechanisms of control as well, ensuring that a relatively small community retains control over transactions (see also Smith [1989, p. 61]).

6. 'Cognitive' should not be confused here with 'mental'. In this context, I take cognitive processes as practical actions producing new representational knowledge. The latter can take various forms, such as calculations, observations, classifications, or narratives, among others.

7. Glossing is defined as a 'prescription with which to search an *actual* occasion of discourse, an *actual* utterance, or an *actual* text' (Garfinkel and Sacks [1970] 1990, p. 75, italics in original). In other words, and simplified, glosses are attempts, made by participants in a situation, at defining 'what is going on here'.

8. In many situations where a transaction is broken, procedural trust has been violated. In other situations, violations of procedural trust are seen as informational; they need to be dealt with. Think here of bargaining situations, where the expectation of regular price decrements by the seller is, say, replaced with price increments. This is breach of trust in Harold Garfinkel's sense (1963), in that some basic assumptions of the bargaining sequence are violated, and this violation has to be accounted for (for instance, as stupidity). Nevertheless, the violation itself has an informational character, in the sense that it generates an uncertainty which has to be dealt with.

9. Oftentimes, the character and features of market exchanges have been worked out by opposing them to ritual gift exchanges. This has been one of the major topics in economic anthropology, and its origins can be found in Bronislaw Malinowski's *Argonauts of the Western Pacific* (1922). Here, Malinowski distinguished between ritual exchanges involving shell armbands and shell disc necklaces, on the one hand, and economic barter on the other hand. The two are never mixed and while the latter is meant to cover living necessities, the former has a ritual character, meant to enhance the social prestige of gift givers. The emphasis on the difference between barter and gift giving was meant, among others, to counter the view that 'primitive' societies were living in scarcity (for a critique of this view, see, among others Sahlins 2000, p. 95), and to highlight an important difference between modern and pre-modern societies: while in pre-modern societies gift-giving is dominant, in modern societies market exchanges become dominant. It would be easy to extend this view as to cover the distinction between contemporary developed societies, on the one hand, and developing societies, on the other (with different forms of gift giving dominant in the latter). This view, in its turn, has been challenged in recent years by the work of Viviana Zelizer (2006), among others, who shows that economic transactions contain elements of gift giving (the economy of favours) and vice versa.

10. Similar strategies are employed by temporary work agencies (see Smith and Neuwirth [2008, p. 80]).

2 Markets as Networks, Groups, and Communities

After having discussed passes and dribbles in the previous chapter, I will focus now on the teams entering the field of transactions, and engaging in plays of games. Players on a team know each other; very often, they know players on the competing team as well: they meet; they exchange stories; they have a common social life. In short, they have relationships. In the present chapter, I discuss relationships in plays of transactions.

It is necessary to do so not only because these relationships affect the ways in which transactions are conducted, but also because the existence and role of relationships, which we intuitively regard as important, does not always resonate with conceptualizations of market transactions or with their contemporary transformations. First, the economic conceptualization of transactions privileges anonymity, not social relationships. If relationships come to influence transactions, the price setting mechanism may become tainted by social factors, such as reciprocal obligations or tradition. It is not perchance that the general equilibrium theory (in its Walrasian formulation)—which I discuss in the next chapter—starts from an idealization of the floor of the stock exchange, where brokers loudly announce the prices at which they would trade, without hinting that they know each other (see Schumpeter [1954] 1994, pp. 1002–3). Of course, real brokers on the floor of the stock exchange do not hint that they know each other, simply because this is so self-evident to them, and made visible in every transaction. Nevertheless, the conceptualization of transactions as anonymous (and of equilibrium as taking place under these conditions) requires a closer investigation of the role played by relationships.

Second, newer technological developments (discussed in detail in Chapter 4) apparently bring transactions closer to the ideal of anonymous transactions. This is the case, for instance, of at least some segments of contemporary online financial markets. One might argue here that the street transactions discussed in the previous chapter were anonymous as well, but in the case of online financial markets we would have near-complete anonymity. Is then this a case where reality finally adapts to a prescient economic model, where social relationships do not play any role any more?

Third, it is necessary to see how social relationships might intervene in the production of informational surprises. After all, following the conceptual scheme of information as uncertainty-increasing surprises, we need to investigate how various kinds of social relationships contribute or not to producing and handling information.

The first issue which needs discussion here is the idea of social relationship itself. In the previous chapter, transactions—the basic analytical unit of the sociology of markets—have been treated as interactions. Approaching them as social relationships is not the same; indeed, different research programmes can be grounded on transactions as interactions or as relationships. In market interactions, relationships appear as the reciprocal orientation and attention of participants mediated by the object of transaction, orientation, and attention, which were bounded in time and space, as well as mutually intelligible. Relationships are 'tagged' in interactions, in the sense that participants display (inherently ambiguous) evidence about the existence and character of a relationship (Goffman 1971, p. 196; Pentland 2008, p. 22). Moreover, with respect to market interactions, social relationships appear as being endowed with a certain amount of variability and uncertainty, since transactions can be interrupted or can lead to different outcomes.

In the perspectives discussed below, however, social relationships are understood as having a much more stable character, as reproducing across time and space boundaries. This understanding can be traced back to at least Karl Marx's argument ([1872] 2002, p. 84) that the value of a commodity is actually determined by the amount of work crystallized in it. Since work is always social, and not strictly individual,[1] it can be seen as determined by the social relationships among groups involved in or depending on economic activities (a definition which covers all of society). Of all social relationships, ownership of the means of production is the most relevant for economic life, creating two social categories: those who have the means of production (capitalists) and those who don't (labourers). These two categories have to relate to each other (Marx and Engels [1848] 2004, p. 8), with the labourers selling their labour power to the capitalists. Social relationships appear thus as durable, legally codifiable positions within and across social categories. They are stable, not necessarily based on interactions, and pervasive throughout society. While ownership of the means of production is primarily an economic relationship, it reverberates in other domains of social activity as well, most notably in the political and the cultural ones, generating relationships of domination and ideology, respectively.

For Max Weber ([1921] 1972, p. 177), class situation designates 'a typical chance of (*a*) the distribution of goods, (*b*) of the external life situation, and (*c*) of the inner life fortune' as a consequence of having goods or qualifications which bring income within the given economic order. Additionally, Weber highlighted status groups (more about which later), as well as households, kinships, neighbourhoods, and political communities as relevant with respect to the distribution of economic goods (Weber [1921] 1972, pp. 179, 219).

This both enlarges and redefines social relationships with respect to economic transactions. Such relationships are not conceived any more solely with respect to ownership of the means of production, but include availability of qualifications and goods which can bring a stream of income. Renting a building, lending money, or giving music lessons can be included here, among others. This expands the sphere of market transactions beyond the production and exchange of material goods. At the same time the categories of relevant social relationships are expanded, so as to include families and communities, among others. Unavoidably, this changes the notion of relationship: while some can be legally codified, they are not understood any more as categorial positions, but as stable interaction patterns, involving sets of tacit, as well as explicit rules, rights, and obligations, together with behavioural scripts.

The question then becomes: how do such interaction patterns, with all the implied apparatus of rules, rights, obligations, and scripts intervene in market transactions? Conversely, the question can be asked: to what extent can market transactions be translated in the terms of the above interaction patterns, including their apparatus (see also Rauch and Hamilton [2001, p. 2])? To take but one question discussed in the previous chapter, that of price equilibrium (or discovery, in interaction terms), it becomes: how do these patterns contribute to price formation?

Markets in Networks

One way of answering the question about the link between transactions and relationships would be to see the latter as enveloping the former. The idea of interaction patterns (or social relationships) as engulfing market transactions is attractive, because it apparently avoids both the determinism associated with strict social-structural positions inherent in the notion of class, and the indeterminism implied in the picture of atomized market actors engaging in transactions according to their expectations about utility and their individual preference orderings. This perceived middle ground between two extremes was expressed in Mark Granovetter's now classic argument (1985) that economic activities (including transactions) are embedded in networks of social relationships. Granovetter (1985, p. 490) defined embeddedness as 'concrete personal relations and structures (or "networks") of such relations' which generate trust and discourage malfeasance. Trust, as a fundamental condition of market transactions, is produced within concrete personal relations because the costs of obtaining, processing, and evaluating stories about transaction partners is always reduced by relationships (Carruthers and Babb 2000, p. 48), while the accuracy and detail of stories is increased. This does not mean that opportunities for malfeasance are not present; they, too, are generated within networks of personal relationships, yet kept in check by trust (Granovetter 1985, p. 491). These arguments are formulated as a modification and extension of Karl Polanyi's argument that economic transactions require trust (Polanyi 1945; Beckert 2007, p. 8), and as a counter-argument to Oliver Williamson's position (1975) that intra-firm organizational arrangements are more important than market transactions because they are more cost-effective (Granovetter 1985, p. 493). A fundamental factor such as trust cannot be reduced to cost-effectiveness issues; moreover, inter-firm transactions depend on personal relationships as well (Granovetter 1985, pp. 496–7).

Before discussing the career of the network concept further, as well as the critiques of embeddedness, it is worth pausing for a short reflection upon networks, trust, and information. In the above account, networks appear as concrete relations—of the type 'who knows who'—which are important exactly because of the trust they generate. Trust here is not understood as procedural trust, of the kind discussed in the previous chapter, but as a sort of routine: knowing, say, Jimmy, means both knowing his routines and being able and willing to accommodate them. This kind of knowledge also enables us to produce stories about Jimmy in a routinized manner. (For instance, Jimmy likes a specific dish, so we'll serve it when we invite him over to dinner, and we will also tell stories about his preferences.) This mutual adaptation and reciprocal knowledge of routines are reinforced by emotional elements (Burt 2005, p. 172). Together with the knowledge of personal narratives[2] (we are able to reproduce at least parts of Jimmy's life narrative, for instance), they constitute trust. Information is seen here as the reciprocal adoption of personal narratives, a process in which these latter may undergo revisions and encounter surprises; discovered malfeasance is a case in point here. Overall, though, surprises are not the rule, but the exception.

This amounts to saying that market transactions take place on the basis of the reciprocal adaptations and routines of economic actors. While this may hold for inter-firm transactions, it is not the case for street transactions such as those discussed in the previous chapter, or for online, anonymous financial transactions. I do not need to know the African peddler's life story in order to buy a handbag from him. Such transactions are based on fleeting encounters rather than on deep engagements with each other and, indeed, the whole logic of street peddling is rather the antithesis of personal commitment between sellers and customers. This situation aside, we encounter many instances where networks of personal relationships can shape transactions and their outcomes; examples here are networks of brokers on the trading floors of stock exchanges (from the pre-automation era), networks of firms from various branches of industry (e.g. Langley 2008, pp. 57–8), or networks of professionals offering their services to the public (such as lawyers, for instance).

A central argument is that networks of personal relationships, being characterized by trust, circulate specific stories about products, prices, and transactions, stories, which are bounded to the trust features of the respective networks and will not be diffused outside. By circulating them, members of the network translate relationships into transactions. Thus, to use Pierre Bourdieu's notion (1994, p. 80), markets have a chiastic structure: the deal of a friendship (what advantage does it bring that I know you?) is the friendship of a deal (a transaction will cement our relationship). Trust as mutual adaptation (see also Burt [2001, p. 33]) is reinforced in its turn by this circulation[3], which mixes up personal stories with data about the economic performance of the transaction partners. Personal, even intimate knowledge about a transaction partner contributes to creating a constraining system of tacit obligations, which in some instances may be more effective than a formal system of governance (in some other instances, it may run counter to the formal system).

Mitchel Abolafia (1996, pp. 49–54), for instance, distinguishes among three levels of control in financial markets: the informal level, provided by reciprocal obligations and tacit rules; the formal level of control, consisting in surveillance and corrective action undertaken by internal committees; and the institutional level of control, located within the formal hierarchies of market institutions (boards of directors, CEO, CFO, and the like). The three levels do not overlap; informal arrangements of control are not entirely determined by institutional mechanisms, nor are they necessarily in harmony with them. This opens up possibilities for traders to commit themselves to informal mutual obligations, while trying to circumvent at the same time formal arrangements for control. Such situations point to the fact that market transactions are not characterized by a unique system of moral obligations, but rather by parallel systems. It resonates with Max Weber's observation ([1921] 1972, p. 383) that the 'free market' is anchored in moral obligations different from those of intra-community exchanges.

In her investigation of the computer industry, AnnaLee Saxenian (1994) has highlighted the importance of informal networks for the success of Silicon Valley entrepreneurs. In a study of the networks through which firms get loans from banks, Brian Uzzi (1999, p. 487) notices that banks employ managers whose job is to cultivate and develop relationships with the upper management of mid-sized firms which are their clients. This involves, among others, acquiring knowledge about the personal life circumstances of the upper management, for the purpose of 'personalizing' the relationship: knowledge about how kids are doing in school, hobbies, sports, etc. This knowledge is mixed up with knowledge about the companies and their financial needs.

In this perspective, information appears as multi-layered narrative constructions (mostly oral),[4] which are intrinsic to processes of mutual adaptations and to the creation of shared routines. From the perspective of the interaction order, transactions such as a corporate bank loan appear as engagements in which actors use organizational structures in order to establish personal relationships, and use personal relationships in order to maintain and control organizational structures. Since such narratives are circulated only within networks, and since they mix personal and organization-relevant aspects, asymmetric information emerges (see also Uzzi and Lancaster [2004, p. 322]); persons situated outside networks do not have access to network-specific organizational narratives. Moreover, external actors cannot evaluate the significance of organizational narratives in the same way in which internal actors can; this significance is tied to personal stories which get their relevance from processes of mutual adaptation.

Narratives produced and circulated in this way influence price formation, in the sense that prices will differ within networks from those applied to external transactions. Brian Uzzi and Ryon Lancaster (2004, p. 340), for instance, find that the prices asked by law firms for complex services tend to be lower within a network than prices for the same complex services delivered outside the network. (This, however, is not valid for routine services, but only for complex ones.) Other factors influencing prices for legal services are board memberships of lawyers (which tends to increase prices) and the status of firms (which also tends to increase prices). This amounts to saying that network-internal mutual adaptations, reached on the basis of oral exchanges, will create price differentials.[5] While this can be interpreted either as reducing transaction costs or as giving clients a certain amount of leverage (Uzzi and Lancaster 2004, p. 340), its character as routine-like storytelling remains uncontested.

An important issue here would be to see how surprises are generated within engagements, based on such storytelling, surprises which may lead to price modifications. Theoretically, if storytelling plays only the role of reinforcing mutual adaptations, network participants could dispense with it once a certain level of accommodation has been reached. This would deprive networks not only of a central element of trust, but also of a price-setting mechanism. Therefore, storytelling would have to regularly produce informational surprises in order to remain a key price-setting mechanism. That surprises are produced is indicated, among others, by the fact that firms can walk away from seemingly secured deals. A relevant instance in this respect is the recent episode of the failed acquisition by Citibank of Wachovia, where the former was abandoned in favour of a deal with a competitor (Wells Fargo). Assuming that networks played a significant role in such a deal, and that routine storytelling was instrumental in the production of information, then obviously this did not maintain network stability in this case (and, in the end did not set the price). It was rather an informational surprise (the competitor's unexpected offer) which did this.

A second aspect is to see how different network characteristics and types affect both network dynamics and price discovery within networks. Networks can be characterized by different densities of social relationships, as well as by different types of relationships; for instance, in some networks (or network regions), relationships are at arm's length[6], while in others they are embedded. In some network regions, relationships are dense, while in others they are ragged—that is, with holes. Arm's length relationships are characterized by sporadic transactions and by weak mutual obligations, whereas embedded relationships are characterized by regular transactions and by an inner governance structure relying on mutual commitments (Uzzi 1999, pp. 483–4). Therefore, the kinds of information circulated within these networks will differ according to their characteristics; an embedded network, for instance, will circulate personal stories mixed with organizational ones in ways in which an arm's length network will not do. Moreover, networks can expand or shrink; their size will be relevant with respect to the mechanisms of social control imposed upon their members, as well as with respect to information.

In his study of the social networks of traders and brokers on the floor of the Chicago Board of Trade, Wayne Baker (1984) examined the relationships between price volatility and network dynamics. On the trading floor, networks of social relationships constitute a system of mutual obligations, which keeps the traders' opportunistic behaviour in check; for instance, market makers will accept to trade with each other only if their counterparts have a high participation in the market (Baker 1984, p. 782). Thus, tendencies to trade with friends, for instance, or sometimes to flout the rules of trading will be restricted. However, such mechanisms of social control can work well only within smaller crowds of traders,[7] simply because they can keep each other within eyesight. An increase in the size of trading networks on the overcrowded floor will make control mechanisms less effective, and will encourage thus more opportunistic behaviour. The effect is that price volatility will increase in larger trading networks, because the social controls which dampen volatility are less effective now. With a continued increase in crowd size, however, networks will tend to break down again into smaller, more manageable crowds, with better control.[8] With that, price volatility will decrease again (Baker 1984, p. 805). While in smaller groups prices can be achieved by negotiation, with the increase in network size competitive bidding occurs. As the crowd increases, however, price volatility increases as well, and as the crowd breaks down under its own size, smaller networks will emerge with dampened volatility.

In this account, networks set constraints upon the traders' opportunistic search for information and action; increased price volatility, for instance, can be seen as an increased informational content of prices (they produce more surprises) leading to action. Smaller networks based on trust and mutual obligations stress routines (like negotiated prices, which then have to be repeated) and decrease informational content. In phases of network emergence—for instance, in developing economies—firms turn first to existing bureaucratic channels to gather information and find transaction partners; once networks are set in place, the influence of formal organizational structures fades, and that of intra-network information increases (Keister 2001, p. 356).

This raises a problem with respect to how changes—that is, novel transactions—emerge within networks. Since mutual obligations are such a powerful mechanism of control in smaller networks, it would follow that the agency of their members is restricted. Networks of dense relationships would then rather tend to stifle innovation. If this is so, then a more advantageous position from the viewpoint of information and innovation would be one at the interface between dense clusters of social relationships. Agents situated between such clusters would then be able to profit from more information and foster more innovative behaviour. Ronald Burt (2005, p. 16) calls these social positions structural holes. An agent situated within a structural hole should be able to gather, process, and circulate more information than one embedded in a small dense network. Moreover, agents situated in structural holes can become network entrepreneurs; they bridge between people on opposite sides of the hole, accumulate social capital from various networks, and are thus able to facilitate social and economic transactions. Ronald Burt (2005, p. 18) considers network entrepreneurs to be an intermediate form between 'the force of corporate authority and the dexterity of markets' (see also Powell [1990]). In other words, they facilitate intermediate transaction forms, which do not have the anonymity of markets or the formality of organizations.[9] While such positions may bring advantages to their holder, they also seem to foster openness to new ideas, meaning mainly that ideas developed within a network stand a better chance of being transferred to another one (Burt 2005, pp. 55, 72). More recent simulations, however, seem to indicate that such structural advantages are conditioned by entrepreneurs holding a monopoly over brokerage activities; in the absence of such monopolies, networks will tend to evolve into bipartite types, which emphasize external over internal ties (Buskens and van de Rijt 2008, p. 393).

From the viewpoint of network dynamics, four types of processes can be distinguished (see also Powell et al. [2005, p. 1139]): preferential attachment (firms get linked to those which have the most links already), homophily (mutual connection of like firms), imitation (firms link to the nodes where others link), and multiconnectivity (search for novel links). In their study of the biotech industry, Walter Powell and collaborators find that during the evolution of the industry over decades, both the nature of network members and their ties change; while during the early phases finding capital (preferential attachment) is the most important aspect, over the life of the field multiconnectivity gains in importance (Powell et al. 2005, pp. 1187–9; Powell,

Koput, and Smith-Doerr 1996). In time, multiconnected firms become centres of preferential attachment, helping thus establish hierarchies within the field.

If we understand multiconnectivity as being supported by a drive for novel connections, and hence for potential informational surprises, then over the lifetime of an industrial field the search for (and the exploitation of) information become essential with respect to firms acquiring central positions. This points to the fact that networks per se, understood as routine-based mechanisms of social control, have a limited potential for explaining the production, circulation, and uses of information in transactions. Closed or quasi-closed networks[10] reduce uncertainties and facilitate mutual adaptation of their members but, since information implies producing uncertainties, it would imply that networks would rather put the brakes on the production of information. Processes such as preferential attachment, homophily, and imitation are not conducive to informational surprises either. One could imagine a situation where routine-based networks of transactions could be quasi-automated; this, however, would increase network vulnerability to unforeseen major events. An example here is provided by networks of economic transactions within former socialist economies, which were to a very large extent routine-based (manufacturing and selling the same product time and again to the same firms). When an event such as the fall of the Iron Curtain came in 1989, they were thrown into a major crisis. It is important to understand how economic crises can act as information producers, constraining actors to become active in novel directions.

One solution here is to stress either the role of structural holes or that of multiconnectivity, which can be understood as a version of the former. However, this raises the question of the relationships among networks, relationships which can take the form of hierarchies, but not only. It also raises the question of the relationships between networks and groups (such as status groups), and of the ways the latter use cultural elements in the production and control of information. Third, it raises the question whether information circulated within networks should be understood only with respect to the allocation of resources (such as money or researchers, in the case of biotech companies, for instance). At the same time, we encounter market forms where networks do not seem to play an important role; a prime example here is that of anonymous, online financial markets. Consumption is another case in point; while we can capture important features of transactions in industrial goods with the network concept, this works less well for the consumer side.

After a period in which the notion of embeddedness has been expanded by including, for instance, issues of political and cultural embeddedness[11] in addition to structural ones (see Zukin and DiMaggio [1990]), critics argued that it offers an externalized view of the social character of economic transactions (Krippner and Alvarez 2007, p. 232; Krippner 2001) and that it cannot capture all market forms. In other words, the networks of social relationships appear as external frames, which support, constrain, and bind market transactions; this can work well as a critique of neoclassical economics, but less well as a platform on which to build a specifically sociological programme in the study of markets. It should not be forgotten here that the notion of embeddedness has been originally developed for analyzing labour markets (Mark Granovetter's initial interest), being transferred later to the analysis of inter-firms relationships, against the background of a growing interest in substituting the notion of network to that of formal organization.

Markets from Networks

One solution to this problem is outlined in Harrison White's work (1981, 2002): instead of treating networks as external with respect to market transactions (the embeddedness view), markets should be treated as hierarchies of networks. The early 1990s work of Harrison White (1992) advanced the issue of market-as-networks, while suggesting some alternatives which do not entirely resonate with it. For White, the main theoretical issue is that stable social orders (a notion which seems to overlap at least partly with that of structure) need to solve the identity problem—that is, the component formations need to keep their identities under control across various, shifting situations. This implies, among others, organizational forms constituted around a dominant principle of valuation ordering. Such forms are interfaces, arenas, and councils, with quality, purity, and prestige, respectively, as valuation principles (White 1992, p. 16). Markets can be interfaces, and also arenas; they cannot, however, be councils, since the latter are based on prestige-oriented shifting coalitions. As interfaces, markets are 'committed to continuing delivery of identity as tangible production ... identified by its quality' (White 1992, p. 30). Retail as well as production markets would come under this category. As arenas, markets operate timing-based selections; examples of these are stock exchanges, and also flea markets (White 1992, p. 31; 2008, p. 99). Forms of social ordering such as arenas and interfaces can in their turn be hierarchically ordered; this is not without consequences when networks come into the picture.

It would follow from the above that these two types of markets are very different—and White (1992, pp. 31, 51; 2008, p. 99) specifically states this. If they are so different, then networks might play different roles in interfaces as opposed to arenas. (It should be also noted here that while both terms allude to the interaction order, this is not what White is preoccupied with; his aim is to find stable relational structures across a variety of empirical phenomena.)

Networks come into picture here as sets of relationships on one side of each interface, which constitutes a market. In a recent reformulation, White (2008, pp. 7–8) partly replaces and partly specifies the concept of network as 'netdom'—that is, as a set of network relationships which circumscribe a specific domain of experience (political, economic, or kinship, among others). In retail, for instance, or in markets for industrial goods (an example which White invokes time and again), buyers do not usually establish relationships among them (this may be more valid for retail than for industrial goods). Producers, however, do, and these relationships are set around 'commitment(s) of producing firms into being peers in a differentiated set, which organizes terms of trade around an induced order of quality among the producers' (White 1992, p. 42). This means that on the seller side of the seller–buyer interface, several other interfaces emerge among networks of firms, which come together within a certain segment of a hierarchy of producers. Thus, the seller side would be represented by a hierarchy of producers' networks, organized into segments. Two consecutive segments meet at the 'commit interface'. These segments produce distinctive flows of products. What counts then within each segment is the revenue–volume pair, and producers must make choices from the available combinations, in such a way as to stay within their respective segments while optimizing the pair (White 1992, p. 43).

Markets, then, should not be seen simply as networks characterized by various types of social relationships, but as hierarchies of such networks, with an emphasis on hierarchy. (Note here, however, that this applies to only one type of markets—interfaces, but not to arenas.) Indeed, White (1992, p. 24; 2002, p. 284) repeatedly uses biological metaphors such as feeding chains or pecking orders in order to stress the fact that a market is a sui generis social phenomenon characterized by emergent hierarchies of transaction networks. This brings us away from the functionalist idea that networks perform certain operations that facilitate resource allocation, such as reducing the costs related to the search for information. In his view, markets are characterized both by intra-network cooperation and inter-network competition; they can be best understood as sui generis phenomena if we take into account that they provide the settings for two modes of valuation (out of three): valuation by quality and valuation by purity (White 1992, p. 32). Interface markets operate according to valuation by quality, while arenas operate according to valuation by purity (White 2008, p. 68). Valuation does not mean here the valuation of transacted objects as an aim in itself. Rather, the valuation of transacted objects appears as a means for valuating and ordering social actors in ways which can be applied across various social settings. A means of finding out valuation orders is 'looking at the story-sets active in the local discourse' (White 2008, p. 67), story-sets which coalesce into narratives. Narratives, in their turn, work as regimes of control, in the sense that they account for 'interaction and switching of identities across different realms in a regime' (White 2008, p. 226). In other words, narratives are discursive means of legitimating markets and of connecting them to other domains of social life, an aspect which will be examined in detail in the last chapter of this book.

Since valuation is a means of establishing identity, and since social order cannot be achieved, maintained, and reproduced without establishing, for all practical purposes, the identities of participating actors, it follows that markets are social arrangements, which create competitive, dynamic orderings across society. These orderings are competitive in the sense that they are achieved by social competitions among participants, meaning competitions on social attributes; for instance, who has the best quality in relationship to volume, as in producer markets; or sorting out, or purification competitions, as seen in flea markets or on the floor of the stock exchange.

This comes very close to the previously discussed notion of valuation as gameworthiness. Nevertheless, while gameworthiness is defined by social attributes displayed during a play of the game (speed, or cunning), Harrison White emphasizes valuation in relationship to price, volume, and quality. An additional aspect which comes close to previous arguments is the notion of markets as hierarchies of networks, which allows us to grasp the situation of a premier league team playing next to, yet separated from an amateur group. Within the hierarchy, different teams engage in different plays of the same game, with different valuation outcomes. Yet, for Harrison White, who works with a notion of hierarchy segments operating each in its own ecological niche, only two adjacent segments can meet at the interface. The example of Venetian peddlers, however, indicates that non-contiguous segments of a hierarchy need not be spatially and temporally separated.

White's arguments appear partly as an elaboration upon, and partly as turning upside down Max Weber's definition of the market as the archetype of rational social action through exchange. In Weber's definition ([1921] 1972, p. 382) markets are competitions in which participants engage each other for exchange chances. In Harrison White's view, such competitions are structured alongside network hierarchies[12] (at least in interface markets) and around a dominating valuation principle (be it quality or purity). At the same time, the market cannot be 'free' in the sense of being unbound by ethical norms (i.e. it cannot be anchored in universal distrust); since it is grounded in the 'formal inviolability of promises' (Weber [1921] 1972, p. 383), and since inviolability requires trust (provided by networks), it follows that mutual ethical obligations may be valid within specific networks, but not necessarily outside them.[13] Trust is understood here as personal, and not as procedural, of the kind analysed in the previous chapter.

Since councils, which are prestige-based competitions, are not the domain of markets, we could say that it is here that ritual gift exchange can be located. Gift exchange also serves to establish individual and collective identities (see

Mauss [1950] 1999, p. 274); this type of exchange is often related to prestige competitions among groups (see also Bourdieu [1980, pp. 168–9]), and it can be located within councils as a form of order.

While markets are conceived as hierarchies, seeing them as regions on a plane determined by volume and quality can yield relevant insights into their dynamics; in addition to ordinary markets, Harrison White (2002, pp. 95–6, 142, 304) distinguishes between crowded markets (where sellers multiply in the same region to the effect of driving each other out), explosive markets (where, in opposition to crowded markets, the growth in sellers results in market size growth), and paradox markets (where valuation correlates negatively with unit cost of production). An instance of crowded markets is the proliferation of coffee chains in a small neighbourhood where coffee culture is not a fashion any more. An example of explosive markets is the proliferation of organic produce shops in a neighbourhood where organic produce is all the rage. An example of paradox markets is provided by novelty stores where the merchandise is perceived as overpriced with rapport to quality.

The key issue though remains how information affects markets as hierarchies of networks. Since the two central notions which complement the network concept—arena and interface—evoke communication modes, it is relevant to know how information is generated and circulated in such hierarchies. White assigns communication a reproductive character with respect to markets; trust as mutual adaptation is maintained through personal narratives mixed with organizational ones, and 'idiomatic discourse for some particular market variety evolves out of anecdotes and longer picaresque narratives' (White 2002, p. 303). Translated in the terms of the interaction order, this means that markets emerge through chains of engagements within networks, as well as through indirect observations among networks. This would go somewhat like this: network members (i.e. managers and other employees of firms sharing a similar production profile) use social occasions (conferences, golfing trips, business meetings, etc.) for swapping stories, both organizational and personal. Additionally, they study documents (memos, business reports, statistics) produced in their own organization, as well as in other organizations. Stories and documents generate familiarity among managers, and hence trust. They also facilitate generating what White (2002, p. 29) calls production schedules, that is, decisions about the production volume at which a firm occupies a position in the market. At the same time, firms occupying different positions in the hierarchy observe each other, even if they do not participate into another network's idiomatic discourse; an example here is provided by high-street fashion firms imitating high-end fashion trends.

All these 'idiomatic discourses', together with indirect observations of what is going on in other networks, help to maintain markets as hierarchies of networks. What is more, observation of existing ties (or of the absence thereof) constitutes in itself a signal about the position of firms within or outside such networks (Podolny 2001, p. 34). The fact that signals are conceived here as having a maintenance and adjustment function, based on the notion that they serve to make distinctions (Spence 1974, p. 11) leaves little room for information as surprises. It is also to be noticed here that such informational surprises could at most trickle down within the hierarchy, as lower situated networks of producers observe higher situated ones and try to maintain their position by adjusting schedules of production. The fashion world is again a case in point: clothing manufacturers observe the collections of high fashion houses, which work for them as surprises, and try to imitate them adaptively (see also Aspers [2006, chapter 4]). What is perceived from outside the network as an informational surprise may be perceived within the network in a totally different way.

This, however, does not solve the issue of how hierarchies of firms confront and adapt to informational surprises such as those triggered by unforeseen events. The credit crunch of Fall 2008 is a case in point here. In spite of the fact that trust (aka mutual adaptation) is taken as the basis for signalling within stable hierarchies of networks, the empirical evidence points to the fact that this trust can unravel pretty quickly. In the above-mentioned credit crunch, members of peer networks lost trust and recalled loans (or refused to extend lines of credit), generating thus a liquidity crisis which confronted firms with informational challenges. The intervention of new, network-external actors (i.e. governments) shattered the expectations on which the banking system (and its regulation) operated. It could hardly be argued that the new intervention came from a structural hole in the banking network; it came from actors (governments, regulators, elected political bodies) which were not part of the loans network.

But we don't need to turn to economic crises to see that a view of markets as stable hierarchies of networks grounded in the reciprocal observation of signals is not entirely supported by empirical examples. Take aircraft manufacturers, for instance; while there is differentiation according to the product, there are only two producers at the top: Airbus and Boeing. Moreover, they do not always seem to work by reciprocal adjustments, but by producing informational surprises targeted at buyers (i.e. airlines) and at each other; for instance, Airbus's double-deckered A380 was countered not with a similar product, but with a surprise: the Boeing 787, a much smaller, streamlined aircraft. The electronics industry seems to work on a similar principle: the iPod and the iPhone are cases in point here. They emerged as surprises and, while imitated, they set the pace not for manufacturers down the hierarchy, but at similar levels of quality and price. Or take nanotechnology: while this emerging industry still has very few concrete products to show, it started by creating informational surprises (in the shape of projected or imagined applications) as a means of attracting financing and of starting long and costly research programmes.

Thus, a couple of issues are raised with respect to the limitations of the markets-from-networks approach. The first issue is that of legitimacy as a basis for informational flows; the second is that of authority, and of the relationships among heterogeneous groups in markets. These issues point to the fact that, in addition to considering networks as part of markets, we must take into account groups as well. Also, in addition to taking into account narratives about production volumes (and personal ones as well), we must pay attention to the social processes through which markets achieve legitimacy. (It is not perchance that the credit crunch brought about heated debates about the legitimacy of markets.)

The significant differences between conceiving markets as networks, on the one hand, and conceiving them as hierarchies of networks, on the other, come better to light if we return to the problem of legitimacy, discussed in Chapter 1. Markets as such have to be tied to other social institutions in a justifiable fashion—that is, both market participants and observers should be able to provide a discursive rationale for market transactions, on the basis of which said transactions can be situated within society at large and tied to other social activities (see also Suchman [1995, p. 574]).

If we see markets only as networks, however, legitimacy appears as superfluous, simply because while members of the network could observe their environment, external observers could be prevented from directly or indirectly observing such networks. This is the principle on which illegitimate and/or illegal transaction networks operate: networks which transact in human beings or body parts, in illegal substances, endangered species, or toxic waste, for instance, erect barriers to observation from the outside. Such barriers, however, would restrict the discursive forms which enclose and circulate information. From the observer's perspective, these networks could hardly be seen as 'swimming in a sea of discourse', but rather in one of silence. Moreover, since—following White—markets are about order and identity, and since the latter implies, among others, putting a face to the world (White, Godart, and Corona 2007, p. 186), it implies that networks alone could not sustain markets. Intuitively too, it is rather difficult to equate markets with networks. (Networks dealing in endangered species exist, but can we speak of a market in tiger penises? If yes, what would be the sea of discourse supporting it?)

An additional issue is that networks not integrated in legitimate hierarchies can become unstable, because of the trust problems they generate.[14] While in relationship to networks trust is mostly seen as mutual adaptation, another of its facets is provided by authority (to be discussed in detail in the following). This means, among others, that network members acknowledge internal hierarchies and positions of authority as legitimate. Network-internal legitimacy is reinforced when the network itself is integrated within a larger, socially acknowledged hierarchy and connected to society at large. This is so because integration and connection to society provides discursive solutions for balancing and/or solving challenges to authority, should any arise. These mechanisms, in turn, endow legitimate hierarchies of networks with more stability. An example here is, among others, provided by challenges to organizational leadership, which can be solved in a publicly sanctioned manner (incompetent CEOs, for instance, can be legitimately forced to step down). In non-integrated networks, however, challenges to authority are more difficult to solve in the absence of public sanctioning, and this can diminish the trust network leaders put in their subordinates, and the other way around. Challenges to authority, as well as control of potential challenges, would then tend to be solved with more violent means. (Think here of networks of illegal traffickers, where murder can be both a means of challenging authority, and of preventing such challenges.) This, in turn, makes such networks potentially unstable.

The situation changes if we look at markets as hierarchies of networks. In this case, direct and indirect observation of other networks becomes essential for sustaining the hierarchy and also for the generation of informational surprises. The need for structural holes, for instance, illustrates this problem; at least sporadic observation must be made possible in order to have such holes, and hence surprises. At least in part, mechanisms of reciprocal observation would involve public spaces as well as a controlled access of the public. Trade fairs, which are public events, and to which the public is admitted on certain days, are a case in point here. Brochures and advertising are another example. Seen in this perspective, the African peddlers and the high-end fashion shops discussed in the previous chapter would be different segments of the same market. Their interaction procedures would be different, but nevertheless they would be observable (albeit in different ways), as an intrinsic feature of their identity.

Markets from Groups

This raises again the question of the internal and external boundaries of such hierarchies; features such as space, time, and status symbols, among others, play here a crucial role. Such features are more difficult to capture with the concept of network, which essentially focuses on personal relationships. However, they can be captured with the concept of status groups, which focuses more on the shared, mutually intelligible and observable features[15] of a group. Moreover, while the network concept usually captures only the producer side, the notion of status group helps us understand the consumer side as well, together with the dynamics between production and consumption. Markets should thus be considered not only as hierarchies of networks, but also as hierarchies of status groups.

These latter, as defined by Max Weber ([1921] 1972, p. 179), are characterized by an 'effectively claimed positive or negative privileging in social appreciation', a privileging based on a combination of several elements, such as lifestyle, education, prestige of origin, or of profession. While money can be an element of privileging, it alone cannot provide the basis for status groups. Status is expressed in (*a*) what Weber calls connubium—that is, marital exchanges (and, more generally, social relationships) within one's own group; (*b*) benefits from association with other groups (or commensalism); (*c*) monopolistic appropriation of privileged chances for acquiring goods; and (*d*) specific conventions and traditions. While status groups can be associated with certain professions, this must not be necessarily so; in Weber's view they are, however, associated with the monopolistic appropriation of chances, in relationships to specific activities. This appropriation in itself is not enough (after all, production and trade in illegal substances can be monopolized as well), but must go hand in hand with observable conventions and traditions, as well as with specific forms of socialization. In other words, symbolic aspects of groups, made visible within society, are essential with respect to monopolization processes.

Pierre Bourdieu (1979), whose work can be partly seen as an extension and elaboration upon the notion of status group, would add here tastes and habits, visible in specific cultural preferences, ways of speaking, body language, or clothes. For Bourdieu, however, status groups are not arranged in a hierarchy, but rather within a multi-dimensional system of differences (called field), which allows participants' groups to position themselves simultaneously in different ways with respect to each other. This multiple positioning makes possible the reciprocal translation of ordering, or valuation principles according to which hierarchies are built along each dimension. For instance, the literary field is constituted by different status groups—that is, groups of writers who reciprocally position themselves along multiple valuation lines: artistic talent, public authority, or income. These valuation lines can be translated into each other. While mystery writers, for instance, deal in the art of money making (low prestige, broader public, higher income), highbrow writers deal in the money of art (see Bourdieu [1992]).

It is not difficult to find examples of status groups in economic life: take the market in law services discussed in the previous sections. Lawyers are status groups not only in that they monopolize certain legal activities, having jurisdiction over a specific body of knowledge (see also Abbott [1988, pp. 88–9]), they also enjoy specific levels of social prestige associated with education, ethos, knowledge, and public authority. They benefit from association with groups such as paralegals, which at the same time appear as subordinated. Another example here is that of stock brokers: during their history, stock exchange brokers differentiated among several status groups, according to their activities on formal or informal stock exchanges (see also Preda [2009b, chapter 3]). The Paris Bourse, for instance, had official, state-appointed brokers, whose transactions were recognized by the French state. Alongside with (and outside) the Bourse a second market existed in Paris, the *coulisse*, whose brokers (the *coulissiers*) had a lower status. Clerks were a subordinated group (not everybody could become the clerk of a stock broker).

We do not need, however, to go back in history to find examples of status groups among brokers; contemporary traders and brokers in financial institutions are (informally) organized along status lines as well. While their evaluation (and pay) is performance-based, competitions for profit lead unavoidably to status effects and to the creation of prestige hierarchies, so that lesser traders will try to imitate (and emulate) 'star performers'. This points towards the fact that not all transactions may follow principles of rationality and efficiency, or be executed according to well-laid plans, but unfold according to the logic of gameworthiness as well. In two recent cases, French banks lost very large sums of money as the result of traders executing unauthorized derivatives transactions while aiming to be recognized by their peers as prestigious.[16]

While economic status groups can and do engender prestige-based competitions, their use of symbolic actions to generate and reproduce hierarchies provides not only legitimacy, but also an interface for interactions with non-economic groups (political, social, or cultural). This is so because by using symbolic actions in order to integrate themselves in society at large, economic status groups necessarily have to redefine themselves and their activities as having relevant non-economic features as well (i.e. political, social, or cultural).[17] This integration allows the transformation of money into prestige; a large donation to an art museum, for instance, can open access to respectable circles, in a way in which wealth alone cannot. An honourable merchant is also expected to be a concerned citizen, a pillar of the community, a supporter of the arts, etc. An example here is provided by the relationships between economic and political status groups, which allow for political interventions within market activities. These political interventions are not restricted to market regulation, but can also take the form of redefining economic activities as having ultimately political goals (and establish thus economic policies).[18] Political interventions can also take the form of forcing or persuading economic actors to take certain courses of action (the mergers of Fall 2008, in the United Kingdom as well as in the United States, are a case in point). Conversely, relationships between economic and political status groups allow for the interest-based intervention of economic status groups in political activities (lobbyism is a case in point here). Other examples are cultural sponsorships performed by economic groups, or activities falling under 'corporate social responsibility', as a way of socially integrating economic activities and interests. It goes without saying, however, that such relationships need not always be harmonious; conflict and tensions can be part and parcel of them.

Moreover, symbolic actions can become themselves a domain of specialized knowledge, monopolized by specific economic groups. In other words, representations of status groups, as well as their output can become a source of economic activities controlled by other status groups. Public relations firms taking over the task of shaping and controlling the media 'image' of economic status groups are a case in point. More importantly, perhaps, the capacity of economic status groups to crystallize around processing the output of other status groups is expressed, among others, in the emergence of various forms of economic expertise (to be discussed in the next chapter) which, in their turn, act as an additional interface to non-economic groups (think, for instance, of the relationships between economic expertise and policy making).

Networks of personal relationships can, of course, exist within status groups. In fact, the prestige defining the latter can act as a control mechanism for access to these networks, for establishing the boundaries among various status groups, and for specifying the communication mechanisms between such groups and the public. At the same time, if we look at organizations, they can be seen in terms of interlinked status groups as well, which coordinate around a common set of relevant activities,[19] within a formal regulatory framework or not. This resonates with the arguments of neoinstitutionalism,[20] according to which organizations deploy symbolic activities, ceremonials, and rituals for maintaining the status quo and for gaining legitimacy (e.g. Meyer and Rowan 1977, p. 341; Davis 2005, p. 154), and that these activities are given priority over maximizing the functional efficiency of organizations. As these activities are key within the organization (maintenance of the status quo takes precedence over efficacy), organizational groups will develop sets of symbols and activities in relationship to their position, resources, and actions. At the same time, since the interface between organizations and society includes an essential symbolic aspect (legitimacy), status groups will intervene in maintaining this interface by cooperating with other groups (for instance, public relations managers). This does not mean that organizational groups are geared towards maintaining only facades: it means that symbolic, status-related activities necessarily intervene in maintaining and reproducing instrumental actions within organizations.

At the organizational level, corporate boards can function as ceremonial groups endowing corporate statements with authority. In their investigation of corporate boards, Gerald Davis and Gregory Robbins (2005, pp. 294–5;

also Zajac and Westphal 1996) find that boards are selected as to project an image of prestige to external observers (investors, among others). Prestigious directors tend to bring along other prestigious directors on board, enhancing thus the reputation of the corporation, but not necessarily improving its performance (Davis and Robbins 2005, p. 307). Policies adopted by corporations, such as the repurchase of own stocks, while not consistently implemented, can also acquire a ceremonial function, reinforcing corporate authority and legitimacy vis-à-vis investors (Zajac and Westphal 2004, p. 450).

Firms use markers of status and prestige not only to position themselves within a system of transactions (i.e. a market for a certain product) but also to make inroads across systems (Podolny 1993, p. 867). Moreover, status affects the revenue margins commanded by a firm's products; a firm can have higher margins on products perceived as high status. Because of this, firms have little incentive to launch products that are perceived as high quality, but have lower status. This is the case in the wine industry, for instance, where the status system (shown, among others in wine appellations) acts as a disincentive for producers to develop innovative wines which might be perceived as having lower status (Podolny 2005, p. 131). A similar situation is encountered in the art market, where dealers price paintings by size within the portfolio of individual artists. Dealers and artists perceive prices as being correlated with status; lower prices, while potentially increasing sales, would lead to a perception of lower status and therefore have to be avoided (Velthuis 2005, p. 177). If we look at the relationship between status and innovation in the computer industry, for instance, high status firms will have fewer incentives to innovate compared with middle status ones, which are active in non-crowded niches (i.e. they do not have many competitors for their product profile). As innovative firms become established, they move up on the status scale and become less innovative (Podolny 2005, pp. 172–3).

Since status is expressed through symbols, it follows that economic status groups would emerge not only on the production side but on the consumption side as well. Here, public visibility is especially relevant. Thorsten Veblen ([1899] 1994, p. 36) noticed that 'in order to gain and to hold the esteem of men it is not sufficient to possess wealth or power. The wealth or power must be put in evidence, for esteem is awarded only on evidence'. For Veblen, advanced capitalism brings about a leisure class, characterized by conspicuous consumption; that is, economic actors who do not need to work in order to earn the existence publicly on show that they can afford to consume time in a non-productive fashion (Veblen [1899] 1994, p. 43). Such a class develops into an internal hierarchy of status groups (Veblen [1899] 1994, p. 77), characterized by symbolic elements, such as taste. This argument, echoed later in the works of Pierre Bourdieu (1979) on taste and distinction, has been more recently concretized in investigations of the material and social arrangements which support conspicuous consumption, that is, public places dedicated to shopping not only as a functional activity but as a symbolic one as well. The emergence of the department store in the second half of the nineteenth century (Zukin 2004, pp. 21; Cronon 1991, pp. 333–40; Miller 1981) and the transformation of consumption into a mass phenomenon after the Second World War (e.g. Cohen 2003) underline the importance of status not only on the producer side but on the consumer one as well.

Consumption-related status segmentation has attracted much sociological attention (see Schor and Holt [2000]; Zukin and Maguire [2004, pp. 174, 193]), including, among others, developments of Karl Marx's arguments ([1872] 2002, pp. 83–6) about the fetish character of commodities and the alienation of workers from the products of their work. This segmentation, however, is indicative of a process analogous with that described by Harrison White for the producer side. Markets do not crystallize as mere networks, but as hierarchies of groups, hierarchies in which status-relevant symbolic activities (related to prestige) play a significant role for transactions. The question then is to examine the relationship between symbolic activities and information closely. Before doing this, however, an additional aspect must be discussed, namely, that of trust in status groups.

Markets, Charisma, and Status

Up to this point, two forms of trust have been discussed in more detail: (*a*) procedural trust (see Chapter 1), characterized by the shared expectations of transaction partners that specific interaction sequences will unfold in the anticipated order. Procedural trust provides transaction partners with the background for eliciting and inferring information about the closure of the transaction. (*b*) Trust as mutual adaptation,[21] characterized by reciprocal knowledge of narratives (including the partners' formulations and justifications of interests). For all practical purposes, reciprocal narratives are accepted as valid and thus support the circulation of organizational data and contribute to network stability.

There is, however, a further aspect, which is related to status groups. Members of these groups can occupy publicly trusted positions without reciprocal knowledge of narratives. Examples here are provided by entrepreneurs, who can be entrusted by members of the public with their savings, for instance, in the absence of any reciprocal, deep knowledge of narratives. When such personal narratives are presented to the public, they can be often in a standard and even superficial format: this is why later 'revelations' can sometimes destroy public trust. The Ponzi scheme perpetrated by Bernard Madoff over four decades is a case in point here. Other examples are provided by other financial scandals of the early twenty-first century (Enron, Lehman Brothers, Royal Bank of Scotland), when trusted executive figures have been publicly discredited by the decisions they have taken. The public relied on the charismatic authority of entrepreneurial figures rather than on close personal knowledge.

Max Weber ([1921] 1972, p. 140) defines charisma as the 'quality of a person, taken to be extraordinary and for which the person is valued as having supernatural, or superhuman, or at least extraordinary powers or characteristics, which are not accessible to anyone, as godsend, as exemplary, and hence as leader'. Charismatic authority is 'alien to the economy' (Weber [1921] 1972, p. 142), in the sense of not using extraordinary gifts as a source of income (thus, a professional clairvoyant, who sells her services, cannot be charismatic). However, charismatic authority is not alien to economic activities and to market exchanges: Weber ([1921] 1972, p. 142) sees it as embodying 'from the perspective of a rational economy, the typical power of the "non-economic"'. This means that symbolic aspects of charismatic authority[22] (the extraordinary) intervene and shape economic activities. Being legitimated, among others, by office (think CEOs), and also by techniques of revelation (think profit forecasts, for instance), or by search procedures (think senior management searches conducted by specialized headhunting firms), charisma is entrenched in economic life (Weber [1921] 1972, pp. 143–4; see also Khurana [2002]). Charisma means then something else than mutual adaptation: it is not necessarily symmetric (one trusts the charismatic persons, but not necessarily the other way round); it can imply subordination (and sometimes imitation as well); it implies accepting narratives, utterances, or judgements of charismatic figures as valid or as unquestionable.

Since charisma stresses the symbolic activities and representations on which authority rests, it follows that economic status groups, with their emphasis on prestige, cannot be entirely separated from it. Such groups can achieve public authority without necessarily building broad networks of personal relationships. Charismatic trust implies distance from the public, control of public appearances and perception, as well as difficulty in accessing charismatic persons. In some cases, achieving charismatic trust implies setting up and controlling justificatory discourses, while restricting access to direct observations. It is what happens, for instance, on the stock exchanges of the nineteenth century, when restricted access to the observation of the trading floor is paired with a legitimatory discourse emphasizing charisma (Preda 2009b, chapter 6). In her study of life insurance, Viviana Zelizer (1979, pp. 125–7) highlights how insurance salesmen had to refashion themselves as altruistic missionaries in their struggle to get public acceptance.

This refashioning succeeded when prestige was coupled with expertise and the marketing of insurance as based on specialized knowledge (Zelizer 1979, p. 142).

Examples of charismatic trust are provided, among others, by the figure of the entrepreneur: Joseph Schumpeter (1943, p. 125; see also Swedberg [2003, pp. 286–7]) considered them to be individuals of 'supernormal ability and ambition'. In the world of finance, instances of charismatic trust are delivered by the figures of grand speculators (e.g. George Soros) who can bring down bureaucracies (the narrative of how Soros brought down the Bank of England in 1992 is a case in point here). Another example is provided by the rise of charisma-based economic transactions, such as direct selling, which do not rely on building complex organizational structures, but on a central figure ('the founder') who sets in place, mobilizes, and controls networks of sales-people understanding themselves not as corporate managers, but as 'followers' of an economic leader (see Biggart [1989, pp. 126–7, 131]). Charismatic figures are not only used in commercials, but in telemarketing as well, where often a glamour figure (from the sports, the movies, or just the gossip columns) promotes her own brand of merchandise (grills, perfumes, cooking sauces, and the like).

'Supernormal ability and ambition', however, refer here to the spheres of legitimate exchange, where entrepreneurs can present themselves to the world in terms of prestige, as means of mobilizing capital and of connecting to other status groups. In the underground economy, however, characterized by closure to public life and observation, entrepreneurs struggle to find business opportunities and rely mostly on small, tightly knit networks of relationships (Venkatesh 2006, pp. 118, 148). Here, the charismatic figures[23] are the moneylenders who in a cash strapped economy control the flows of (more or less legitimate) money.

Charisma serves not only to legitimate the social position of specific status groups, but their modes of profit as well. In his examination of the ways in which institutional traders legitimate their bonuses, Olivier Godechot (2007, pp. 79, 103) emphasizes two basic mechanisms. The first is that of regarding profit (made by the traders for the bank) as an object or good without a master, free floating around and waiting to be appropriated. Traders do not appear to consider themselves as employees of the bank but rather as entrepreneurs using existing institutional infrastructures in order to find and appropriate profits. The second mechanism is that traders regard themselves as endowed with will, on the grounds of which they compete for appropriating profits. This justification of bonuses on the basis of sheer will points towards charismatic authority as an intrinsic feature of trading, and to status competitions on the trading floor as unavoidable. As discussed above, several recent scandals, related to fraudulent transactions, seem to confirm such competitions.

Status and Information

While legitimating the social position of status groups, charisma acts as a connectivity interface, through which groups can relate to each other. This has important implications for how information is produced, circulated, and used. Statements, utterances, data, and narratives issued by members of status groups are endowed with prestige and authority; in other words, prestige appears not only as a private feature of such groups, but is transferred to interactions in public as well. Seen in this perspective, a public statement made by a status person will have a different value from the same sentence uttered by a non-status person. An utterance about gross profit will have a different value when formulated by the chief financial officer of the respective company than when formulated by a junior accountant, or by a secretary. This means that statements are not simply representations of external states of the world; depending on the circumstances of specific utterances, they can be judgements (i.e. endowed with authority). Their status as information cannot be separated from this endowment. When such statements are 'leaked', a non-status source (e.g. the secretary) can be endowed with authority exactly on the basis of the 'leaking'. The play with legitimate and illegitimate procedures can intervene in hierarchies of prestige. The same applies for 'anonymous' sources. While anonymity would never be trusted in an official public statement about profits (the person making the statement must occupy an official, specific, and legitimate position), anonymous leaks can be trusted.

Conversely, public statements can discredit the authority of an entrepreneur and damage her charisma exactly because they have been openly made, uttered at an inappropriate time, or made in public and not leaked to the public. When a now defunct Icelandic bank took a large stake in a British investment bank, the CEO of the latter received enquiries from the British takeover panel. According to the CEO's declarations in the media, 'they wanted to know...why our price has risen so rapidly over the past couple of days. So I laughed and said, "I think you'll find the reason is that Mr. Einarsson, the chairman of Kaupthing, said two days ago, like an idiot, that he was going to make a bid for Singer and Friedlander"' (Lewis 2009). This also points out that making public utterances is a feature of gameworthiness, and that competitions can unfold along the lines of making cunning, shrewd, or subtle statements, competitions which are directly relevant for the players' charisma.

Since status groups have the property of connectivity[24], statements made by members of other groups can be absorbed and processed as informational surprises. They will be received as consequential judgements, and not simply as utterances about the state of the world. Consequentiality means here that the recipient group can use interpretations and judgements of a statement in order to project future courses of action. The fact that external authoritative statements can be absorbed by status groups expands the 'sea of discourse' beyond the limits of a network of personal relationships, and highlights the role of charisma in producing and circulating information.

Some recent examples should illustrate this. While many have closely followed oil price movements, perhaps nobody has followed them more closely than traders on the New York Mercantile Exchange (aka the Merc), where future contracts for about 500 million barrels are traded daily. In early June 2008, while many drivers were cutting down on car use and the decrease in gasoline consumption was already apparent to traders, the price shot up by more than $5 on a single day, and by almost $11 the following day. According to Merc traders, this had nothing to do with supply and demand, but with two news items (Lowenstein 2008). The first item was comments about inflation made by Jean Claude Trichet, the President of the European Central Bank (ECB). The second was a comment by an Israeli cabinet member about the necessity to attack Iran. Neither the president of the ECB nor the members of Israel's cabinet are members of the status group of Merc traders. Yet, their statements are endowed with authority, because they are perceived as coming from members of relevant, that is, connective status groups (political in this case). Because of this authority, the statements themselves are perceived as judgements; an utterance about inflation made by the President of the ECB is not the same as an identical utterance made at the family dinner table by, say, a worker in the automobile industry.[25] Being public judgements, statements can be processed by other status groups as informational surprises—that is, as increasing uncertainty, but at the same time as providing the ground and justification for actions (i.e. trades).

Another example here is the deep plunge taken by the pound sterling after the Governor of the Bank of England stated at a Leeds business conference that a recession in the United Kingdom was likely (Wearden and Seager 2008). In this case, currency traders took the statement not as a probabilistic one (which could have been made by almost any person reading the newspapers), but as an authoritative judgement on the economic situation, a judgement which became information and allowed them to project a course of action. An authoritative statement about the likelihood of a recession, made at a provincial business conference, can anticipate its surprise effect. This is why we witness slips of tongue and 'carelessness' sometimes: utterances intended to trigger certain effects by pretending negligence.

Yet another example is provided by the case of Paul Berliner, a former trader with a Wall Street brokerage firm, who in April 2008 was charged with fraud by the Securities and Exchange Commission (SEC 2008). The charge was that the trader had disseminated a false rumour about the bid price offered by a private equity group (Blackstone) for the shares of a corporation (Allied Data Systems). What Paul Berliner did was to send instant messages to traders at hedge funds and brokerage firms about this bid price (which was substantially lower than the officially announced one). From the recipients' cell phones, the announcement made its way into the media, and the stock price of Allied Data Systems experienced an intraday decline of 17 per cent. This brought Berliner (who had shorted the stock)[26] an alleged profit of over $26,000 within one day (which he was forced to return). Relevant here is that the utterance appears to have been circulated as being endowed with authority, and hence as a judgement. This endowment allows additional layers of authority to be added to it: after being circulated through instant messaging among traders, it finds its way into the media, from where it returns to traders, this time bearing additional authority. It is its character as a judgement which makes it into information—that is, into a surprise able to come back to traders in an objectified form. Such rumours cannot be started by anyone: they have to have from the start an initial authority, or justification, upon which further layers can be added. This also indicates that authority can be laminated (Goffman 1974, p. 82)—that is, different layers of charisma can be added to statements while these are repeated and circulated around, reinforcing thus their judgemental character.

A more general consequence to be drawn from these examples is that information is not provided by signals or messages, which are neutral with respect to senders and receivers. Information is inextricably linked to authority: it emerges as judgements legitimated by the charismatic features and the prestige of their authors.[27] Even data (such as price or volume data) can be information only insofar they are tied to an authoritative source. A second consequence is that charismatic features have to be displayed in order to endow statements with the necessary authority, allowing them to work as information. The display of charismatic features goes hand in hand with symbolic activities. This is why many utterances are formulated within ceremonials such as press conferences or business conventions. Conversely, utterances can be planned as slippages and maladroitness, making pretended clumsiness into a feature of gameworthiness.

If we look at status symbols as such, they provide the charismatic support for authoritative judgements rather than constituting information per se. Changes in prestige-associated symbols (sudden or not), can, however, become information. Such changes constitute informational surprises against which the authoritative character of judgements has to be revised. Rituals of public elevation or of degradation can play a significant role in this case. An example in this sense is provided by media stories during the financial crisis of 2008–9. In one of these stories, Richard Fuld, the former CEO of Lehman Brothers (the failed investment bank) was punched in the face at the company gym by a Lehman employee. This ritual of degradation, which undermines authority and credibility, revises the prestige hierarchy: after this incident, statements coming from the former Lehman CEO will have a different degree of authority. With respect to status, then, we can distinguish at least two aspects: (*a*) data, utterances, or stories which derive their surprise character from the charismatic authority with which they are associated; (*b*) data, utterances, or stories which rearrange prestige hierarchies, establishing new authorities or sending established ones into oblivion.

Against this background, we can re-examine the argument about markets as status competitions as follows: both the hierarchy of networks approach promoted by Harrison White and Joel Podolny's status ordering view competitions as limited by relatively stable positions within niches and hierarchies. Evolution along the pecking order is slow and step by step (i.e. niche by niche); evolutionary jumps are improbable. (We should remember here the explicit biological analogies.) In this model, crises rarely happen. If we take the latter into account, however, as informational surprises which reshuffle hierarchies of prestige and authority, not only at the individual level, but at group and organizational level as well, then status competitions acquire an additional dynamism. More investigation is needed here about the ways in which informational surprises can create prestige vacancies, and with them opportunities for market actors to gain new positions in terms of charismatic authority. That this can happen over relatively short periods of time is highlighted by crisis events.

Markets from Communities

In addition to networks and status groups, there is a third form which should be discussed here, namely communities.[28] Usually discussed in political sociology, the concept of community was seen initially as occupying the middle ground between state and society (Toennies 1971, p. 65). In addition to this, however, community was conceptualized as different from the end-rational association, but nevertheless related to exchanges of goods and services, namely, as based on common elements, in which mutual services are grounded (Toennies 1971, p. 64). Common elements can be shared interests and passions, values, as well as living together in the same household.

Communities can crystallize around economic activities, such as household management (e.g. a community of flatmates) or state-imposed contributions (e.g. the community of taxpayers); they can build around voluntary contributions as well (e.g. the community of donors to an art museum). Communities can also build around market-oriented activities—for instance, communities of small agricultural producers who market their products together (see also Weber [1921] 1972, pp. 207–8). We encounter communities built around Internet transactions, such as eBay, around transactions in specific objects (e.g. stamp collectors). Some communities can crystallize along gender and ethnic distinctions, while others don't; for instance, some investment clubs[29] are gendered, while others are not (Harrington 2008).

Characteristic for communities is that they do not necessarily imply the existence of deep ties or direct relationships. While some communities are based on arm's length relationships or on shared identity markers (e.g. gender, sexual orientation, ethnicity, or age), it is not always necessarily so. A community of stamp collectors, for instance, can cut across gender, age, or income distinctions. What characterizes a community in the last instance is the common orientation provided by a shared interest. In the case of economic communities, the basis is provided by a 'rule of association, according to which . . . goods and services necessary for social action are raised' (Weber [1921] 1972, p. 207). It follows from this that the form of market transactions in which economic communities engage, their definition, and character will be determined by the said rule of association. Thus, while a family and a group of flatmates are both household communities, their rules of association would be different, and therefore the mutual transactions in which they engage would be different as well.

Rules of association, however, have an exclusionary character. They establish the conditions under which individuals can become members of the community in question. In this sense, communities imply status, in the sense that they are centred on specific activities or interests, which oftentimes are endowed by their practitioners with charisma. This, for instance, is the case of communities of musicians or painters. While this does not always lead to hierarchy building among communities, the fact that communities imply criteria for inclusion or exclusion (linked to the rule of association) means that the types of transactions they engage in will have different significance according to whether the counterparts are community members of not. This, in turn, can lead to the emergence of multi-layered, transaction-relevant ethical commitments, not very different from those discussed by Mitchel Abolafia (1996) with respect to bond traders.

In her study of monetary and non-monetary transactions within families, Vivian Zelizer (2005a, pp. 220–1) highlights that family members engage in monetary transactions and income management in ways which do not necessarily affect family solidarity. Families appear both as loci of economic calculation and of boundary negotiation; distinctions between what is legitimate as a monetary transaction and what is not are established within the practical actions of the household community. Economic calculation and boundary negotiation are also related to power relationships and constraints, undermining thus the assumptions of altruism on which economic conceptualizations of families are based (see also England [1993, p. 46]). We can contrast such cases with that of homeless newspaper sales discussed in the previous chapter. These sales situations may incorporate gift exchanges as well, but overall they leave little room for an *ex ante* negotiation or redefinition.

Sellers can hardly ask to keep the change as a gift. Family transactions can ground such redefinitions in the reciprocal moral commitments inherent to family life: offspring can request to keep shopping change as pocket money; demands for the execution of unpaid household chores can be justified with respect to mutual obligations of help.

Negotiations and redefinitions of activities are also characteristic for the ways in which investment clubs make decisions. The flow of decision-making is often defined by conversational dynamics—that is, by whether specific stocks are discussed at a start of a meeting, in the middle, or towards the end (when tiredness has settled in and members are prepared to go home). Decision-making is also shaped by situational definitions related to the perception of the members' own activities, as well as by their own personal experiences with products of the companies (Harrington 2008, pp. 53, 93). It appears in this case that the interaction dynamics of investments communities generates definitional settings and personal narratives against which informational surprises about a company can be elicited.

While investment clubs can be seen as face-to-face communities, electronic transactions have generated virtual communities as well, in which participants do not meet in physical spaces, but nevertheless abide to the same rules. Charles Smith (2007, p. 3) argues that communities enable participants to 'take the role of the other' in the absence of direct contacts or ties. In doing this, communities achieve (sometimes by negotiation) common definitions of the objects being transacted, and of their own activities. An example in this sense is provided by the way in which Internet advertising space is sold: its value is established as links to search words, which in their turn can be priced differently according to communities of users (Smith 2007, pp. 15–16). Additional examples are provided by communities of users whose common interests help establish markets for specific technologies: in the case of the Moog synthesizer (Pinch and Trocco 2002), the market for this electronic music instrument emerged as a consequence of professional and amateur musicians adopting it, or composers writing for this instrument, among others. While several versions existed, with different degrees of technological sophistication, the model which gained broad acceptance was the one which attracted diverse communities of users, such as professional and amateur musicians. Other, more sophisticated models were adopted primarily by avant-garde composers, creating thus a special niche.

This points to the fact that the emergence of market niches, as well as their ordering (hierarchical or not) is not influenced solely by producers, but also by communities of users, their activities, and the communication modes specific to each. It also points to cultural features of communities, which are irreducible to economic transactions, but nevertheless are essential for the constitution of demand; making music, in the above example, is not reduced to commercialization. Quite the contrary: many of the musicians who adopted the synthesizer had a non-commercial attitude. Neither was making music seen simply as a leisure activity in these communities, but rather as something more profound, which had to do with cultural identity. This brings us back to the issue of legitimacy; in markets, demand for certain goods and services do not simply cover a need, but can connect to (and be influenced by) domains of human activity which are non-economic. Such aspects are emphasized in more recent research on the links between community-building and economic development, research which stresses civic orientation and collective responsibility as sources of social capital encouraging economic development (e.g. Portes and Mooney 2002, pp. 309–10).

Circuits and Communities

Another special instance of communities, which also shares some features with status groups, is provided by circuits of commerce. These are defined by sets of social relationships and shared economic activities, accompanied by a common accounting system, shared understandings, and boundaries between members and non-members (Zelizer 2008, p. 2). Circuits of commerce have their own accounting systems, which cannot be reduced to mental constructs, but are material technologies (see also Chapter 4); groups exchanging goods and services based on local currencies, tokens, or vouchers, for instance, are instances of such circuits. The use of specific accounting technologies, tied to specific monies, reinforces particular systems of trust, where personal and objectified trust forms become mutually reinforcing; members come to trust each other because of the shared accounting system, and trust the latter because they trust its users as well. The identity of such circuits comes to be defined by their exchange practices and the media supporting them.

Circuits are meant to supplement and partly replace the notion of hierarchy inherent in the conceptualization of markets as status groups. Yet, if they are different from hierarchically arranged groups, circuits of commerce are different from markets as well, most importantly perhaps because they do not imply the notion of competitive exchanges intrinsic to the definition of markets. With that, circuits appear more as a particular instance of communities; Viviana Zelizer (2006, p. 30), for instance, includes caring connections among circuits of commerce.

At the same time, the notion of circuits ascribes less relevance to the issue of economic rationality or calculability: within circuits, egoism and selflessness, gift giving, and advantage taking mix up. Moreover, circuits of commerce help explain how groups develop a particular 'ideology' or 'discourse' which justifies their economic activities. This is something more difficult to explain with the notion of network, but intrinsic to the concept of institution (discussed in Chapter 5). Since circuits have their own accounting units and systems (see also Zelizer [2005c]), and since an intrinsic feature of such systems is the (narrative) justification of exchanges and expenditures, circuits can develop worldviews and narrative justifications of their activities. In this respect, they are not unlike status groups, which also have legitimating accounts based on their special character.

Markets from Informational Surprises

I will now turn to a concrete example showing how markets are created from surprises, and how communities emerge around them. At the same time, this example prefigures some of the key topics investigated in the following chapters, such as expertise and the role of market technologies. The case study discussed below is also a very explicit one, in the sense that it concerns the creation of a market for surprises. Sold on at least two continents (Europe and North America), but probably best known in Continental Europe, surprise eggs have been a favourite of children for more than three decades. In Europe, they are sold in supermarkets and convenience shops, among others, for less than one euro. While their packaging may differ slightly across countries, surprise eggs are hollow chocolate eggs each containing a plastic capsule of about 4 cm (ca. 1.57 in.) Inside the capsule are small plastic figurines; sometimes they are cast, and sometimes they will be assembled from components, according to instructions. Several figurines will usually form a series; some series are licensed from popular movies or comic characters, and some are in-house inventions. The surprise eggs are produced by a chocolate manufacturer (Ferrero AG, based in Frankfurt, Germany), who in the post-Second World War scarcity years came up with the idea of selling individual pralines (instead of the more expensive box) and chocolate spread as a substitute for the more expensive solid chocolate bars (Kleipa 2004, pp. 3–5).

The surprise eggs have found keen buyers not only among children but among adults as well. These latter are interested not so much in the hollow chocolate egg as in the plastic figurines, which have become collectibles. Indeed, adults can be often seen in supermarkets buying dozens of eggs at once and trying to guess from the weight of each egg the figurine it might contain. A figurine such as the Happy Hippo, for instance, sold in 2003 for 50 euros (Kleipa 2004, p. 13). There are catalogues listing all the available figurines, akin to those listing art objects. While auction catalogues stress the genealogy of ownership, the surprise egg catalogues stress appearance and rarity. Because production errors occur from time to time, a few copies of a figurine might differ in colour, and this makes them even more expensive.

Complete series of figurines and intact figurines sell for more than used or incomplete figurines. The whole Star Wars series, for instance, can sell for hundreds of euros. Completeness means here that the plastic capsule and the assembly instructions are part of the package, and they must be intact as well. Figurines are sold on eBay, and also at flea markets and car boot sales, usually neatly arranged in transparent plastic boxes. Collectors consider the most important criteria to be (in this order) completeness, conservation state (this will enhance the figurine's lifespan), rarity, period (the catalogue provides data about the years in which the figurines were produced), and popularity (Kleipa 2004, pp. 32–3). Similar to art lovers, collectors of surprise eggs can specialize in specific periods or characters; for instance, they will collect only figurines produced in the period 1999–2000, or only figurines wearing a hat. (Due to large volume production, a year contains many series of figurines.) Moreover, collectors have developed a special vocabulary for each component of a figurine, including elements of packaging and assembly instructions.

We are confronted here with two interdependent transactions: transactions in surprise eggs and transactions in collectible figurines. On the first market, adults represent a large proportion. Irrespective of this, the logic of this market is that of informational surprises: adults and children alike buy the eggs not for the quality of the chocolate, but for the toys inside. The second, collectibles market processes these surprises according to a series of criteria, which are not entirely different from those of the art market: figurines are catalogued with information about production year, appearance, components, and the like. They are displayed in cases, and careful handling has an influence on the price. One of the aims of this processing of surprises is to identify further surprises: that is, pieces which are rare, either due to manufacturing errors (e.g. painting Darth Vader's costume blue instead of black) or due to limited production numbers. In its turn, the chocolate manufacturer exploits this by announcing in advance that certain figurines will be produced in limited numbers, so as to increase egg sales.

The market for collectible figurines is not framed by any institutional arrangements, formal organizations, or legal contracts. As mentioned above, figurines are sold at car boot sales, flea markets, or over the Internet. This market resembles more an amateur soccer play taking place in a meadow than a premier league game in a state of the art stadium. Yet, this does not prevent the amateurs' play from expanding at national and international levels, developing its own forms of expertise, and its own material arrangements.

Taken in themselves, manufacturing the figurines probably costs only a couple of cents (the whole egg sells for less than one euro). The prices at which they trade among collectors are much, much higher. These prices are not justified with respect to quality of execution or to aesthetic criteria (there is widespread agreement that aesthetics is not the strongest feature of the figurines). Prices are justified with respect to completeness, conservation, and rarity. Since complete and well-conserved figurines are rarer to come by than used ones, the first two factors are meant to increase the rarity of a piece; a truly expensive Happy Hippo, for instance, will have all its intact packaging and assembly instructions included and maybe, for good measure, some part painted in the wrong colour as well. Rarity, which can be seen here as an informational surprise (of the kind 'oh, this exists!'), is not legitimated aesthetically, functionally, or historically, but as an autonomous valuation criterion.

The routines and material assemblages set in place by the community of collectors are meant to work towards the identification and preservation of such informational surprises. The manufacturer, in turn, regularly provides collectors with new surprises. The capacity to produce new figurines is an important element in the reproduction of these transactions. The market of collectible plastic figurines does not work towards the allocation of any resources, or towards fulfilling any need, material or aesthetic. Yet, why does it exist then? Of course, one could argue that this market works as a community of collectors ready to invest money, time, and effort in this activity and engage in transactions. At the same time, it is a community willing to engage in competitions based on the ability to identify, control, and preserve informational surprises. The skills required by membership in this community point towards this: the ability to guess the possible figurine from the weight of chocolate eggs, the knowledge of series produced in the past, the ability to keep the packaging intact, and so on. It is also a community engaging in competitive social valuations, where the ability to identify and preserve figurines (including the packaging), to guess the contents of chocolate eggs from their weight, to painstakingly and doggedly assemble whole series, to incessantly search for that rare manufacturing accident are as many indicators of gameworthiness—that is, social attributes acknowledged as such by peers. In this perspective, the market for surprise eggs is perhaps less about very small, cheap pieces of plastic than it is about showing one's specific gameworthiness.

With that, we have come closer to a further sociological specification of markets, albeit not a final one: markets are (hierarchies of) groups, networks, and communities competing on gameworthiness-relevant information—that is, by producing, identifying, and handling informational surprises in relationship to socially relevant attributes. Production, identification, stabilization, and control of surprises occur in specific interaction formats. This applies to informational surprises related to selling corporations as well as to selling handbags or hollow chocolate eggs. Informational surprises, together with the related skills and knowledge, are different for a handbag sold on the pavement from one sold in a high fashion boutique; hence, markets can contiguously coexist even when the artefacts they are related to are apparently so similar.

Information and Market Structures

Summing up, this chapter has investigated markets as social structures, distinguishing among three basic formations, namely, networks, groups, and communities—with circuits as an intermediate formation (see Table 2.1).[30] The theoretical argument, however, has been that a conceptualization of markets as networks leaves open important questions, which can be better answered with the concept of status groups. The hierarchies intrinsic to markets are neither clear-cut nor static; they can be characterized not only by evolutionary change, but also by rapid transformations, which can happen as a consequence of crisis events.

Hierarchies are maintained and reproduced by interaction forms including, among others, gossip, stories, dramatic performances, rituals, or casual exchanges. Private and public utterances (including media representations of such utterances), visual representations (of people and artefacts), and numerical data are also among the resources and tools of these hierarchies. This is not to say that all public and private utterances, representations, or data are information. First, information implies judgement—that is, it is endowed with an authority—which makes it inherently asymmetric. Second, information generates uncertainty (i.e. produces surprises) requiring further action. At least two types can be distinguished here: (*a*) group- and hierarchy-relevant information and (*b*) transaction-relevant information. The first type is geared towards the maintenance or realignment of relationships within and among groups, while the second is geared towards the initiation, stabilization, and completion of transactions. In this sense, the second type of information can be constrained by the first, although there are degrees of freedom as well. These degrees of freedom emerge when there is relative interactional

Table 2.1. Markets as social formations

Formation type	Primary communicational features	Primary trust features	Primary ties
Networks	Personal narratives	Mutual adjustment	Deep ties Arm's length Inter-network holes
Status groups	Prestige symbols Symbolic communication	Charismatic trust	Prestige-based hierarchy Authority
Communities	Virtual communities: mediated, interest-based communication; negotiation Face-to-face community: reciprocal adjustment; rules of association	Virtual communities: weak adjustment Face-to-face community: rule-based adjustment	Virtual communities: common orientation to object; infrequent ties Face-to-face community: orientation to rules

separation of the two types: for instance, gossip at a party (which may generate information of the first type) may be relevant for, but does not overlap with a transaction conducted next day between the gossiping partners. Second, as it has been exemplified in the previous chapter, the character of transaction-relevant information also depends on the moment when it is generated in the interaction sequence. This placement within the sequence cannot be determined by relational information. An auction room can be full with members of the same status groups (who may also know each other), yet this will not determine who bids what at which moment in the auction sequence, and in reaction to whom.

Both group- and transaction-relevant information can be laminated—that is, additional layers can be added to both (see Table 2.2). A judgemental statement about a relationship within one group can be commented upon, a comment that can become information in itself. Price data used in a transaction can also be commented upon, a commentary which in principle has the capacity of reorienting the course of the transaction. This means that the dynamics of market information is unforeseeable (we can have expectations, but we cannot forecast when a comment will be made, for instance); self-supporting (new comments will be generated all the time); recursive (comments will be made about comments); connective (non-economic groups can make transaction-relevant comments); under-determinate (we cannot foresee reactions to comments); and polythetic (information can be the object of market transactions, but also of ritual gift giving).

In the following chapter, I will examine the issue of comments and their role in market transactions. With that, I mean in the first place a specific kind of commentaries, namely, expert ones. Market transactions seem to be accompanied by a variety of forms of expertise, which constantly intervene in the said transactions, an expertise which includes, among others, conceptualizations and models of market information. It is now time to turn to investigate closer how forms of economic expertise are constituted and the roles they play.

Table 2.2. Types of market information

Features of market information	Subtype 1: relational information	Subtype 2: transactional information
Unforeseeable	Mostly face-to-face	Face-to-face or mediated
Self-supporting	Supports, but does not determine transactional information	Can be bought and sold
Recursive		Can be converted into relational information
Connective	Subject to gift exchange	
Under-determinate		
Polythetic		

☐ **NOTES**

1. Work is not strictly individual, in the sense that it is the product of the division of labour, which creates interdependencies among individuals and groups. Thus, each individual's work depends on the work done by others. In this perspective, work appears as a social relationship and not as an activity determined by the intrinsic capabilities of any individual.

2. 'Narrative', in the way it is dealt with in this approach, means a variety of conversational forms (like personal storytelling), as well as written forms of communication (e.g. e-mails). From the viewpoint of the interaction order, however, we can say that networks of personal relationships are supported mainly by engagements and staged performances.

3. According to Roland Burt (2001, p. 41), personal stories are not so much appreciated for their informational content per se, but because they reinforce the actors' reciprocal predispositions.

4. This resonates with Harrison White's viewpoint (2000, p. 118) (discussed in the following) that markets are constituted in a sea of discourse. While at the first sight this could be seen as adding another layer of embeddedness (i.e. communicational embeddedness), White's position is more sophisticated.

5. A similar situation is discussed by Alan Kirman (2001, p. 177) with respect to fish markets, where some buyers are loyal to specific sellers, while others shop around; the result is price differentials for the same commodity.

6. This notion is somewhat similar with Mark Granovetter's notion (1973, p. 1361) of weak ties, which involve less time spent together and less emotional commitment between participants. Granovetter takes weak ties to be characteristic rather for inter- than for intra-network relationships.

7. It should be added here that the spatial organization of the trading floor shapes the size of crowds. Caitlin Zaloom's ethnographic study (2006, pp. 60–1) of the CBOT shows that the shape of the trading pits (octagonal, with stairs descending onto a lower trading platform) makes it difficult for traders to relate to everybody in the pit in the same way. Traders will compete for dominating positions, from which they can see and be seen by as many participants in the pit as possible. The crowd dynamics (i.e. the varying number of participants to whom a trader relates in the pit) is thus a function of the competition for dominating places.

8. John Levi Martin (2009, chapter 3) makes a similar argument, albeit theoretically: inter-actional demands grow exponentially with the size of the group. However, cliques are a dominant structural form in everyday life. Consequently, a group which grows in size will tend to break down into cliques.

9. This does not preclude the fact that networks are active in organizations as well. Indeed, some of the research on networks in economic settings at least partly replaces the notion of organization with that of network, in the sense that the investigation of formal aspects of organizational processes recedes in favour of examining how informal network-based exchanges within organizations overlap with inter-organizational transactions. This has also to do with the fact that the neoinstitutionalist approach in organizational sociology replaces the study of organizational formal rationality with that of rituals and discursive processes which reproduce organizations (see also Meyer and Rowan [1977]; Lounsbury and Ventresca 2003), while effective transactions are rather network-driven.

10. Network closure should not be exclusively understood as restricted access and limited number of participants. Networks can be topically closed as well—for instance, networks

within an industry branch are focused on specific topics (e.g. production technologies, sales strategies), while being closed to others. This can make development and adaptation of substantially new technologies, for instance, difficult. This is the problem of resistance to innovation, which can be endemic in closed networks.

11. Roughly put, political embeddedness means that market transactions are shaped by political institutions, agents, and interests. Cultural embeddedness, in its turn, means that transactions depend on customs, rituals, and rules with a local character, as well as on (loosely defined) discourses which contribute to group identities. There is thus, for instance, a 'Chinese way' of doing business, distinct from a 'German way', and so on. This, however, doesn't change the fact that cultural or political factors are seen as external constraints with respect to transactions. The problems related to the externalization of social factors with respect to transactions are not solved by these distinctions.

12. White (1981) and, echoing him, neoinstitutionalist sociologists as well (Fligstein 2002, p. 63) see markets as 'self-reproducing role structures', which include status aspects.

13. Anthropological research points out that systems of reciprocal obligations are differently structured according to whether exchange partners belong to the group or not (Carrier 1996, p. 219).

14. This does not mean that such hierarchies do not offer the possibility of attaching illegitimate or illegal transactions to them. Going back to the example of the Venetian handbag peddlers discussed in Chapter 1, we can see how they can coexist in the public space with high-end shops as part of a hierarchy regarded by the public as legitimate, even if some of its players are not lawful.

15. Note here again that observability is not restricted to such features being directly observable. Fashion shows, for instance, are directly observable to only a few. They are indirectly observable through accounts, stories, photographs, commentaries, and so on.

16. See Nelson D. Schwartz, 'A Spiral of Losses by a "Plain Vanilla" Trader'. *New York Times*, 25 January 2008; Nicola Clark and David Jolly, 'French Bank Says Rogue Trader Lost $7 Billion'. *New York Times*, 25 January 2008; James Kanter, 'Charges Are Sought Against French Trader'. *New York Times*, 28 January 2008; Doreen Carvajal and James Kanter, 'A Quest for Glory and Bonus End in Disgrace'. *New York Times*, 29 January 2008; Nelson D. Schwartz and Katrin Bennhold, 'A Trader's Secrets, a Bank's Missteps'. *New York Times*, 5 February 2008; Matthew Saltmarsh, 'French Bank Suffers $807 Million Trading Loss'. *New York Times*, 17 October 2008.

17. In anthropology, this transformation is captured in the analysis of rituals of exchange meant to consolidate symbolic power.

18. In a recent editorial piece published in the *New York Times*, the investor Warren Buffett (2008) resurrected the 1980's slogan, 'buy American', as a way of expressing trust in the US economy. This is a reformulation of an economic activity (investing) as having an ultimately patriotic goal.

19. An understanding of organizations in terms of groups does not exclude the material aspects of organizational life. Organizational groups deploy activities involving the manipulation of artefacts and can use the latter in order to establish status distinctions (see here Bechky [2003]; Callon and Muniesa [2005]; Beunza and Stark [2005]). Moreover, price discovery in organizations depends to a large extent on material arrangement for displaying and memorizing data, among others. These aspects will be discussed in detail in the following chapters.

20. Since neoinstitutionalism emphasizes status- and legitimacy-relevant activities within organizations, activities that are deployed by status groups, it follows that markets can be

seen as inter-organizational (aka inter-group) interfaces. However, because status groups have the property of connectivity—that is, they can link with other status groups from outside their field of activity, markets as interfaces would necessarily provide connection points for non-economic groups as well (political, social, or cultural).

21. Trust as mutual adaptation can become legally codified, in the form of fiduciary trust—that is, the obligation of an agent to execute the instructions and to act in the best interests of the principal. Such a legal obligation would be difficult to conceive without the assumption of adaptation—that is, the agent must adapt to the interests and viewpoints of the principal.

22. Weber ([1921] 1972, p. 142) counts sponsorship, generously tipping waiters, donations, baksheesh, as well as blackmailing among the forms of charisma-based economic activity.

23. Following Weber, charismatic figures need not have positive connotations. We should not forget that blackmailing and robbing are counted by Weber among charisma-based economic activities.

24. An example of connectivity among status groups is provided by a recent episode, when the Tory shadow chancellor, George Osborne, apparently attempted to elicit party donations from a Russian oligarch at a social meeting hosted in Greece by a British hedge fund manager from the Rothschild family (Watt and Wintour 2008). We encounter here members of different status groups (political, economic, and financial) who meet socially and 'discuss' political and economic affairs. That status plays a significant role, which goes well beyond networks of relationships, is revealed by the reasons for why the donation story was leaked to the media. Apparently, the shadow chancellor, in gossiping about a rival, had 'behaved disloyally, improperly and has conducted himself in a shabby and dishonest manner' (Watt and Wintour 2008, p. 4). Another example of connectivity is provided by venture capitalists, who entertain ties with politicians, as well as with scientists. Some venture capital firms are closed to investors who come without recommendations and without the required reputation. A recent report described a prominent venture capital firm as 'a mutual-interest society of wealth, knowledge and connections, and even if you wanted to, even if you begged, you couldn't invest with them' (Gertner 2008).

25. While the media plays a significant role in circulating such utterances and adding to their authority, this does not change the fact that it is the charisma of the author, by force of his or her position, which endows the utterance with authority and trust. After all, an unknown person interviewed on national television in prime time and uttering the same statement would not have had the same effect upon the traders.

26. This refers to the practice of short selling—that is, selling a stock without owning it. The seller (acting on the assumption that the stock price is going down) borrows the stocks, sells them, and then buys them back at a lower price and returns them to the lender.

27. It should be noted here that authorial prestige can be transferred upon technologies, and can be tied to the procedural trust incorporated in technological assemblages. This will be discussed in detail in the following chapters.

28. Sometimes, communities are equated with networks of social relationships, the only difference being that the former manifest affectivity (see Segre [2008, p. 9]). In this case, we would face the difficulty of explaining how certain networks can develop affects, while others don't. Additionally, the cases of the Internet, or of symbolic communities indicate that such affects are not always present. It is rather a shared orientation and/or interests which are relevant here.

29. While investment clubs have a formal structure, provided by statutes, legal codification, and hierarchy, among others, they are nonetheless communities; members can leave them at will and are not obliged to make participatory contributions (e.g. they can be present at meetings without participating in discussions). It should be mentioned here again that Weber treats (formal) associations as communities.

30. Authors such as Charles Perrow (2002, p. 24) distinguish between markets, hierarchies, and communities as separate socio-economic formations. However, since from a social-structural viewpoint markets can be conceived as involving group hierarchies (including networks), as well as communities, the distinction between markets and hierarchies has not been maintained here.

3 Markets, Information, and Economic Expertise

A soccer match involves not only teams on the field, but also commentators; sports journalists and the public observing the play make incessant comments upon what is going on in the field, before the play, while this latter unfolds, and after the play. Not only that, the players themselves make comments upon the play while playing and also before and after the play. The play of the game always includes the comments upon the play. Similarly, plays of competitive transactions include comments and judgements upon what is going on, comments which very often are clad in the mantle of expertise.

The fact that comments are authoritative sends us back to the issue of status groups. I have argued in the previous chapter that within markets status groups possess the property of connectivity—that is, they can link up with non-economic groups, drawing upon the resources and activities of these latter, as well as influencing them. Examples in this sense are provided by the connections among market groups and political or scientific ones (think scientists participating in venture capital, or politicians being lobbied by business groups), or among market groups and socialites.[1] Connectivity also applies to groups specializing in the production, circulation, and processing of informational objects, without these groups being directly involved in market transactions. Such groups—called for practical purposes informational—can maintain direct connections with market groups, or can connect with political ones, for instance. Analysts employed in investment banks, as well as government-employed economic experts (e.g. in economic think tanks), are cases in point here.

The existence of informational groups can be explained by the properties of market information: its laminations, recursive features, and polythetic character make it possible for groups situated outside market transactions to operate in the production, dissemination, and processing of additional levels of market information. This happens because relational and transactional information cannot be entirely controlled by its authors, and because additional layers of information can be fed back into market activities.[2] These additional layers generate then surprises in the market, multiplying possibilities for action. In this perspective, information does not decrease market uncertainty, but rather increases it, eliciting thus responses from the involved actors.

At least the following informational groups can be distinguished here:

1. Groups specializing in the production and dissemination of relational and transactional information as merchandise—that is, groups which engage in producing and selling informational objects, creating thus additional market layers. Service providers such as Reuters or Bloomberg, but other news agencies as well are to be counted among them.[3] Rating agencies are also a case in point.

2. Groups specialized in the production and distribution of information within market settings, in relationship to or as part of the transacted entities. Economic analysts embedded in corporations, or financial analysts working in investment banks should be counted among them.

3. Groups embedded within non-economic organizations, and which are specialized in the production and dissemination of economic information as subordinated to the goals and activities of the larger organization. Economic experts working for governmental or international agencies are examples here.

4. Groups which produce informational objects as a self-contained goal, not necessarily targeted at immediate applications.[4] This is the case of academic economic science.

5. Groups specialized in the production and distribution of market information for broader publics: financial and economic journalists are examples here.

6. Groups specialized in the production and distribution of relational, social, and object-relevant information for broader publics, information which while not immediately related to market transactions, can become relevant for them. Gossip, technology, art, sports journalists, or literary critics are examples here. While the judgements they produce are not immediately oriented to transactions, they can become transaction-relevant. An article by an art critic, a review by a literary critic, or a sports commentary can influence the price of artwork, the advance on royalties for a future novel, or the transfer price of a soccer player, respectively. For instance, the professionalization of opera singers and the transition from a patronage to a market system in the eighteenth century included the circulation of news about singers, as well as the emergence of opera criticism, useful when negotiating fees (Rosselli 1989, p. 26).

7. Groups specialized in the production of artefacts which can become informational and integrated in market transactions. Software engineers are a case in point here. While these groups do not produce information in the same way in which economists or analysts do, they produce objects which can incorporate and display information to market participants. These groups can develop a special relationship with market groups, which will be detailed in the next chapter. It suffices to notice here that, while connected to specific

market groups (think venture capitalists in the software industry), techno-logical groups can become directly involved in transactions, by taking over roles previously performed by market groups (such as brokers).

What is characteristic to all these groups is that they produce information as particular objects endowed with specific properties. In doing this, they employ a variety of cognitive tools, knowledge, and skills. The production of information cannot do without these tools, operations, and skills. While market groups have been conceived as producing and circulating mainly oral information within transactions (or within transaction-relevant interactions), informational groups manufacture solid-state information, so to speak. Moreover, such groups can lay a legitimate claim to being particularly suited for the production of information. They can claim to possess whatever is necessary in this production, yet others do not have.

Since networks of personal relationships are present within informational groups as well as within market groups, it follows that we will encounter here the same types of social relationships: deep ties, arm's length relationships, as well as structural holes among networks. Therefore, similar phenomena are expected to appear here, such as informational innovation coming from less dense regions of networks, or cascading imitations down the hierarchy of niches. However, since informational objects are only to a limited extent commodities—in the sense that only some of the above groups directly engage in transacting them for money—and have a series of distinct properties, we should expect phenomena like imitation, for instance, to be rather restricted. This also has to do with the fact that informational groups are professional groups, where a key component of status is originality. (Economists or analysts have to be original, to distinguish themselves in order to maintain their position.) This limits imitation efforts, among others.

If status characteristics apply to market groups, there is no reason that they should not apply to connected informational groups as well. We would encoun-ter then similar prestige- and resource-based hierarchies both within each category and among categories of informational groups. This would affect for instance groups of economists (who have their prestige hierarchies), of financial analysts (who are rated by publications such as *Institutional Investor* or the *Wall Street Journal*), or of economic journalists (working for the *Financial Times* carries more weight than working for, say, the *Evening Standard*). We shall also expect competitions for gameworthiness, similar to the ones taking place in market transactions, albeit along different valuation criteria. That informational groups are competitive in this sense is indicated by the contests taking place periodically, and culminating in the crowning of the financial analyst of the year, distinguished publication awards, career awards, and the like.

At the same time, these groups are ranked among themselves: being an academic economist carries a different weight from being a chart analyst, for instance. By being ordered along hierarchies of prestige, which resonate onto the informational products of these groups, they confer additional legitimacy to market transactions. An analysis of market trends for instance, published in a respected newspaper, sets another layer of legitimacy upon the actors, institutions, and processes in question. Additionally, there is the legitimacy conferred by judgements upon the features of market transactions. Conversely, an analysis can also delegitimate economic transactions. All in all, this means that informational groups produce not only informational objects with a narrative character (e.g. the newspaper description of a merger), but also judgements upon market transactions.

The fact that informational groups are ordered along hierarchies indicates that the products of their activities, as well as their oral statements will be endowed with different degrees of authority. A statement about inflation made by, say, the chief economist of the Bank of England will carry more weight than the same statement made by the chief economist of a provincial savings institute. Since they are endowed with authority, informational products will be taken as judgements. Yet, not only will judgements carry different weights, but they can also be contested or judged upon in different ways. A research paper may be signed by a prominent economist, but be judged by audiences as a poor product.

All this points to several issues which need further unpacking: (*a*) informational groups act as professional or quasi-professional groups, having at least partial, institutionally sanctioned control over their domain of production, as exemplified by access, training, and certification, among others. (*b*) They act as expert groups, using specific cognitive tools, knowledge, and skills, and with access to and control of specific cognitive resources in the production of information. (*c*) They engage in competitions, as manifested in the specific judgements they make about their own products, and in the claims made by their publics. (*d*) Being solid-state, informational products can be transferred and put to use in market transactions, changing the latter, or can become the object of transactions themselves.

I will now discuss these aspects one by one, starting with jurisdiction.

Informational Groups and Jurisdiction

Professional groups are characterized by jurisdiction—that is, by a specific link between the claims of the groups and the work they perform (Abbott 1988, p. 20). By claiming a unique authority to perform certain tasks and services, professional groups can also lay claim to a monopoly over their activities, to public payments, to self-regulation, or to specific mechanisms of education and certification. In short, jurisdiction implies that professional groups ask society to recognize the unique character of their cognitive structure (Abbott 1988, p. 59). This recognition, which automatically implies legitimacy, is grounded in specific social structures and institutions, such as professional associations, schools, contracts with public bodies, and so on.

Seen in their evolution, information-related professional groups can be broadly divided into two categories: those oriented to qualitative tasks and those oriented to quantitative ones. Qualitative-task areas, such as librarians, documentarists, or archivists, developed and expanded in the nineteenth century in relationship to the expansion of government (which produced documents to be stored and managed), as well as in relationship to the development of technologies for storage and for office work (the typewriter, or the catalogue system—see Yates 1994). Other qualitative-task areas, such as journalism, remained less well defined and tied to activities such as public relations or advertising (Abbott 1988, p. 225); recently, they too have been affected by technological developments (see also Boczkowski [2004]). Quantitative-task areas evolved on a somewhat different path, due not only to a specific impact of technology, but also to specific relationships with the government, among others: thus, statistics and accountancy were shaped not only by their ties to government, but also, especially after the Second World War, by technologies developed initially by and for the military. While cost management and marketing were weakly developed at the turn of the nineteenth century, they changed from the 1950s on, when a new profession arose, namely, the management specialist (Abbott 1988, p. 238).

The evolution of market-related informational groups, while relatively recent, is marked by attempts to establish various degrees of jurisdiction over their production and dissemination of information. The nature of this jurisdiction is determined not only by the technologies they employ and the character of the cognitive work they perform, but also by their ties with market groups, the competition they encounter, and the claims they make about their informational products. Providers of transactional information, such as Reuters or other news agencies, established themselves early in the nineteenth century, in relationship to efforts at transforming news into a commodity. These efforts were conditioned to a large extent by the available technology (submarine cable telegraphy became commercially viable only towards the end of the nineteenth century), as well as by attempts at expanding on a global scale (Winseck and Pike 2007, p. 338; see also Standage [1998]). From the start, providers of transactional information (like telegraph companies) geared their activities towards businesses which remained their primary customers. In many situations, jurisdiction initially implied the state granting commercial information providers a monopoly over the commercialization of news within a certain territory, monopoly which was rescinded only much later and not without tensions.

The establishment of commercial information providers led to the emergence of several hierarchically interconnected and sometimes gendered professional groups. For instance, initially telephone operators were mainly women, because their pitch of voice came clearer over the wires (see, for instance, Bertinotti [1985]; Downey [2000]). At the same time, new status groups emerged, such as telegraph operators (who had to learn the Morse code) or courier boys (Downey 2002, p. 40). This indicates a professional dynamics which continues to the present day, when IT workers are in charge of maintaining the technological infrastructure of markets, for instance. Initially, to a certain extent, providers of informational hardware (and skills) were separated from information providers, in the sense that telegraph companies, for instance, did not produce and own the messages which were being transmitted. This, however, has to a large extent changed; nowadays major information providers in financial markets, for instance, own the software and the data being accessed by clients. This points to an additional aspect of jurisdiction: the fact that data has the legal status of an owned commodity (for the origins of this legal status, see Preda [2009*b*, chapters 3–4]; Abolafia [1996, p. 59]).

For other informational groups, however, it is not so much the legal status of data as a commodity, or the technological infrastructure supporting its dissemination which are decisive with respect to jurisdiction, but successful authority claims, directly related to the properties of the informational objects these groups produce. This appears to be more the case for professional groups who do not directly engage in market activities, but want to establish themselves within existing institutional arrangements (like higher education, for instance), or to establish an object as informational, before bringing it to the market. Laying claim to a domain of activity—and to the associated informational objects—implies among others successfully mobilizing different kinds of authority (scientific, political, or economic), as well as occupying central positions within the institutional framework in question. This, in turn, requires using institutional resources and constraints in skilful ways, fending off contestations and marginalizing opponents. In addition, the standardization of informational objects facilitates their diffusion and use, reinforcing thus the jurisdictional claims of the groups producing them.

In Europe, statisticians have a longstanding relationship with the state; already in the early nineteenth century, the state's administrative practices were incorporating statistics. With statistics offices often being attached to trade ministries, the systematic gathering of economic statistics and the formation of academic bodies were initiated (Desrosières 1998, pp. 153, 167, 173). Statistics, however, were not particularly trusted by economists; it was engineers intervening in economic activities who, in the 1920s and 1930s, established the conjunction between statistics and economic theory and introduced it into higher education (Desrosières 1998, p. 164). At about the same time, the US Corps of Engineers began routinely introducing cost estimates into their analyses as a way of justifying their projects for the US Congress not only in technical terms, but also in utilitarian ones. This regime of justification helped projects being pushed through Congress and conferred a new authority—that is, economic, in addition to technical—to the US Corps of Engineers (Porter 1995, pp. 154–5).

In the case of chart analysts, for instance, gaining jurisdiction implied establishing the product of their activities as informational—that is, as susceptible to being used by traders as a tool in transactions. The first chart analysts—who were originally stock brokers—mobilized scientific and business authorities in order to represent their product—charts—as informational, and as relevant for conducting transactions (Preda 2007, pp. 53–4). They used, among others, public endorsements by successful speculators for their charts, and marketed publications dedicated to chart analysis as a way of promoting their authority. Thus, chart analysis became established in the absence of any institutional framework to support the education and certification of analysts. In the United Kingdom, financial and economic journalists gained jurisdiction in the nineteenth century by distinguishing their authority from that of fiction writers (until the 1820s, the distinction was unclear), and by promoting financial writing as factual, in opposition to fiction. This implied, among others, forging alliances with statisticians and with academic economists, gaining dedicated space in newspapers, and finding employment in government agencies, such as the India House (Poovey 2008, p. 353). After financial journalism became a distinct branch of journalism, it started combining the presentation of numerical data with narratives, representing finance as 'a culture unto itself, as a law-governed, natural, and—pre-eminently—safe section of modern society' (Poovey 2002, pp. 22–3). Parallel with the mobilization of various forms of authority, product standardization is another way of gaining jurisdiction; credit scoring agencies, for instance, marketed a labour-intensive, custom tailored credit-scorecard system to provincial banks during the 1950s, offering them a standardized quantitative way of making decisions about credit applications. In the 1980s, data gathering and processing was also standardized, facilitating the diffusion and consolidation of credit agencies, as well as increasing their authority (Poon 2007, pp. 293–5).

For academic economists, however, jurisdiction requires not only establishing an informational product which can be endowed with global authority (in the form of a model, together with the corresponding research methodology), but also establishing such a model as dominant within academic institutions. While chairs in political economy were already established in the eighteenth century (Fourcade 2006, p. 161), the object of economics remained contested for a longer time. For instance, formal models of market exchanges competed with home economics and with institutional economics (which provided an account of the historical development of socio-economic institutions, in their relationship to the state) as the object of investigation for the economic science (Swedberg 2008; Yonay 1998). Up to the Second World War, outsiders such as literary critics or poets could intervene in economic debates and formulate programmes with impunity: economic policy was not considered a matter exclusively for experts trained in economics. Academic economists promoting formal models of market exchanges were able to gain jurisdiction by expanding and consolidating their position in academia, a process which took place mainly after the Second World War. Among others, this went hand in hand with them being able to establish an informational product which was more standardized than other approaches (and hence more easily transferable), with gaining important positions in academia, as well as with establishing strongholds within governmental bodies. This dominant position was reinforced with the accrued prestige gained in public and institutional spheres, not least by establishing a dedicated Nobel Prize in 1969.

Gradually, formal economists gained a greater influence in policy making, by occupying official positions (in sectors of government) which were formerly occupied by other professionals, such as lawyers (see Babb [2001]). This echoes earlier developments, where in nineteenth century France, for instance, formally trained economists established themselves as an academic profession by displacing other professional groups engaged in economics, such as lawyers and scholars (see Zylberberg [1990]). Internal displacements within academia, coupled with establishing positions within political bodies (government, think tanks), were accompanied by an increased capacity of transforming further fields into an object of investigation for the economic science.

A good example here is provided by the way in which finance was brought into the field of economics. During the nineteenth century, conceptualizations of price variations were not undertaken by economists, but by educated stock brokers, in works situated at the boundary between investment advice and academic treatise (see Jovanovic and Le Gall [2001]; Preda [2004]). Academic economics continued to more or less ignore finance until the early 1960s, when academics working at the University of Chicago and MIT, respectively, introduced stochastic analysis to the study of price variations. New, specialized journals (as well as manuals and anthologies) were published, and PhD students were recruited, who then went to occupy prominent positions in academia. This went hand in hand with the increased use of computers, which provided the technological support for stochastic analysis. Intellectual developments of the early twentieth century were now represented as the intellectual tradition of financial economics, centred on the thesis that markets are efficient. The formation of a canon within the new subdiscipline (i.e. within financial economics) was accompanied by the elaboration of a canonical history, which assembled an intellectual tradition out of authors who until then had been more or less neglected (Jovanovic 2008).

Overall, professional groups establishing jurisdiction over market-relevant informational objects and activities apply combinations of the following strategies:

1. They establish the status of their domain of cognitive production, either as a commodity, as a tool for the use of other groups (e.g. state bureaucrats, engineers), as a truthful representation of economic entities, or as a combination thereof.
2. They establish public authority by setting up institutional structures which control admission and progress within the profession.
3. They forge links with other groups (state bureaucracies, market groups), links which create an audience for their products and confer them additional authority.
4. They gain definitional control over the object of their cognitive production, by occupying dominant positions within the institutional structures of production, by generating disciples, and by marginalizing or displacing competing groups, among others.
5. They legitimate their informational products by reference to representations of tradition and of intellectual authority.
6. They create specialized vehicles for the dissemination of products to audiences (e.g. publications), vehicles which are endowed with prestige.
7. They standardize products, making them transferable across audiences.

The products of expertise, as well as expert skills, can be the object of commercial transactions: when experts can successfully claim jurisdiction over the uses of their skills and the dissemination of their products, both skills and products can be made into commodities, leading thus to the emergence of new markets. This is true not only of economic experts but, more generally, of the professions which establish social closure over a domain of activity. Examples here are medical and legal services, and also the sports or the arts (think of the markets for soccer players or for opera sopranos, for instance). While markets in expert services and skills appear to be highly stratified and prestige-based, they attract inevitably additional layers of expertise which produce information relevant for these stratification processes. If we take the market for opera singers, for instance, where specific skills and knowledge are hired in a highly stratified and competitive system (there are relatively few sopranos, for instance, in the higher strata of Covent Garden or La Scala), opera critics appear as providing an additional layer of expertise (with its own jurisdiction) relevant for the dynamics of the transactions through which opera singers get contracts.

While features such as the above certainly pertain to how jurisdiction is established and maintained, there are additional, content-related elements which are relevant. We need to look not only at the dynamics of market-relevant expert groups, but also at the dynamics of market-relevant informational products. What do these products look like and how do they intervene in transactions? Therefore, we need here a closer examination of expertise and its outcomes—that is, of how informational products are generated and positioned with respect to market transactions.

Theories of Markets and Expertise

A theory of market equilibrium, an analysis of stock price volatility, or a credit risk analysis are products of expertise—that is, they are generated using specific sets of cognitive operations, skills, and tools. Expertise appears as 'a kind of possession, certified or uncertified, of knowledge that is testified to be efficacious and in which this testimony is widely accepted by the relevant audience' (Turner 2003, p. 25). But the relevant audience is never a unitary one; in fact, forms of expertise may have more than one audience. With respect to science, we can broadly distinguish among the following categories of audiences: audiences which come from the same (or similar) expert groups (say, physicists); audiences which come from other, yet connected groups; and less well defined audiences which overlap with segments of the broader public. While the first kind of audience may be persuaded by the argument of the truth claims made by an expert, other audiences must accept these claims as true on different grounds. Yet, the acceptance of truth claims of science by further audiences depends on the universal acceptance of the legitimacy of the scientific community (Turner 2003, p. 25).

We can order types of expertise along a continuum, according to their legitimacy in relationship to audiences. At the one end of the continuum then would be science expertise such as physics, which enjoys universal acceptance. A second type of expertise is granted legitimacy only within a restricted audience (think theology or astrology here). The third kind would be that of bodies of knowledge which create their own followers (think chiropractors, although we can find examples from the world of finance as well). The fourth kind of expertise is one designed to speak to a specific kind of audience (think here social work expertise). The fifth kind, related to the fourth, is made by experts who speak to a bureaucratic audience (Turner 2003, pp. 27–8; Collins and Evans 2002, p. 252).[5]

The truth claims made by a financial economist with respect to her model, for instance, will have to persuade an expert audience on veridicality criteria which are internal to that audience. Other audiences, such as that of investment bankers, or of financial journalists will have to accept the claims as true on grounds different from the first audience. In other words, the community of expertise of financial economists is based, among others, on knowledge of cognitive operations, skills, and tools with which a theoretical model is produced, as well as on knowledge of (and agreement upon) the standards to which these tools and skills should be applied. Moreover, this community includes knowledge of past or competing applications and their results, of 'intellectual traditions', of the 'intellectual puzzles' the community agrees upon as worth studying, and so on. This community-specific knowledge, partly explicit and partly not, will allow the truth claims of the model (presented, say, at an academic conference) to be judged according to community-internal standards of adequacy. Such standards, however, are not the standards of the community of financial journalists or investment bankers, who would then position themselves with respect to the truth claims on different grounds (e.g. the model can be used in understanding a practical problem, or for devising financial instruments, and so on).

An example in this sense is provided by economic journalists recently discovering Ariel Roubini, the NYU economist, as the one who made accurate predictions about the financial crisis of Fall 2008. Characterized as a 'respected, but formerly obscure academic' (Mihm 2008), Roubini's predictions were dismissed by academic peers because they apparently lacked the kind of formal modelling which was the norm within the community of academic economists. Financial journalists related to Roubini's claims based on their relevance for discussing the crisis events of 2008.

While it could be said that economists enjoy universal legitimacy, other economic experts address specific audiences and, therefore, do not have unlimited legitimacy. This would be the case, for instance, of chart (or technical) analysts, whose claims are at odds with those of financial economics. Chart analysts do not enjoy authority within the academic community, and their theories are routinely dismissed by the latter. Another case in point here would be government economic experts, such as those active in making growth forecasts or in diagnosing the state of the economy. Financial journalists, in their turn, enjoy legitimacy only for specific types of claims vis-à-vis their audiences; for instance, while their narrative of economic events may appear as authoritative, in referring to economic forecasts they resort to the authority of academic economists or of analysts. This points to the fact that claims made for models, statements, or economic data have different degrees of authority, depending not only on the epistemic community of the claimants, but also on the audiences they address.[6]

The authority enjoyed by economic theories with respect to audiences, as well as their status (as representations or as something different) cannot be considered without taking into account how these specific explanatory models and conceptualizations gain dominant positions within the community of academic economists. A dominant position within an epistemic community, one whose aim is systematically producing knowledge about a phenomenal domain, always implies the dominance of a certain definition of that domain and of the relevant phenomena. In other words, a dominant theory or model of market transactions will always include a definition of markets as an object of investigation, on the basis of which relevant elements will be separated from non-relevant ones. Such a model will also include definitions of the elements of that domain, distinctions among categories (for instance, between principal and secondary elements, or features), and definitions of relationships. This sends us to the argument formulated by Michel Callon and Fabian Muniesa (Callon 2007*b*, p. 140; Callon and Muniesa 2005, p. 1231), according to which in order to become subjected to market exchanges, entities have to be defined as such. This definition (what Callon calls framing), together with the separation of features considered as irrelevant from the viewpoint of transactions (an operation called disentanglement), is what theoretical market models do.

Market Transactions in Economic Theory

In order to understand how this authority works, then, we need to understand the definitional shifts within theoretical market models, as well as the relationships between these shifts and claims of authority. In the following, I take readers through a review of the conceptual changes which made the notion of information into the centrepiece of formal models of market transactions. In a further step of the argument, in the discussion of the performativity thesis, I will examine how these models are used in economic practice. One of the fundamental changes within economic theory is the nineteenth century transition from political economy to the marginalist paradigm. Political economy was conceived as the science of collective wealth: Adam Smith's chosen title for his main work, the *Wealth of Nations* is an apt illustration, as is Karl Marx's conceptualization of class as the basis of wealth. The discipline's emergence in the early eighteenth century, and its evolution up to the mid-nineteenth century includes redefinitions too: from the association with moral pamphlets and fiction writing, characteristic for the early eighteenth century, to a conception of political economy as an 'analytic instrument designed to investigate hypothetical cases' (Poovey 1998, p. 323). While political economy dominates the period 1700–1860s,[7] starting in the 1870s a new theoretical approach emerges first in Britain and France (with Stanley Jevons, Léon Walras, later Alfred Marshall, the Italian Vilfredo Pareto, and the American Irving Fisher as the main figures), an approach which emphasizes the formal treatment of market transactions as equilibria of demand and supply, and the role played by marginal utility, costs, and profits, respectively. Markets appear thus as grounded in competition, and price formation as being approximations of an ideal state in which perfectly competing, isolated economic agents meet each other (Schumpeter [1954] 1994, p. 1002).[8]

This implies a whole series of redefinitions: conceiving market exchanges in terms of price equilibria and competition, and real markets as approximations of pure competition among atomized agents requires conceiving economic exchanges as a matter of individual decisions (therefore, of agency), prices as the most important piece of information on which agents act, and the domain of the economic science as something related to human action (and not to providence, for instance). Moreover, conceiving market exchanges in terms of individual actions means separating the economic from the political, extricating the state from the medley of transactions, in which it found itself all too often in real life, and subsuming the variety of market transactions to a unique, abstract formulation. Political economy, however, did not see economic phenomena as a matter of individual agencies, but rather as closely related to developments in the natural world, and to relationships among social groups. Human reason (and hence agency) was not treated as distinct from the body, and was not seen as reducible to decision-making (Schabas 2005, pp. 101, 141). Neoclassical theory abandoned historical research as a mode of investigating market exchanges, while stressing its own apolitical character (Schabas 2005, p. 151). It oriented itself to the natural sciences, particularly to physics (thermodynamics), for the conceptualization of price movements (Mirowski 1989, 1994), and to biology for legitimating markets as responding to particular needs within society.[9] While political economy included attempts to search for answers to the problem of class relationships (as manifested in the domain of economic exchanges), neoclassical economics excluded moral judgements from its domain of expertise, and abandoned any attempts to offer an answer to the issue of class relationships. Instead, it formulated a programme of model building, where formal, normative models would guide economic policy, and would reveal a level of reality situated beyond everyday life (Breslau 2003, pp. 404–5).

This was made possible, in part, by the fact that during the 1860s, shortly before the marginalist revolution, energy physics had made its way into physics manuals and was becoming a dominant metaphor for the description of the physical world (Mirowski 1989, p. 217). While analogies with biology justified the idea of markets performing specific economic functions, individual actors could be conceived as similar to particles, and utility as similar to energy. Prices then would be akin to vectors in a force field, determined by marginal utility, which gives expression to individual desires (Mirowski 1989, p. 224). The state of equilibrium is akin to the centre of gravity, where the natural (aka the market) price will be found (Mirowski 1989, pp. 238, 240). In this perspective, atomized individuals signal each other their preferences (aka desires) via prices and quantities; coordination within society is thus ensured by the 'invisible hand' of the market, in the sense that individual actors can now reciprocally observe their preferences and take decisions accordingly. This presupposes that market agents are oriented primarily towards the satisfaction of their desires; all they need is to decide upon the ways in which they can maximize (or optimize) this. Decision, in this case, would mean selection of the appropriate courses of action according to a template of rationality shared by all, and also according to individual preferences. Failure to share this template would almost automatically, even if gradually, eliminate individuals from market participation, since their choices would be punished (they would lose money). This, in turn, reconfirms that markets function as self-sustaining allocation mechanisms.

Information, Signals, and Prices in the Theory of Markets

Against this background, in the 1930s the notion of information made its entrance in economics. The person credited with highlighting its importance for allocation processes is Friedrich von Hayek, who at the time was involved in heated debates about the feasibility of a centralized, planned economy, as opposed to capitalist market economies. In those days, the debate was not a purely academic one: communism was triumphant in the Soviet Union and its declared economic goal was the instauration of a planned economy, as a more just and efficient alternative to market capitalism. The idea of planning, however, implies that a central agent (the government) allocates resources to all economic agents and manages the distribution of goods. In order for this to work, argued Hayek, such an agent would need knowledge of all the actions of economic agents, as well as exhaustive knowledge of their specific circumstances. Moreover, the central agent would need to know how to use this exhaustive knowledge of all specific circumstances. This type of knowledge is different from scientific theories, implying a great deal of experience-based actions, some of which cannot be completely formulated (Hayek 1976, p. 80). The utilization of knowledge, however, is not given to anyone in totality (Hayek 1976, p. 78). Therefore, it would be futile to think that a central agent can allocate resources and distribute goods in an efficient manner.

In what amounts to a reformulation of Smith's idea of decentralized coordination—the invisible hand (Streissler 1994, p. 48)—Hayek argued that individual economic agents need knowledge of prices for their decision-making (Hayek 1976, p. 57). It is this decentralized knowledge, made possible by market transactions, which allows the dynamic coordination of market actors through their interactions. This argument, however, is not without contention. Starting from the same notion of the invisible hand, Léon Walras, for instance, had argued that market economies need an 'invisible auctioneer' similar to the broker on the floor of the stock exchange: an impartial agent which centralizes and distributes information. For Hayek, however, it is the irreducibility of situational knowledge to information which makes this impossible; while a presumably impartial agent can centralize information, it could never centralize the specific knowledge of a myriad of economic situations the auctioneer is not part of. Dispersed economic actors can do this much better, since while communicating with each other they share diverse experiences and build up shared expectations. In this perspective, economic processes appear as grounded in knowledge; markets can be seen as knowledge-based competitions, while political interventions (such as regulations) require (explicit) knowledge about the economy as well.[10] Yet, knowledge is not information; while economic processes can be seen as anchored in specific forms of knowledge, this does not yet make information into a key theoretical concept. The shift from knowledge to information came within the context of particular debates about the 'invisible hand'.

Prices (i.e. numerical data) become information, as well as a mechanism for coordinating the distribution of information (Hayek 1976, pp. 84–6).[11] This is one of the sources of the idea that markets work analogous to giant switchboards, where price signals circulate from node to node, without the intervention of a central operator. Economic agents, then, have to choose among alternative courses of action based on the information contained in and carried by prices: economic calculus becomes then 'the pure logic of choice' (Hayek 1976, p. 84). The picture of the economy becomes thus one of dynamic order (or what Hayek calls a catallaxy), where society adapts to changes in particular circumstances not only by allocating resources to a 'unitary order of ends' (Hayek 1978, p. 183), but also by revising this order of ends. In this order, competition is valuable not for its own sake, but 'only because its results are unpredictable' (Hayek 1978, p. 180). This means that competition can change not only the results of allocation but also the order of ends for this allocation (Potts 2001, p. 214), in a way that a central agent cannot. In other words, markets as systems of competitive exchanges produce surprises with respect to goal-oriented allocation of resources, as well as with respect to how these goals are ranked.

Market Information and Efficiency

If prices qua numeric data are information, then their dispersion in the market can be seen as a measure of the actors' ignorance, leading thus to increased searches and diminished returns (Stigler 1961, p. 214). Conversely, the value of information would be the amount by which this reduces the expected cost of a buyer's purchases (Stigler 1961, p. 221). Another way to avoid costly searches for information and to reduce uncertainties would be economic organization (Stigler 1961, p. 224; Akerlof 1970, p. 499); organizations create the procedural rules and the social relationships which allow market actors to reduce their cost of information: gossip at the water fountain can provide valuable information at a lesser cost compared with acting in isolation. Note here, however, that the meaning of this kind of information differs from that of prices as information.

Price concentration in the market is then the opposite of ignorance: by being able to observe prices in a centralized and unitary manner, market actors get the same type of information. This does not exclude temporary deviations, for instance, that in some situations some actors will get relevant information before others. Overall, though, and in the long run, no specific group of actors will consistently get relevant information so as to extract and advantage in transactions, time and again. This can be seen as the impossibility of the monopolistic exploitation of information (Stigler 1961, p. 223), to the effect that in an efficient market trading on the available information will fail to provide an abnormal profit (Dimson and Mussavian 1998, p. 94). Market efficiency[12] implies the following:

1. Price observation has to be publicly accessible. One can have a monopoly on price data, and charge for access to it. But one needs to provide other market actors access to this data if they are to trade starting from it. In other words, there has to be a public for price data observation, even if this public is not to be confounded with the general one.

2. There have to be shared procedures for translating information into prices. This means that stories, gossip, the interpretation of data, and the like, have to find their way into prices by means of interactions of market actors (see also Stinchcombe [1990, p. 11]). How these types of information find their way into prices can be seen in at least two different ways. The first is the one mentioned above, namely, that there have to be set interaction procedures which cannot be monopolized. There is no such thing as a monopoly over how to gossip; a group can monopolize for some time some gossip content, but not how to gossip. In this perspective, market efficiency would mean the public availability of sanctioned procedures of market interaction. Therefore, market efficiency implies not only the public availability of information, but also the public availability of procedures through which this information is interpreted and translated into prices (see note 12 for a definition of efficiency).

Another way of conceptualizing the translation of information into prices is by postulating certain characteristics of market actors qua rational actors. The assumption that all economic agents exhibit the same characteristics (i.e. rationality), and therefore should be treated as all alike enables formal modelling (Mirowski 2007, p. 211), while diverting attention away from the interactions of market actors. The key postulate here is that market actors have rational expectations, meaning that they use all relevant information correctly, because they know the structure of the market model, its values, and parameters (Le Roy 1989, p. 1595). While they may not share the same information they share knowledge of the market model, and this allows them to calculate in the same way. Central among these expectations is that future returns on investments are unpredictable; the conditional expectations of an event (t + 1) contingent on a previous one (t) do not depend on the information available at t (Le Roy 1989, p. 1590). Therefore, the future cannot be predicted from the past (Le Roy 1989, p. 1613). Being a rational market player would then mean sharing knowledge of the market structure, being driven by self-interest and calculating based on the premise that the future will not necessarily be like the past. In real life, however, actors act based on anticipated retrospections—that is, based on their assumption that the future will be similar to their past experiences.

The assumption that rational actors share the knowledge of the same market model, its parameters, and values has been accompanied by postulating a distinction between market players who share this knowledge and those who do not; these latter are deemed to be noise traders, whose demand is determined by factors other than the expected return on the investment (Dimson and Mussavian 1998, p. 98; Le Roy 1989, p. 1612). In financial economics, noise traders are deemed to be those situated outside the organizational contexts of trading firms and brokerage houses, lay market participants supposed to have a lesser grasp of the market. More generally, a 'noisy information structure is one in which not only can one signal occur in several states, but also several signals can occur in the same state' (Birchler and Bütler 2007, p. 20). This means that the same classifications and categories can be used by market actors in different ways, and that observable data can be associated with states and events in more than one way. In other words, there is no fixed set of rules for unambiguously matching observable data with states of the world. This means at least two things: first, if prices circulate information, this latter must also have at least some features different from the prices themselves. Prices draw the attention of economic agents to something else; they trigger processes that are irreducible to mere price data, and act as a stimulus for market actors to search for other kinds of information as well. These searches can be observed by third parties and interpreted as signals about the participants' plans or intentions (see also Machlup [1984, p. 48]). In the Arrow–Debreu commodity model, for instance, market actors need information about the time and place of availability, the probability of delivery, as well as a technical description of the commodity (Boehm 1994, p. 160).

Moreover, the very existence of market transactions points to the fact that not all market players hold the same information (i.e. the same data and the same stories interpreted in the same ways). Transactions require differential information: this latter is conceptualized in financial economics as a consumption set (the actors' choices), together with a utility function (a ranking across these choices), and the partition of a probability state of the world (discrete states where these choices will be realized with specific probabilities) (Krasa and Yannelis 1994, p. 883). Thus, different preferences, together with the actors' different positions in the market (implying that these preferences will be realized with different degrees of probability), lead to differential information. In its turn, this forces actors to cooperate—that is, to exchange information in a truthful way (Krasa and Yannelis 1994, p. 884)—in order to realize their choices.

Differential information can also be seen as distinctions relevant from the viewpoint of the observer. Distinction signals, in their turn, can be indices marking unalterable characteristics of the person (e.g. height), or they can be manipulative attributes (e.g. dress) which send to an unobservable social category (e.g. class). Seen in this perspective, it is not only prices which signal, but other observable items as well (see Spence [1974, p. 107]; [2002, p. 434]). Michael Spence (1976, p. 592) explicitly defines information as 'what I call signals, taking the seller's point of view, others have called screening or sorting, looking at things from the buyer's standpoint'. Signals, thus, can be seen as tools employed by observers to construct social categories. With that, signals become intrinsic to deploying action routines which ignore indexical knowledge (i.e. which stereotype other actors). An example here would be ignoring the particular situation of a credit applicant and making the judgement based on socio-economic categorization. The problems brought by stereotyping (i.e. inaccessibility of particular, yet relevant knowledge) are acknowledged as intrinsic to asymmetric information (Akerlof 2002, p. 413).

Theoretically, then, from the perspective of economics the issue is investigating how price equilibria are reached on the basis of imperfect signals—that is, of observable elements which produce categories and classifications which are neither unambiguous nor shared by all participants in exchanges.[13] Beliefs in such categories are self-confirming, meaning that the categories themselves are empiry-resistant. This resistance also means that equilibria can be achieved at different prices—that is, there is no unique point where supply meets demand (Spence 2002, p. 437; Rothschild and Stiglitz 1976, p. 641). Moreover, actors have to invest in the signals they send—an apt illustration here would be buying a new suit for a job interview.

Shifts in beliefs can result in new equilibria; such shifts arise in informative situations (Hirshleifer 1975, pp. 526, 529). The picture we get is that of differentiated sets of categories and classifications which serve as props for action. While these categories are not entirely shared by all, actors stick to them by virtue of routines. Yet, such categories are subjected to uncertainties. Uncertainties offer opportunities for action or speculation (Feiger 1976, p. 684), so that actors will tend to value uncertainties and to keep them for themselves first (and speculate and act on them). This, in turn, increases the asymmetry of signals, which, in its turn, is a source of further uncertainties, etc.

Prices, Information, and Market Automation

Another, and perhaps more important implication of prices as the key market information stems from them being amenable to mathematical operations—that is, to transformations according to fully specifiable sets of rules. This, combined with the assumption of rational market actors—who should calculate, implement, and evaluate their decisions according to fully specifiable rules as well—leads to conceptualizing markets as sets of algorithms performing functions such as data dissemination and communication; order routing; order queuing and execution; price discovery and assignment; custody and delivery arrangement; clearing and settlement; and record-keeping (Mirowski 2007, p. 211). Such rules can be transferred upon computer technologies; the actions of individual market players can be viewed as subroutines of these technologies (Mirowski 2007, p. 212). Such a view is anything but far-fetched, if we take into account that in the past two decades or so electronic platforms have integrated the trading of heterogeneous assets (it has become reality to trade, say, currencies and commodities futures on the same interface). The main issue, then, becomes one of mechanism design—that is, of devising rules (aka the software programs) for optimizing allocation processes. This resonates with the view of actors' rationality; if it can be shown that this rationality is hardwired—that is, embedded in neurophysiological processes—actors would almost automatically follow trading algorithms. With that, market issues become programming issues—not incidentally, two recently developing subfields of economics are neuroeconomics and engineering economics (Schull and Zaloom 2008; Mirowski 2007, p. 215).

The historical roots of the preoccupation with conceptualizing markets as algorithms processing numerical data can be found in a particular kind of allocation problem, which arose during the Second World War. Fighter pilots had the task of shooting down enemy aircraft while using a scarce and expensive resource—bullets. Enemy aircraft, in its turn, had unpredictable trajectories, and was difficult to shoot down. During the war, against the background of practical problems related to tracking aircraft with guns, operations research was established as a set of analytical techniques for processing meaningful, informational patterns out of data signals. At the end of the war, the RAND Corporation was established (Mirowski 2002, pp. 208–9; 2005), which, during the Cold War, contributed significantly to developing game theory and its applications in the social sciences (particularly political science and economics).[14] In a way similar to that of discovering a hit point while flying the aircraft and aiming at the enemy plane, a price point could be discovered based on computations—that is, a price at which buyers and sellers will converge. This would avoid inefficiencies related to lengthy and costly processes of trial and error.

After the Second World War, a series of factors contributed to the consolidation of the notion of thing-like economic information, even though economic actors weren't conceived any more as adhering to the same static decisional template. When applied within economic theory after the war, operations research helped reorient models away from the idea of a natural price equilibrium to that of dynamic equilibria. At the same time, game theory promoted a concept of rational, calculative economic agents engaged in strategic games; these games could be ordered along types, according to their rules and their possible outcomes (e.g. the dictator's game, the prisoner's dilemma, etc.—see also Olson [1965]; Strahler [1998]; Von Neumann and Morgenstern [1944] 1992; Gintis [2000]). Actors engaged in market games acted strategically, following rules of action (which could be entirely spelled out), and made decisions based on the signals they received from their counterparts. What is more, these actors adapted their reactions to the signals they received—that is, they learnt during the game (Mirowski 2002, pp. 371, 377). In other words, strategic actors respond to informational inputs (aka signals) by modifying their behaviour—that is, by incorporating new information in their calculations.

The understanding of market behaviour shifted to strategic (i.e. calculative) reactions to external events. Since the rules of the (market) game could be completely spelled out (and were therefore entirely formalizable), and since information as signals was formalizable too, it followed that, in principle, it was possible to conceive of markets as sets of algorithms for allocation decisions (Mirowski 2002, p. 541, 2007).

It could be well argued that this brings us back to the very problem Hayek sought to fight: there would be little difference, if any, between the centralized allocation of resources by a central political agent, on the one hand, and the allocation of the same resources by a central computer system, on the other. Thus, while contemporary attempts at market automation see themselves as continuing Hayek's legacy, in the very end they undermine Hayek's central idea of the distributed character of knowledge.

Philip Mirowski's answer to this is that instead of a single, centralized computer system we would have a network of differently automated markets, or markomata circulating information inputs (Mirowski 2007, p. 231).

The implication is that actors will behave differently according to the transaction rules contained in the trading algorithm. The actors' searches for information and their reaction to it will be different; for instance, in a double auction market, the players' informational behaviour and decision-making will be different from a Dutch auction market.[15]

This amounts to saying that instead of devising a single trading algorithm, markomata should operate based on various algorithms, in order to achieve specific local functions and objectives (Mirowski 2007, p. 228). This appears as a translation of Hayek's postulate of the situational character of the knowledge employed by market actors. (How markomata would deal with the tacit and only partially formalizable character of this knowledge is not answered yet.) The question then becomes whether a meta-market emerges, that is, a competition among markomata. Mirowski (2007, p. 237) answers this question in terms of evolutionary adaptation and mutation (which does not exclude competition). Market automata will evolve then in terms of computational complexity (and expand as well), by producing new types of algorithms adapted to the trading situation. Concretely, this would mean that what was previously regarded as non-tradeable entities would be transformed into tradeable ones, based on devising new sets of rules for trading them. A more recent example is provided by the auctioning of bandwidth for mobile communications (Mirowski and Nik-Khah 2007): while a couple of decades ago bandwidth was not regarded as something tradable (but falling under the control of the state), more recent technological developments, as well as advances in the design of trading mechanisms (together, it should be added, with a new attitude towards economic policy, as well as with lobbying on the part of corporations) have transformed it into a tradable entity.

The rise of experimental economics (see Friedman and Sunder [1994]; Guala [2005]) and later of behavioural economics (see Wilkinson [2008]) complicate the picture, in the sense of introducing imperfections into the strategic behaviour of economic agents, imperfections due to psychological or to neurophysiological (i.e. hardwired) biases (e.g. Schull and Zaloom 2008). Whether they are seen as hardwired or not, such imperfections can be cognitive; for instance, (psychological) predispositions to weigh positive and negative news differently, or memory failure, or simply fatigue distress. They can be related to cognitive phenomena such as framing and anchoring (Ricciardi 2008, pp. 100–2), meaning the format in which a situation is presented, or the inclination to stick to a belief which might not be true. They can also be of emotional nature: phenomena such as arousal and affects (fear, overexcitement) can impede upon decisions (see Strack and Deutsch [2004]). They can also be perceptions of fairness, of reputation, of trust, of status, or of gender (e.g. Chen and Gazzale 2004; Bolton, Katok, and Ockenfels 2005; Eckel and Wilson 2007). These imperfections, however, affect strategic decision-making only in the sense of introducing predictable deviations from the standard game model, deviations which can be factored into this model. This means that it is possible to improve market algorithms by factoring in social–psychological biases—indeed, what has happened in recent years is that market-relevant informational systems are redesigned in such a way as to respond to such biases. For instance, in auction markets such as eBay, as well as in online financial markets, categories of trader reputation are built in, based on projections of how they will affect trading decisions, projections done on the basis of economic experiments (see, for instance, Harris [2008]; Bolton, Greiner, and Ockenfels [2008]).

The above principles, even in the present summary overview,[16] highlight the fact that information is conceived as observable, thing-like signals, from which unobservable entities can be deducted (I cannot directly observe other people's desires except from their market decisions, and hence from prices). They also highlight that the processing of these signals would be automatically ensured by all market participants being oriented towards maximizing (or optimizing) utilities and by general adherence to the template which adapts means to ends (allowing, of course, for some individual failures and corrections). Not only that this separates the domain of market exchanges from that of political actions, for instance, or from that of family commitments, or of traditions, but it also introduces specific definitions of the individual, and of prices, as the basic assumptions allowing a formal modelling of price equilibria. Prices are seen as the basic form of market information. The behaviour of market actors is calculative, in the sense that they maximize (or optimize) their utilities under given constraints, by adapting (and allocating) available resources to these ends.[17] Moreover, questions of social value are separated from questions of utility: economic theory is concerned only with the latter.

Having provided this overview, it is now time to examine how models incorporating these principles are put to use in practice.

Information, Market Models, and Performativity

For a long time, formal economic models have been criticized by sociologists for not being realistic—that is, for not taking into account how real market transactions work. With the rise of experimental economics, it looks like finally economists have taken the criticism to heart, albeit preferring the insights offered by psychology to sociological ones. Irrespective of this, the charge of being unrealistic is grounded in the assumption that theoretical models have a representational character—that is, models of exchange and of price equilibria depict (even if in a simplified fashion) relationships and characteristics which are to be found in actual transactions. When talking, for instance, about the actors' preference ordering, we would expect, based on this representational assumption, to find such ordering in real-life transactions. When talking about calculations made by agents, we would expect to find in real life people laying out strategic plans for shopping, or making cost and benefit analyses when buying a handbag, for instance. The fact that, instead of this, sociologists encounter people haggling, or not interested in doing any comparison, has contributed to the accusations of unrealism.

During the past decade or so, the discussion about the representational character of economic models has been replaced by one about their performative features, a debate in which passionate adherents of this concepts have faced some equally passionate critics. This time, the tables have been turned, in the sense that from being unrealistic, theoretical models have been characterized as being too realistic—not in the sense of an accurate representation, but in the sense of generating the phenomena they describe. The point of contention, therefore, is whether we can endow market models with the powers of creating that which they talk about. This, of course, has broader consequences: by endowing models with such powers, we would also ascribe the latter to the groups which create these models, namely to economists. This is a weighty assertion, which deserves close attention.

The notion of performativity was established by the philosopher of language John Langshaw Austin (Austin 1962) as a tool for analyzing classes of utterances which are not true or false, because they do not have a representational character. Instead of representing states of the world, these utterances create or modify them. In order to do so, however, certain conditions have to be fulfilled, which Austin called felicity conditions; these relate to the appropriate social circumstances and reciprocal orientations of participants. An utterance such as 'I hereby pronounce you man and wife' will be performative within a marriage ceremony, when uttered appropriately by a priest or a civil servant endowed with the corresponding authority. The utterance, however, will not be felicitous if uttered by small children while playing with dolls.

With the notion of performativity, Austin highlighted that the effects of utterances should be considered within their social context, taking into account the parties involved (speakers, hearers, and audiences), as well as the resources, constraints, and shared understandings of the situation. A general discussion about the representational v. the performative character of utterances is of little productivity without taking into account all the above elements. Depending on them, one and the same utterance can have substantially different characteristics and effects. An additional lesson to be drawn here is that utterances are not disembodied: they have a material form, decisive for their effects: they can be oral or written, on paper or in electronic form, and all these factors count with respect to their properties and effects.

Applying this to the case of economic models, then we need to take into account how they work in particular circumstances, at least in the context of their production and that of their use. Moreover, we need to take into account their concrete material form; in science, theoretical models are less abstract than we might think, in the sense that they are produced and circulated in specific shapes, and these shapes are consequential with respect to what the models do (see Livingston [1999, 2006]; Knorr Cetina and Merz [1997]). In experimental economics, for instance, theory production involves complex assemblages of computer rooms, questionnaires, flyers for recruiting test subjects, advertisements, monetary rewards, software for processing results, and so on. The design of these assemblages itself rests on a series of assumptions about behaviour in a controlled environment, the understanding of and reactions to questions, or the irrelevance of subjects' interactions in the computer room. (Participants in the experiment might share these assumptions with the experimenters only in part.)

If we look at the producer side—that is, at how theories are generated and put to use by economists, we can see that authors do not necessarily treat their models as having representational character. Authors of formal models in economics are careful to disentangle their agency from the objects they have produced, so that these latter appear as having a trajectory of their own, independent of the economists who have produced it (Breslau and Yonay 1999, p. 329). Yet, this autonomous trajectory does not mean that the model reproduces (more or less) exactly real relationships existing among economic actors, or that it depicts market exchanges as they take place. Neither do economic models start from empirical observations, which are then inductively processed into generalizations.

What formal economic models do is arrange abstract elements into relationships which are taken as plausible constructs and, in a second step, can be brought into relationship with selective observations (Yonay and Breslau 2006, p. 377). In their ethnographic investigation of how formal modellers work, Daniel Breslau and Yuval Yonay highlight the importance of 'prefabricated' objects, legitimated within the academic community, which work in ways similar with the off-the-shelf instruments used in natural science laboratories (Breslau and Yonay 1999, p. 325). These objects are endowed with authority, and modellers combine and adapt them to the study of specific problems, which in their turn are perceived within the community as legitimate theoretical problems, and ranked according to importance. 'Prefabricated' objects can be 'households', or 'individual agents' (Yonay and Breslau 2006, pp. 368, 377), which do not have to resemble real individuals (there can be only two kinds of households, or of individuals in a model), but are abstract entities endowed with postulated properties, and which, within the model, will react according to these properties. Through combinations, prefabricated objects are used to build 'microworlds' (Yonay and Breslau 2006, p. 377) which are then matched to selective bits of reality by means of (more or less vaguely) defined conventions. These bits of reality, in their turn, are mostly represented by statistical data, taken as a proxy of individual and collective behaviour.

We can go back to the analogy with plays of the soccer game here: in soccer, the chalkboard is a tool used among others by sports commentators, managers, and fans alike in order to analyse the game. It consists of a wooden board or an electronic screen reproducing the spatial scheme of the soccer playing field. On the board, the positions and movements of players are drawn as numbers, dots, and arrows. As such, the diagram of a play sequence on the chalkboard does not represent the interactions in the field. These latter are too complex and contain too many verbal and non-verbal elements to be reducible to arrows and dots. The chalkboard is rather a tool with the help of which a microworld is assembled from prefabricated elements, and used to comment and make judgements upon players and teams.

Economic models can be seen as analogous to the chalkboard in soccer: they are something more, and different than simply 'discourse'. While communities of (academic) economists master the metaphorical language which comes attached with the circulation of these models (at conferences, public debates, during interviews, journal articles, and the like), and while these communities also master the justificatory accounts and argumentative structures put to work in debating competing models, these latter are not simply stories about economic reality. (They can and usually are accompanied by stories, but are not reducible to them.) In the same way in which a chalkboard drawing is a plausible alternative to a soccer match, these models create alternative plausible constructions, which afterwards, based on conventions, are judged upon their compatibility with reality. In this perspective, models are not only endowed with epistemic authority within the academic community (some models will be more successful than others), but this authority will be extended beyond that community. Hence, models are authoritative, plausible microworlds, alternative to reality, yet connectible to it. Models can be brought and used in economic settings not as representations, but as action tools, exactly because of their character. They tell real, situated actors what could be other than it is in that actors' situation.

This has several important consequences: models are used exactly because they are endowed with authority, and this authority has been disentangled from the personal features of their authors. Representations of alternatives to the real world are used as action tools. Such uses go beyond the boundaries of academic communities which develop models; implemented in concrete contexts of action, these models can change the said contexts. Consequently, we have to examine how models (and elements thereof) are used outside communities of economists as well.

Performativity and User Communities

A now classic example of how the use of abstract models outside the academic community changes economic transactions is provided by the ethnographic study of a French strawberry market (Garcia-Parpet [1986] 2007). Up to the early 1980s, the strawberries produced in the Loir-et-Cher region of France were considered of inferior quality compared with those coming from southern France. The region's growers (organized in cooperatives) sold their products through a network of personal relationships (and through middlemen), aided by the local Chamber of Agriculture. The producers themselves delivered the strawberries to wholesale buyers, and payment was delayed until the strawberries were sold to retailers, and from there to consumers. In 1981, the Chamber of Agriculture hired an adviser with formal training in economics, who suggested the implementation of an auction market, and helped the Chamber of Agriculture write the rules of the auction, according to the economic theories he had learnt. The chamber persuaded the largest strawberry growers to participate in this market, organized training sessions for producers, intensified efforts to create a quality label for the local strawberries (countering perceptions of inferior quality), standardized packaging (500 gram plastic baskets), and installed the infrastructure (building, parking space, and auction room with computers) for the auction market.

Once the auctions took off in 1982, middlemen were gradually eliminated, because they did not have enough cash to participate. In time, networks of personal relationships were dismantled, not without frictions. On the buyers' side, only the bigger, cash-rich shippers could take part in the strawberry auctions. On the producers' side, other crops were partly replaced with strawberries, and bigger growers consolidated their positions. The auctions led to a rise in strawberry prices, to an improvement in the quality of the produce, to the creation of new administrative structures (the council managing the auctions, a source of prestige and authority), and reinforced the growers' links with the local banks. At the same time, not all cooperatives participated in the new auction system, which was perceived as eroding their control over the distribution of agricultural produce.

In this case, the replacement of sales networks with a centralized auction market was accompanied (and even preceded) by significant additional efforts at changing the public perception of the local produce. At the same time, the installation of a new system was less the direct application of a specific abstract model than a creation which, while following a general idea present in economic theory, went hand in hand with educational measures, the creation of bureaucratic control mechanisms, and product standardization. Local bureaucracy (the Chamber of Agriculture) was instrumental in pushing forward this model, and retained control over it.

Another example of how abstract economic models become performative comes from the field of financial economics. A central body of theoretical work here is provided by the options pricing theory—namely, a formal model allowing the calculation of prices for options contracts[18] based on a limited number of variables (such as the underlying price and volatility). While options trading had existed since the eighteenth century, in spite of repeated, yet ignored bans and prohibitions, until the early 1970s there was no formal model (aka set of equations) according to which the price of options contracts could be calculated. Efforts had been underway since the 1950s, but various financial economists worked with somewhat different sets of variables and assumptions in their models (as is often the case in science).

The general background of these efforts was provided by the random walk hypothesis—the assumption that past movements in securities prices cannot serve as a basis for predicting future movements. Formulated in 1900 in a PhD thesis by Louis Bachelier, a French mathematician, it was rediscovered in the late 1950s and 1960s (see Cootner [1964]). In the late 1960s and early 1970s, three academics—Fischer Black, Myron Scholes, and (initially independent of them) Robert C. Merton—developed a pricing model simple enough to be used with the available price and volatility data (MacKenzie 2006, pp. 127–37). At the start, there were wide discrepancies between the options prices generated by the model and those generated in real trading in the pits of the Chicago Board of Trade, one major exchange dealing in options.

At this point, several elements intervened: the Chicago Board of Trade (CBOT) was engaged in a competition with the New York Stock Exchange for acquiring new business, and wanted to persuade the Securities and Exchange Commission (SEC, the US regulatory body) that options trading had nothing to do with gambling, and was not disreputable. In its efforts to persuade regulators, the CBOT turned to financial economists (MacKenzie 2006, pp. 147–50): the mobilization of academic authority benefited from the existence of a theoretical model able, in principle, to calculate options prices. At the same time, Black, Scholes, and Merton persuaded traders in the pits of the CBOT to use their theoretically generated prices. This was facilitated by the fact that options price tables were printed out on computer sheets, which could be rolled up (so that a few rows of prices were visible) and taken into the pit; the traders could glance at the theoretical prices while trading. The CBOT traders' community was a close-knit one (most traders belonged to the same extended families), and they jealously guarded their privileges. Traders had an interest in taking control over this new tool, not necessarily because of its predictive powers (which initially weren't there), but because they didn't want others to access it.

In time, the use of computer sheets with theoretical prices led to the convergence of actually traded prices with the computed theoretical values. This happens, argues Donald MacKenzie (2006, p. 165), because 'there was a homology between the econometric testing of the Black–Scholes–Merton model and the trading floor use of the model in "spreading"'. When traders used the model according to the accompanying instructions, they looked for deviations from the implied volatility against strike price, which was a flat line, and tended to trade on these observed deviations, which—they said— would have been arbitraged anyway.[19]

This means that the concrete uses of price data generated by the formal model—uses which depended on the material shape of the data— introduced another observable element in trading, another piece of information to which traders adjusted their transactions. This element was taken as significant because it was endowed with academic authority, and also because it was perceived—at institutional and individual levels—as a useful tool in persuasion efforts. It was something which should be kept under control as well. Thus, the fact that the uses of theoretical price data generated real options prices which confirmed the data depends on several social factors at institutional, group, and individual level: the uses of the model as a tool in policy making efforts; attempts by privileged groups at controlling it; the introduction of a new observational element on the trading floor, an element which constitutes information and which traders used in their transactions. At least these are the crucial elements which account for what Donald MacKenzie (2006, pp. 16, 164–6) calls 'Barnesian performativity', among others, in order to emphasize the fact that theoretical models are more than discourse.

In other cases, the use of statistical data and modelling can lead to the formalization and standardization of rights, which are transformed into a tradable entity. This is the case of fishing quotas, among others: the introduction of statistically modelled quotas in the 1970s has restricted access to a resource previously seen as available to all (ocean fishes). The formalization and standardization of fishing rights has made them into a tradable commodity, restricting access to and consolidating fishing activities (Holm and Nielsen 2007).

Academic economists, however, are not the only experts building models which then become influential within markets. Management theorists, usually located within business schools, develop organizational models which, while not necessarily formalized, can prove influential too. Paralleling to some extent the rise of model-based economics after the Second World War, management science increased its influence once business schools (where it was located) raised their prestige in the 1950s and 1960s (see Khurana [2007]). The organizational and managerial models developed in business schools addressed not only academics, but also managers employed by corporations, which dominated the economic landscape after the Second World War. These models had to provide a justificatory framework—understood as a set of definitions, accompanied by a specific language—with the help of which managers could make sense of their presence and activity not only within the corporation, but within society at large as well (Boltanski and Chiapello 1999, p. 51). In addition, models provided rhetorical strategies, visualization techniques, sets of numerical data, as well as judgements upon enterprises. Akin to formal economic models, these judgements were based not on in-depth knowledge of particular organizations, but rather on microworlds assembled from heterogeneous elements (rhetoric, visual schemes, and so on). Endowed with authority, managerial models fitted well the preoccupation of corporations with selecting charismatic managers (see Khurana [2002]): in the 1960s, one of the main problems debated in the organizational literature was how to motivate managers (Boltanski and Chiapello 1999, p. 100). Thirty years later, this problem persisted within the broader framework of motivating all corporate employees.

Since corporations were confronted with practical problems and tasks (e.g. crises, mergers, expansion, links among internal units, and the like) which resonated immediately in managerial activities (and hence in managerial identity as well), management theorists incorporated change, instability, and critique in the new concepts they were promoting. Not dissimilar with the fashion industry which regularly launches new collections, managerial models launched fashions such as 'diversification', 'focus', 'trust', or 'networks' (Boltanski and Chiapello 1999, pp. 129, 131). Endowed with authority, these fashions were adopted by managers because they provided a justification for their activities, and also because, by following them, managers could distinguish themselves from their competitors and predecessors. The adoption of managerial fashions led to concrete organizational changes, such as the rise of chief financial officers within corporations or the increased influence of institutional investors (see also Zorn et al. [2005, pp. 270–1]; Fligstein [1990]). As managerial fashions spread through imitation, they increased their influence within organizations.

Counterperformativity

The notion of performativity may unwillingly suggest that models can create markets; in none of the examples above, however, was this the case (for more examples, see for instance MacKenzie [2009, p. 30]; Didier [2007]; Breslau [2007]).[20] Donald MacKenzie and Michel Callon are careful to avoid this suggestion, and MacKenzie (2006, p. 263) stresses that the notion of perfor-mativity should not be exaggerated, and should not lead to a neglect of the cultural factors, social structures, and political institutions which shape markets. Callon (2007a, pp. 321–2) emphasizes as well that the notion of performativity is meant to avoid the conflation between formal models and representation. Rather, what happens is that theoretical models, or parts thereof, are mobilized by users in specific situations, at institutional, group, and individual levels. It is the interplay between institutional factors (political as well as economic), group interests, and individual action routines which lead to changes in systems of competitive transactions. Moreover, in none of the above cases was a market 'created' from nothing; rather, what happened was that transactions were remodelled, gained in intensity, and were set in a new institutional frame, with specific effects not only upon prices, but also with broader social effects.

The perceived conflation between economics and the economy, together with internalist accounts of game-based experimental economics implying the latter's epistemic superiority (Guala 2001), and a perceived neglect of social factors in the analysis of the links between academic economists and the business worlds, have prompted critics of the performativity notion to revisit the ways in which models are used in decision-making, such as auctions (Mirowski and Nik-Khah 2007). Procedures based on theoretical models can be used not only as interventions in market transactions, but also as legitimating tools for decisions taken on grounds other than the particular suitability of a specific model. In the case of radio frequency auctions in the mid-1990s, regulatory bodies worked with professional game theorists not necessarily because theirs were the best procedures, but because they lent authority to decisions influenced by specific interest groups. This reminds us that the uses of formal economic models include rhetoric as well, and that the prestige they are associated with can be used as a legitimacy tool.

What is more, the use of formal models can contribute to the unravelling of market transactions, as seen in crises and crashes. This is a situation where models can become counterperformative; instead of contributing to market expansion, they contribute to market contraction. Donald MacKenzie (2006, pp. 191, 205, 211; 2005) considers that there are several factors which con-tribute to counterperformativity. First, formal pricing models work on the assumption that the world is fairly regular—that is, that price variations will take place within a certain range, and that market actors will expect prices to form within this range. In other words, exceptional, unique events are not factored in the model—or, better said, were not factored when the options pricing model became dominant in the 1980s. Traders, however, can factor the assumption of catastrophic events into their actions and price their trades accordingly. Initial price declines will lead to selling futures and options at lower prices, which will feed back into the stock market. This can lead to sales pressure evolving into a downward spiral, where theoretical (lower) prices and actual (even lower) prices reinforce each other.

An additional factor can be imitation: large, authoritative, and particularly successful firms using a specific model will be imitated in their trades by other, smaller or less prestigious firms. These latter may not even have access to the proprietary model used by the prestigious firms, a model which can be jealously guarded. It suffices, however, to observe what trades these prestige firms are doing and imitate them. Imitation will leave no counterparts in the market to take the trades put forward by the more prestigious firms. Without counterparts, the trades will be offered at modified (lower) prices and the margins on which firms trade can be called in.[21] This can lead to a liquidity crisis and to markets unravelling. Examples of such crises are provided by the collapse of Long-Term Capital Management (LTCM, a now extinct major hedge fund) in 1998, or by the banking crisis of Fall 2008, when several major banks in the United States and in the United Kingdom had to be rescued by public interventions (see also MacKenzie [2008]).

In these examples, the actions of actors, as well as the data they use appear as being endowed with authority, in a way which sends us back to the notion of charisma explored by Max Weber (see Chapter 2). Traders will imitate LTCM's trades because they are charismatic, or will use theoretical prices in their trades because they have come to ascribe certain properties to them (after a period of accommodation), or associate them with the charismatic authority of their academic authors. Problems emerge when this charismatic authority is suspended, or when it unravels under its own weight. (Needless to say, after their failure, the LTCM partners, many of whom had an academic background, did not fully recover their reputations.)

Another notion which can be used in investigating the links between formal models and crises is that of overflow, put forward by Michel Callon (Callon 1998; Callon and Law 2003; Muniesa and Callon 2007; Callon 2007b, pp. 143–5). Callon stresses that in order for models to work they must disentangle the economic from the non-economic—another way of saying that models include definitional features (through their assumptions about the entities they incorporate). In their practical use, though, models become re-entangled—that is, the ways in which data are put to work in practice may be influenced by the interests of concrete market actors, by their relationships, and so on. This makes concrete uses of abstract models depend upon local circumstances, which in the end undermine the models' practical stability. This is the overflowing of models—the ultimate instability and indeterminacy of their practical uses (Callon and Law 2003, p. 12). Consequently, formal economic models cannot be seen as antidotes to economic crises, but rather as elements which under specific conditions can increase instability.

The Uses of Non-Academic Expertise: The Case of Economic Analysts

In addition to formal economic models, we need to consider the uses of non-academic expertise as well, and the ways in which they intervene in market transactions. Not only have such forms proliferated over the past decades, but they also seem to play a considerable role, at least in the public perception. Analyses and forecasts of economic events and processes, for instance, are nowadays a constant presence in the media.

If we take a closer look at the work of economic analysts, we will encounter a highly differentiated, complex field. There are securities analysts, who in their turn come in at least two flavours: technical (or chartist) and fundamental. While the claims of technical analysts are at odds with the tenets of financial economics (see Preda [2007]), they have become a fixture of the markets' institutional structures. But there are also buy and sell side analysts: while the former work for institutional investors (such as fund managers), the latter usually work for brokers and write research which is circulated to clients. Additionally, there are credit analysts (Poon 2009), risk analysts (Power 2005), country and industry analysts, among others.

The products of analyses, as incorporated in research reports, are usually a mix of visual objects (charts, diagrams), numerical data, and text. Ethnographic studies of how analysts produce their reports (Mars 1998) show that these are designed to fulfil a double role: diagnose the state of the investigated entity, and make a forecast of its future evolution. While analysts employ a whole range of off-the-shelf instruments (statistical models and formulas) not dissimilar to those used by academic economists, they also try to assemble direct observations of the entities they analyse (such as corporations) by making visits, buying and testing their products, or talking to employees. Additionally, they study and comment on business data, budgets, charts, and statements made by the entities they study. These heterogeneous elements flow together into the 'spreadsheet', supposed to be unique and to condense the knowledge gained by the analyst. The spreadsheet appears as an epistemic instrument (Mars 1998, p. 270), in the sense of being a machine for the production of judgements, one honed to the particular skills of the analyst. At the same time, it is an observational instrument: the spreadsheet processes and translates external economic entities (such as an enterprise) into an object which is internal to the procedures of investigation (Kalthoff 2005, p. 78). On the basis of this transformation, analysts will become able to compare different economic entities, formulate judgements, and make forecasts about them.

The spreadsheet allows analysts to produce stories about the entities they investigate, stories which will then be disseminated to clients. Such stories play a multiple role: they legitimate the analyst as the holder of a particular body of knowledge; they appear as a special product geared towards end users; and they are an important instrument for making forecasting statements, as well as for judging 'the market'.

Stories here should not be understood as classic narratives with plot, development, and characters (although these elements may well be present in various combinations). Nor should they be understood as having a representational character, in the sense of plotting the real world of economic transactions onto a sheet of paper. Stories are objects which combine numerical data, visualizations, and rhetorical elements into alternative, yet plausible microworlds, which allow authoritative statements. They filter and reassemble elements from the broader world of economic actions; they make both judgements and epistemic claims. From the users' point of view, these microworlds contribute to introducing unexpected elements in action, elements which are continuously revised, expanded, and adapted. Because the field of analysts follows the logic of differentiation, each analyst has to produce original stories, different from those of the competition. Stories about the same entities compete against each other; from the perspective of users they appear as informational surprises, and they require additional judgements about their plausibility.

Of course, analysts can produce different stories (with different judgements) for different audiences, according to the webs of concrete business interests in which they are embedded. A concrete case examined by Richard Swedberg (2005) is that of high-tech analysts in the late 1990s: the analysts formulated contradictory judgements, some meant for a broader public, and some meant for those in the know. These cases, which together with others led to changed US legislation separating analysis from brokerage, raise questions about the ethical character of public statements and recommendations formulated by analysts. They show once more than these are not mere representational statements, but judgements which are taken as orientation for action.

This situation is similar with that of economic forecasters, who also use heterogeneous instruments in order to produce objects supporting 'stories' (Evans 2007, p. 695; Reichmann 2006)—that is, authoritative judgements used to establish expectations and draft further courses of action. Like analysts, forecasters use networks of personal relationships (coming from government, from academia, and from the media) and draw on the judgements circulated within; they also feed their own judgements into these networks. They employ a variety of analytical, quantitative techniques and tinker with bodies of data, combining off-the-shelf elements into unique assemblages. In this context, forecasting appears as the activity of 'postcasting' (Mars 1998, p. 139)—that is, of projecting expectations within a preassembled frame which fits the projection.

Moreover, the process of economic forecasting, as well as that of analysis, cannot be separated from their dramatizations, geared towards specific publics and following the logic of informational surprises. The press conferences held by forecasters and analysts (Reichmann 2006, p. 135), the morning calls, the interviews, and the public statements are as many occasions seen by practitioners as intrinsic to what it means to forecast and analyse, respectively. Forecasters appear to be aware of the symbolic character of the data they present, and of their impact on audiences. Data on gross domestic product, exports, productivity, or inflation are perceived as defining collective economic identities. In this perspective, economic expertise includes platform performances akin to those of market transactions.

A closer ethnographic look at how users deal with the analysts' recommendations reveals that opportunities for use are already embedded in the institutional structures of trading; in investment banks, for instance, traders and analysts have regular morning meetings (Mars 1998, p. 400). In hedge funds, analysts and traders sit in front of adjacent screens (MacKenzie 2009, p. 42; also, Beunza and Stark 2005, pp. 91–2). Additionally, analysts and their clients exchange conversations on a variety of social occasions. Yet, in spite of all these institutional opportunities, traders do not slavishly follow the opinions and judgements of analysts; some traders may declare that they are not interested in hearing the analysts' argumentation, but only one main storyline (Hasselström 2003, p. 68; Bruegger 1999, p. 83), which usually takes the form of a judgement. A more recent example of such a judgement is brought to us by the media: discussing (supermarket chain) Sainsbury's rise in profits in the first half of 2008, 'in a note to clients, JP Morgan analyst Alastair Johnson described the results as boring, but added: "But boring is good in these markets"' (Teather 2008).

Nevertheless, institutional engagements such as morning meetings or (more or less formal) discussions between analysts and traders serve as an arena in which, sometimes in contradictory form, locally agreed situational definitions are achieved; in the language of analysts and traders, these are 'views' (Mars 1998, pp. 404–9; Bruegger 1999, pp. 71–3) on the basis of which future courses of action can be projected. That the interaction with analysts is deemed by traders as necessary (in spite of the latter not always accepting the analysts' diagnostic) points to the fact that epistemic objects are contrasted and combined with the traders' accounts of practical actions in order to achieve, in a collaborative fashion, expectations and projections of action. 'Views' are accompanied by 'big pictures'—that is, by accounts of the 'world' and of the 'market' based on combinations of epistemic objects and practical, personal experiences of past trading.

The fact that cognitive operations require shared definitions, mutually confirmed observations, and common perspectives indicates that the cognitive processes out of which information is produced are not just a matter of psychological biases, of the kind discussed in behavioural economics. Cognitive processes are essentially interactional and irreducible to deviations (i.e. biases) from a standard model of rationality or to mental processes (e.g. Watson and Coulter 2008, pp. 11–2). Distributed cognition[22] (see MacKenzie [2008, pp. 46–8]; Callon [2007a, pp. 337–8]; Beunza and Stark [2005, pp. 91–4]; Hutchins [1995, p. 175]) appears to play an important role in the production of 'views' and 'pictures'. Distributed cognition means that paths of action are generated by collaborative work grounded in observations, classifications, and calculations, work which, as argued above, draws not only on experiences of trading, but also on epistemic objects. Since this collaborative work is always task-bound and done in heterogeneous groups, it follows that it will not generate the same results across various trading locales. Even if we assume that the same (or similar) epistemic objects are used, different groups will combine them differently, and the results will be 'views' and 'big pictures' which cannot totally overlap. This explains the continuing market dynamics: people trade with each other not based exclusively on needs (or utilities), but also on competing 'views'.

One effect of such views, analysed by Ezra Zuckerman (1999; 2004), is that analysts use categories to classify the securities they analyse. Securities can be classified (i.e. ascribed to a certain industry or economic activity) in multiple ways; an airline stock, for instance, can be ascribed to the transportation industry, and also to the tourism sector, or to retail (due to in-flight sales, among others). While some securities are classified in consistent ways by analysts, others have multiple, inconsistent classifications: that is, analysts tend to disagree on the categories to which they belong. Securities which are classified in multiple, inconsistent ways have more volatile prices (and trade at a discount) compared with those ascribed to clear cut categories (Zuckerman 1999, p. 1424). Securities markets can be seen then as consisting of several zones, according to whether securities are classified by analysts in a clear cut, consistent manner or not. Some market zones (those with coverage coherence) will be characterized by lower price and volume volatility, whereas others (with coverage incoherence) will be characterized by higher volatility (Zuckerman 2004, pp. 424–5). Because the interpretive models vary in the zones with coverage incoherence, these variations would be information in itself, and would contribute to higher volumes and frequency of trading, and hence to higher volatility. Investors would then tend to assess these (i.e. the analysts') judgements against each other in practical actions. Similar effects of classifications can be encountered in the film industry, as well as in online auctions (Zuckerman and Kim 2003; Zuckerman et al. 2003; Hsu, Hannan, and Koçak 2009). This line of argumentation, again, runs against the representational character of the analysts' work, and promotes a picture of markets as based in a 'self-recursive dynamics' (Zuckerman 2004, p. 405).

Expertise and Market Information

In light of the above, economic experts do not appear as information inter-mediaries (see Bruce [2002]; Fogarty and Rogers [2005]), in the sense of collecting, arranging, and distributing already existing pieces of information, available in the outside world, but which market players were too busy to take care of. Rather, economic experts appear as producing objects (or micro-worlds) which embed judgements about economic entities and their relation-ships. These objects can be the abstract models of economic theory, the products of risk, credit, or securities analysis, statistical indicators, or reces-sion forecasts. Objects are informational not in the sense of reducing uncer-tainties, but rather in that of increasing them, as a starting point for further action.

The notion of object used throughout this chapter is meant, among others, to draw attention to the material character of economic knowledge and expertise. What experts produce are not disembodied manifestations of the 'analytical spirit' or intellect but rather concrete, material objects endowed with specific properties: research papers, reports, forecasts, and the like, which in their turn are used in specific contexts and in specific interaction formats. This production implies specific knowledge skills and specific cog-nitive operations. Among the skills which can be counted here are the ability to read an equation at a glance, the ability to comprehend something like 'elasticity' without much pause for thinking, or the ability to see a diagram as the elasticity curve, for instance. Epistemic objects are packaged together with a specific rhetoric which enables their use: argumentation structures, con-cepts, and persuasion strategies are intrinsic to them. Additionally, the pro-duction of epistemic objects is anchored in specific cognitive operations, such as observation, calculation, or classification, understood not as mental, but as practical operations following community-specific standards of validity and reliability.

These objects are not representational: they do not mirror an external reality. Rather, the activity of economists appears to be somewhat similar to that of physicists, who have traditionally served as the former's inspiration. Like physicists, economists have an 'object-oriented epistemics' (Knorr Cetina 1999, p. 79), consisting in the production of informational entities, which can then be used in various contexts. The notion of performativity, discussed in this chapter, is meant to emphasize this aspect.

Epistemic objects can be about alternative, relevant microworlds, endowed with temporal dimensions. They can be about what happens to entities in a world of transactions different from, yet regarded as adjacent to the real one. This includes showing, among others, what the price of an option contract would be as derived from a restricted set of specific assumptions about the features and behaviour of transaction partners. As such, this rather increases uncertainties with respect to real courses of action. (What if some part of my world comes a bit closer to that microworld?) It is informational because it opens new possibilities for further action (e.g. trading options at a theoretical price instead of based on past habits). Such microworlds can be projected into the future or can incorporate the past (modelling with historical economic data is a case in point here). Their use implies the appropriation of specific skills, of a specific language, as well as specific attitudes on the part of users. In other words, increased use of epistemic objects in transactions—objects endowed with authority—propagates specific knowledge, skills, a specific rhetoric, and specific attitudes. Using these objects means accepting their authority.

Seen in this perspective, epistemic objects are used to investigate, project, and implement (new) courses of action. This can include the generation of new financial products or the modification of existing ones, as exemplified by derivatives markets. It can also include judgements upon how the world is ordered (e.g. classifications of securities), or about how it will evolve (forecasts), about who is creditworthy, and the like. Because they help project courses of action, epistemic objects are intrinsic to maintaining market dynamics.

In the previous chapter, the social structure of markets was discussed in terms of status groups and hierarchies among groups. This view can be extended now by including status groups of experts within markets structures: experts establish jurisdiction upon the production and diffusion of authoritative epistemic objects used in competitive transactions. These products are endowed with (charismatic) trust, which may be connected to, but is irreducible to interpersonal trust. Their uses cannot be separated from institutional contexts, from interests, and from the resources market actors operate with. The production and uses of these objects require material assemblages—devices and techniques on which transactions are grafted, which trace their boundaries, stabilize, and reproduce them across various settings. Indeed, most of the studies discussed in this chapter have stressed time and again the role of material devices. Generally put under the banner 'technology', they play a very significant role with respect to information. In the same way in which a soccer match cannot take place without a ball, or outside the materiality of the playing field, of its markings, boundaries, goalposts, etc., market transactions cannot take place outside the materiality of the relevant technologies, which I discuss in the next chapter.

⬜ **NOTES**

1. A story circulated in the media a couple of years ago recounted how Sanford Weill, the then CEO of Citigroup, used his social connections in order to secure places at an elite Manhattan preschool for the children of a top analyst (Mead 2002).
2. This is not to say that attempts at controlling information do not exist: quite the contrary. Status groups systematically attempt at controlling the information they produce. Full control, however, is not possible; attempts at fully controlling the circulation of information are at odds with the requirements of group connectivity.
3. While it can be argued that news agencies produce and circulate statements about world events, these statements are not simply representations of the world, but consequential judgements. They are interpreted with respect to their relevance for relationships among market actors (be they countries, organizations, or individuals). Thus, while few economic actors would be interested in hurricanes as such (which is interesting stuff for meteorologists), they are interested in the implications of hurricanes for the economic relationships of the affected entities (as measured by increased needs, reduced production, diminished trade capabilities, and so on).
4. This is not to say that fundamental economic research cannot have concrete applications. The nucleus of economic knowledge, however, remains the generation of meta-informational surprises.
5. Harry Collins and Robert Evans (2002, p. 254; Evans 2005) also distinguish between contributory and interactional expertise. The former designates the capacity to make a substantive contribution to the field, while the latter designates the capacity to interact 'interestingly' with field participants. It is especially the second type of expertise which makes possible communication between scientific communities and various types of audiences.
6. We can also encounter instances where the authority of academic economists is not acknowledged by other expert groups. For instance, financial analysts can dismiss abstract models as detached from reality, or as simplistic. In online anonymous markets, traders can ignore theoretical prices computed by available mathematical models, and use other, non-theoretical tools in their trading.
7. It should be noticed here that the evolution of sociology as a science follows a not dissimilar trajectory, from the analogy with literary criticism in the early twentieth century to its reshaping as a positive science from the 1930s on (Schryer 2007).
8. This is not to say that neoclassical economics is the only economic theory at the end of the nineteenth century; its competition includes the Austrian School, as well as institutionalism, and, to a certain extent, political economy. The neoclassical synthesis, which incorporates ideas developed by the Austrian School (such as the role of information) becomes dominant after the Second World War, by perfecting the formal approach to market equilibria, among others.
9. The analogy between society and a living organism allowed for the conceptualization of economic phenomena as fulfilling specific functions, modelled on the circulation of blood, and justified the application of statistics to the analysis of economic phenomena (see Alborn [1994]; Ménard [1980]; Breton [1992, p. 32]).

10. For Marx ([1872] 2002, p. 596), science as an autonomous force is integrated into the work process. This means not only engineering science but also management, accounting, and economics. If we extend Marx's argument to economic exchanges in general, it follows that the products of scientific activities (including economics) can be integrated into market exchanges.

11. Prices work as a mechanism for coordinating the distribution of information not only in market transactions but in the organization of economic life more generally, where they are tied to the ownership of the means of production (see also Streissler [1994, p. 55]); the estimated price per share of a publicly owned corporation, for instance, conveys information about the perception of the risks associated with the corporation's activities and about the decisions of the management.

12. While market efficiency has been part and parcel of orthodox economic theory for a long time, it has been increasingly questioned since the 1980s. Economists distinguish between at least three forms of market efficiency: (*a*) the weak form, according to which prices fully reflect the information implicit in the sequence of past prices; (*b*) the semi-strong form, according to which prices reflect all relevant information that is publicly available; and (*c*) the strong form, according to which prices reflect information that is known to any market participant (Dimson and Mussavian 1998, p. 94). Many argue that the semi-strong and the weak forms of market efficiency are more plausible than the strong form.

13. According to Michael Spence (2002, p. 445), a world of perfect information would be one where all the actors' attributes would be directly observable—for instance, where we could tell at a glance who is honest and who is not. This, in turn, would mean that the rules for reading honesty or diligence etc. at a glance are fully specifiable and amenable to formalization.

14. It should not be believed that only economic theory has been influenced by problems and themes emerging during the Second World War and connected to the military. Sociological research as well has been influenced to a considerable extent by war-related issues (see, among others, Orr [2006 p. 57]; Fleck [2007]).

15. In a Dutch auction, the auctioneer begins with a high asking price, which is sequentially lowered until bidders emerge. In a double auction, buyers and sellers simultaneously enter competitive bids and offers, respectively.

16. The complex evolution of economic theory after the Second World War cannot be entirely captured in this summary discussion; aspects like labour economics, or the economics of international trade, among others, cannot be discussed here. Irrespective of this, though, the notion of information centres upon price data; the behaviour of economic actors can be deduced from price data patterns (after a stochastic processing) exactly because market actors are modelled on a singular template (the ends–means rationality).

17. Sociologically speaking, the problem of calculative economic agents can be traced back to Max Weber's ([1920] 1988, p. 7) analysis of Western capitalism as being characterized by calculation, expressed in the rational organization of the enterprise, the separation between labour and capital, between household and enterprise, and the rational accounting of costs and benefits. For Weber, however, calculation is not determined by an abstract rationality template, but the result of changes induced by particular social institutions (religion). This resonates in contemporary research programmes such as Michel Callon and Fabian Muniesa's (2005; also Callon [2007*a*]), who see markets as calculative devices—that is, as sets of rules and artefacts which constrain actors to economic calculations.

18. Option contracts provide the right, but not the obligation, to buy or sell a financial security at a given price on or before a specified date in the future.

19. The strike price is the price at which the option contract is exercised. Arbitrage is trading which profits from price discrepancies (e.g. buying and selling the same security on different markets).

20. At the same time, performativity is not the same with self-fulfilling prophecies, the concept made popular by Robert King Merton (1968). While self-fulfilling prophecies imply contagion of beliefs, performativity means the modification of action settings through the concrete uses of formal models.

21. Financial transactions are usually leveraged—that is, they are conducted with mostly borrowed funds and only a small portion of the money is paid down when securities are bought. The rest will be paid later at a set date, or when the securities are resold.

22. The notion of distributed cognition has recently been criticized for not really renouncing the notion of cognition as mental operations (essentially of a calculative nature) taking place in a sociocultural environment (see Button [2008]). This notion—and its critique—are relevant especially because it has been transferred into the study of markets, mostly in the work of Michel Callon and Donald MacKenzie.

4 Technology and Market Information

In her book on the Chicago Board of Trade (CBOT), Caitlin Zaloom (2006, pp. 54–5, 74) describes how the traders fought over (and resisted) the introduction of computerized trading, only to find themselves later in an environment which didn't resemble at all the trading pits of the CBOT: impersonal office spaces with rows of computer screens, where the deafening noise of the trading pit had been replaced by computer clicks. Instead of facing each other standing, traders now sat next to each other facing computer screens. While this shift is meant to illustrate the growing role of computers in transactions, it also highlights the fact that markets have technology as an intrinsic component. This has led scholars to argue that markets can be conceived as 'socio-technical agencements' (MacKenzie 2009, pp. 20–1; Callon 2007b, p. 140) or as scopic systems (e.g. Knorr Cetina 2005; Knorr Cetina and Preda 2007). Distinctions such as that between network markets and flow markets (Knorr Cetina 2005, p. 39) are meant to emphasize, among others, the role played by technology, a role which cannot be easily grasped in terms of networks.

In the previous two chapters, markets have been treated in terms of how groups—be they directly involved in transactions or in the production and dissemination of expertise—deal with transaction-relevant information. In this treatment, however, technology has raised its head at almost every step, be it in the form of communication technologies, of epistemic objects, or of the spatial configuration of transactions. Market tools and technologies are present everywhere; it would be a mistake to see them as restricted to a few sophisticated domains. Not only are they ubiquitous, they are also crucial in transactions; if we look no further than money, this medium of exchange takes concrete material forms which are consequential for how transactions unfold (and which will be discussed in detail here). It is time now to take a closer look at how technologies work in relationship to markets and information; before doing this, however, we need a short discussion of how technology is dealt with in economic sociology.

Technology and Social Action

Technology has been increasingly paid attention to by sociologists since the 1980s, in relationship to a critique of technological determinism, seen as a progressivist account of modern societies, an account in which social action and institutions are causally influenced by the invention of machinery. In this account, technological advances shape society, while more and more efficient technologies replace lesser ones. Technology comes to be seen as the answer to social problems and as a guarantor of progress. Critics have questioned the progressivist approach while highlighting, in numerous case studies, the more complex role played by technology in society (see MacKenzie and Wajcman [1985]; Layne [2000]; Grint and Woolgar [1995]; Bijker, Hughes, and Pinch [1987]).

While the sociology of technology initially paid little attention to markets and economic exchanges, it drew on a tradition of thought which is directly relevant for these. In arguing that technology should not be seen as mere lumps of matter formed by the will of its inventors, sociologists invoked Marx's ([1872] 2002, pp. 70–1) argument that commodities (and tools and technologies as well) can be seen as embodiments of abstract human labour and as incorporating concrete labour processes. In discussing how capitalist exchange becomes possible, Marx argues that the exchange value of commodities is given by them incorporating abstract labour; since labour has a social character, commodities incorporate existing social relationships. The social character of artefacts, however, is obscured by them appearing as having an autonomous existence (Marx ([1872] 2002, pp. 84–5). This social character means that objects circulating in market transactions incorporate specific skills (employed in their production) and require at the same time skills from their users. At the same time, these objects are the outcome of specific social relationships; their use will generate and reproduce sets of relationships different from those of their production and circulation. Marx's argument was resonated later, and in a different context, by Émile Durkheim ([1915] 1965, p. 440), who saw objects (such as those used in rituals) as incorporating practical knowledge, as associated with social distinctions, and as requiring the same from users.

If the skills incorporated in objects demand skills from their users, a process of mutual adaptation can occur, in which the skills inscribed on bodies will synchronize to those incorporated in tools (see also Mauss ([1950] 1999, p. 365). It is not difficult to find examples of mutual adaptation from various domains of work, where the manipulation of tools requires specific skills, and existing skills, in their turn, require specific tools. In addition to this, the manipulation of objects creates specific temporal structures, made visible, for instance, in the rhythms with which human actors respond to machines. Such temporal structures can also be visually articulated, contributing to organizing human activities and social relationships (think, for instance, of how work time is visualized on punch clocks in factories). Moreover, the manipulation of tools and technologies can generate social institutions; the skills required in their production and use, for instance, can become part of jurisdiction building (see also Bechky [2003]), where professional groups fence them off to outsiders. Expert groups can arise in relationship to the production, distribution, and use of technology, accompanied by institutional arrangements related to education, work, and commercialization.

Technology can incorporate not only skills (understood mostly as tacit, embodied knowledge), but also cognitive operations. In building machines, for instance, engineers and scientists tinker with models and blueprints (see Henderson [1998]), make calculations, classify objects, store data, and project the ways in which they expect the technology will work. At the same time, technologies generate epistemic objects (these can be figures on a screen, curves, or acoustic signals, among others) which need to be observed, classified, calculated, stored, and memorized. These cognitive operations unfold in interactions; they require shared situational definitions, common perspectives on how machines are working, and coordination and confirmation of observations, among others. The coordinated use of technology results in what Edwin Hutchins (1995, pp. 195, 220) has called distributed cognition—that is, in the division, distribution, and conduct of cognitive processes[1] in interactions among task participants.

At about the time when the sociology of technology was taking off, sociologists of organizations became aware of the issue of tools and technology, and began investigating their impact on forms of work, organizational uses and responses to new technologies, organizational roles, and innovation, among others. While earlier work concentrated on how automation technology leads to standardization of work processes (e.g. Blau et al. 1976), later studies have highlighted how the technology-driven horizontal distribution of expertise challenges organizational roles and hierarchies (Barley 1986, 1996), or how technology generates new risks for organizations (e.g. Vaughan 1996; Perrow 1999). Studies of work processes in organizations have highlighted not only how reputations are built on technical skills and the ability of technicians to retain control of a situation in the work with machines, but also how control can elude human actors (e.g. Orr 1996, pp. 144–5). At the same time, studies of interaction with computer technologies have radically questioned the notion of action plans being incorporable in technology, actions plans which make the reactions of human actors previsible (e.g. Suchman 1987; also Rawls 2008a).

Closer to the issue of markets, historical studies of communication and information technologies such as the telephone and the telegraph have highlighted the changes induced in organizations by the emergence of writing technologies, the gender-specific character of new professions arising from communication technologies, as well as the ability to overcome spatial and temporal boundaries with the help of technology (e.g. Yates 1986; Bertinotti 1985; Flichy 1995; Stein 2001).

Based on the above, a series of technological features in relationship to organizations can be distinguished, features which are relevant for the sociological investigation of markets as well:

1. Tools and devices can be seen as standardizers—that is, as elements of 'frozen labour' with specific uniformities which, in their turn, require uniform skills, operations, and activities in organizational work. Because they create uniformities, standardizers are prone to commensurability and quantification (see also Espeland and Stevens [1998])—that is, they provide the possibility of generating metrics for comparing and evaluating entities which were seen previously as distinct, or for reclassifying such entities. A standardized work process, for instance, can be divided into different phases and, based on their uniform character, performance metrics can be produced; it becomes possible to compare and measure how various persons perform the same phases of the same process. Metrics can bring with them formal rules, or protocols, and increase the degree of control over processes and activities (Stinchcombe 2001, pp. 51–3; Vollmer 2007, p. 582). Moreover, at the organizational level, when processes are standardized, it becomes possible to produce metrics which compare the performance of various organizations. Risk metrics are a case in point here (see Power [2007, pp. 66–9]); they help compare and assess the risks incurred by corporations which at first sight may look very different from each other. This also means that standardizers support the production, storage, circulation, and use of new data, which in their turn require specific skills and abilities, a specific language, and specific sets of assumptions.

2. Standardizers can be transferred across various locales without losing their properties. Their transfer and implementation into a new locale will require that the human actors manipulating the technology will need to learn the skills and language required by it and, in time, will internalize the associated assumptions. Thus, the transfer of standardizers, or 'immutable mobiles' (see Latour [2005, p. 227]) will also standardize the skills and abilities present in various workplaces, will make them recognizable as such, and will encourage commensuration. The transfer of standardizers can take place as economic exchanges (creating thus a market in a specific technology) or as collaborations (the transfer of tools and instruments in science is a case in point here). At the same time, the creation and expansion of standardizers can be a medium for economic exchanges as well. This is what happens when money as a medium of exchange becomes standardized.[2]

3. Transferring standardizers across locales encourages network-building[3], such as the networks between producers and users of technology. A music

technology like the synthesizer, for instance, spread by building ties between networks of musicians and the manufacturers of this technology (Pinch and Trocco 2002). The transfer of standardizers can also raise jurisdictional issues, related not only to who is entitled to produce and distribute technologies, but also to use them and how. (Probably one of the clearest examples here is that of military technologies and the markets thereof.) Jurisdictional issues can come to the fore in debates about the legal status of technologies, of their outcomes, and the limits of their use; a more recent example is that of music downloads and sharing, where digital formats were defined as ownership and subjected to market transactions. Another relevant example here is that of the legal status of financial price data, which nowadays are sold to market actors by specialized financial services such as Bloomberg and Reuters. This wasn't always so: until the early twentieth century, price data were not seen as the ownership of a particular corporation (see also Preda [2009*b*, chapter 3]). Thus, technologies, as well as the objects or states generated by them, can contribute to the emergence of new markets: digital music formats, digital game formats, price data, or e-books are examples here, together with digital music players, games consoles, or digital reading devices such as the Kindle. At the same time, technology can support new formats of market exchanges: eBay, as well as Internet retailers are a case in point here.

Jurisdictional issues can be related to boundary-marking. In the same way in which the status and uses of technologies and their products can be subject to legal definitions and regulations, technology can be used to mark boundaries, in association with legal definitions or not; for instance, in organizations technology can be used to mark spatial and temporal work boundaries, among others (think of punch clocks). But technologies and tools can also be used to mark the boundaries between work and home, for instance, between organizational and family life, or between work time and private time (see Nippert-Eng [1995, pp. 162–3]).

   4. The notion of standardizer might give the impression that technologies relentlessly work towards reducing uncertainty (and, indeed, technology has been often understood in this sense). This is based on the idea that the skills necessary to handle tools and technologies have become routinized. In fact, the uses of technology cannot be reduced to learning and applying a couple of routines—this would amount to nothing but a version of the determinism criticized by sociologists of technology.

Technologies can create uncertainties as well as reduce them. This is valid not only for emerging technologies, which require learning new skills, but also for established ones, which can generate uncertainty. There are numerous examples of malfunctioning technology, common in everyday life. Additionally, technologies produce objects (such as data) which can be uncertain themselves, requiring new modes of (re)action from their users. To come back to the example of electronic music, these modes are not restricted to learning new skills, but also include producing musical pieces of a new genre, which didn't exist before. This creativity can be seen as a way of dealing with the uncertainties generated by new technologies. Closer to markets, price data generated and distributed with the help of technology shouldn't necessarily be seen as reducing uncertainty, but rather as increasing it, and requiring thus from their users new ways of dealing with them. Thus, technology can be seen not only as a standardizer, but also as a generator; it generates uncertainties with which users have to cope (see Preda [2006]), by taking new paths of action.

Another side of the creative, agential use of technology is that this latter can be endowed with symbolic aspects, different from the functional ones implied by the notion of routine. In organizations, for instance, technology can be used for legitimating or for consolidating the authority of specific groups, and not necessarily for efficiency purposes. This sends us back to Max Weber's distinction among forms of authority, discussed in the preceding chapters: technology cannot be exclusively and a priori ascribed to means–ends rationality and to bureaucratic authority; it can be used for consolidating and disseminating charismatic authority as well, or for symbolic or legitimatory purposes, at personal or at organizational level. An example in this sense is provided by the ways in which organizations use mass communication technologies in public relations, not necessarily for the purposes of establishing transparency, but for those of achieving legitimacy.

Markets, Information, and Technology

The general features of technology discussed above admittedly cover only a very small portion of research done in the area, but prepare nevertheless the ground for a more specific discussion of technology in relationship to markets and information. Tools and technologies can occupy in markets at least the following positions:

1. They set up boundaries for market transactions. These include artefacts, tools, and technologies for erecting spatial and temporal boundaries, in relationship or not with legal definitions and regulations.

2. Objects, tools, and technologies mediate transactions. Money, in its different material forms, belongs here. But not only money: online technologies, for instance, are a medium of transactions too. Here, material forms of money can become integrated into the broader medium; electronic money, in the form of debit, credit, and electronic transfers is intrinsic to the technological

medium in which transactions take place. Think of eBay or Amazon payments here, where paying cash is impossible, while a variety of electronic monies— debit, credit, PayPal, electronic transfers—are accepted.

3. Objects, tools, and technologies provide epistemic objects for market transactions, in the form of data generation, circulation, memorization, and retrieval. In the previous chapter, market-relevant epistemic objects were discussed mostly as (formal) models which intervene in market transactions. Models, however, cannot work without data, such as price, volume, or time. They are generated, distributed, and stored with specific technologies, irrespective of whether these latter are computer-generated or hand-written tables.

4. Objects, tools, and technologies provide the backstage support for market transactions, in the form of organizational infrastructures ensuring (calculative and legal) market accountability. Clearing systems executing inter-bank payments, accounting offices computing cost-benefit analyses, or audits belong here. All these technologies have at their core data storage, tracking, and retrieval systems, market memories without which these operations would be impossible.

5. Objects, tools, and technologies used in (1)–(4) can become themselves the object of market exchanges, and thus generate new transactions. Money is not only a medium of exchanges, but its object as well: currency markets are a case in point here. Computer hardware or fibreglass cable is sold or leased to market traders, for instance.[4] Data systems are enabling transactions, but they are bought and sold as well. Data, images, stories, and the analyses thereof are bought and sold in specialized markets too. This is valid not only for financial markets, but for other kinds of markets as well: to give but one example here, firms specializing in geological exploration rely on data gathering and processing technologies, and sell these data to corporations such as mining and oil companies (for a history of this data gathering, see Bowker [1994]). Not only that, markets with specialized providers in price data exist, but the analysis of price data is the object of market transactions too; the same goes for market-relevant news.

In markets, tools and technologies act as standardizers, but not only. They do not merely serve to support regular forms of transactions which can be implemented across various locales. Tools and technologies are generators too; they produce new uncertainties, in the form of information, opening thus avenues of future action. In geological exploration, as well as in financial markets, technology may standardize skills, but it will also produce data which in themselves are uncertainties requiring further action. While geologists may operate similar spectrometers in different parts of the world, data produced by the devices can still appear as surprises, requiring action. A trader may be able to use the same computer systems in Chicago as well as in London, but the data flickering on the screens will still be surprises, not foreseeable on the grounds of having acquired operational skills with trading software.

The production, implementation, and uses of market technologies imply not only specialized skills and abilities, but also cognitive operations, and the objects they generate are epistemic objects, used to make judgements and thus information. As such, they are subjected to jurisdiction. Jurisdiction is tied to expertise and to the activities of status groups claiming various forms of entitlement to these objects. This can be entitlement to produce or disseminate them, and also to add new layers to them through expert interpretation and commentary. Thus, market technologies and the objects they produce provide an interface for status groups active in markets to link in with other status groups specialized in the production and dissemination of technology. Sometimes, as we shall see in the following, this can lead to the blurring of group distinctions, with technology groups becoming market actors in their own right. Being status groups, those involved in market-relevant technologies will use symbols for establishing their legitimacy within organizations and within society at large, symbols tied to the technologies they control. Thus, at organizational level and within society at large, market technologies will be endowed with symbolic aspects as well.

On the basis of these arguments, I will examine now how the dimensions of technology presented above intervene concretely in shaping markets.

Technology and the Boundaries of Markets

As argued in Chapter 1, markets establish boundaries with respect to society at large, and also to other social institutions. Spatial and temporal boundaries occupy a key place here; where and when to transact are issues not simply relegated to shared tacit understandings, but also codified in regulations, and inscribed in the material environment and associated technical devices. Walls and doors, windows, fences, gates, punch clocks, tables and indicators, neon signs, and many more devices mark the boundaries of markets.

Distinctions between the inside and the outside, inscribed in concrete, steel, and glass, allow not only for marketplaces to integrate into society at large, by signalling their legitimacy (you put a neon sign on a legitimate shop), but also offer connection points for less legitimate (or even illegal) economic transactions. Not only can spatial technologies trace boundaries between legitimate and illegitimate transactions, but they can also change the character of the objects being transacted as well. Spatial separation can lead to standardization, creating thus categories of merchandise which can be more easily traded, over larger geographical spaces. In nineteenth century Chicago, grain sent to the city by farmers was mixed together and stored in elevators, leading not only to complaints about low quality, but also contributing to falling prices. Worried about the latter, the Chicago Board of Trade introduced different quality grades which were stored separately, and appointed grain inspectors to ensure that the operators of grain elevators did not flout the regulations (Cronon 1991, pp. 118–19). With this standardization, the CBOT gained additional jurisdiction upon links in the supply chain which were previously outside its control.

Material technologies of tracing space and time boundaries also make jurisdiction, as well as status differences visible; one could say that they send signals to observers about who is entitled to do what actions. In other words, they play a role in establishing jurisdiction- and status-relevant routines. In the example of high-end fashion shops, analysed in the first chapter, spatial technologies of presenting store fronts to the public, their inner architecture, as well as the display of goods, contributed to the formation and display of such routines, in the sense that it is mostly those used to 'moving around' in such an environment who enter these stores. In her ethnography of the Chicago Board of Trade, Caitlin Zaloom (2006, pp. 25–33, 38–41) shows how the architecture of the building was planned in such a way as to integrate into the city, while working at the same time as a symbol of prosperity and economic power. It was not merely functional architecture (after all, this was a commodities exchange), but a stately symbol of the economic might of the institution. The same can be said about the architecture of the New York Stock Exchange, or that of the former building of the Paris Bourse (the Palais Brongniart), both made to look like Greek temples.[5]

On the inside, the trading halls were designed in such a way as to allow maximum visibility and possibilities for movement (eliminating inner columns). At the same time, spaces were clearly marked for traders, clerks, runners, and telephone operators. Traders, for instance, stood in octogonal pits, while clerks had rows of desks at some distance from the pits. This spatial arrangement not only made jurisdictions visible (only traders were allowed in the pits, while runners had to wait on their borders, for instance), but it also shaped the organization of trading activities and structured the production and distribution of information. While informational surprises were produced in the pits, they drew on resources situated outside (a phone order could trigger a surprise, for instance) and were channelled and processed through specific spaces. The same can be said here about the distinction between trading time and clearing time,[6] where the technologies and rules for measuring and recording two different temporal categories were located in different, though close spaces.

At a more macroscopic level, spatial divisions marking jurisdiction over market activities lead to a concentration of institutions and actors in specific urban spaces, which become interconnected. Data flow among these spaces, and support activities are arranged around them. Alternatively, spatial divisions can emerge, where support activities are moved to other, geographically distant spaces, which nevertheless are linked in via communication technologies. These spaces and the corresponding technologies of data processing and transfer constitute a 'world of markets' which is not coextensive with 'the world' as we perceive it. Spatial concentration and differentiation in market activities can contribute to the standardization of data, processes, and skills and to the technological specialization of channels through which it is circulated. While data and processes become standardized, they also become available only through specialized channels, as a means of ensuring jurisdiction.

At the same time, spatial concentration of market-specific technologies (and especially of data transmission and processing technologies) can be accompanied by professional concentration and by the space-bound emergence of specific cultural circuits, understood as worldviews and justificatory rhetoric stemming from these groups (Thrift and Leyshon 1994, p. 316; Thrift 2001, p. 428). Cultural circuits can resonate in spatial changes within organizations, promoting semi-public spaces of 'creative interaction' or buildings intended to facilitate collaboration between scientists and marketers ('idea incubators', or 'spinoffs'—see also Thrift [2006]).

Other examples come from the spatial concentration of financial markets in a few global cities—that is, in geographically dispersed spaces (e.g. the City of London, downtown Manhattan, Tokyo, or Zurich) which nevertheless coordinate with each other via communication technologies and develop own time structures (see Sassen [2001, 2005, 2006]). Financial actors in these cities have easier access to specialized communication technologies, data providers, as well as to informally circulated stories, to rumours, and gossip. They have easier access to networking activities and can connect easily to members of other status groups (from politics, or from management, for instance). While back office activities can be moved to geographically distant places (think call centres or accounting offices in South Asia), they stay nevertheless connected with the main centres of finance and adapt their temporal rhythms to the requirements of trading activities (e.g. 24/7 availability, ability to retrieve and send data on request, etc.). Spatial concentration, accompanied by division of labour and interconnectedness is valid not only for financial markets, but for other types as well: think high-end fashion markets, or markets for computer chips. Both operate on a similar principle of concentration and division, with the design and prototypes executed in a few urban spaces (where know-how, skills, data, and technology are concentrated) and manufacturing taking place in other, geographically separated spaces.

Money, Markets, and Information

If technologies of space and time divide and connect, enabling thus the circulation of objects and tools across marketplaces, there is at least one class of objects and tools which epitomizes this circulation in and across markets: money. Nothing has money's capacity for linking together different markets, and for making commodities flow through exchange circuits. Consequently, its connections to market information need special attention here.

Money, understood as 'one of our essential social technologies' is usually seen as performing four economic functions: medium of exchange, store of value, means of settlement, and measure of value (Ingham 2004, p. 3). While formal approaches in economics model these functions based on the assumption that in their absence a series of inconveniences would result, they have been relatively slow in integrating money as an independent variable. In classical economics, for instance, Léon Walras's model of the general equilibrium operated on the assumption of generalized barter, not on that of monetary exchanges (Lewis and Mizen 2000, pp. 52–3). Versions of the general competitive equilibrium from the 1950s (like the Arrow–Debreu model) did not provide a place for money either (Lewis and Mizen 2000, pp. 92–3; Roberts 1991, p. 538; Milgate 1989).[7] Economists realized in the 1950s and 1960s that this assumption led to inconsistencies and modified models accordingly (for instance, by taking into account that increases in the quantity of money influence demand, all other things being constant). Under the growing influence of game theory, the dominant model of market exchanges has consisted of given sets of participants, their beliefs about each other's characteristics, the order in which they act, the information available during decision-making, the possible actions available at decision points, the physical outcomes resulting from each possible combination of choices, and the valuations of these outcomes (Roberts 1991, p. 540). This did not leave a special place for money as a medium of exchange or as a unit of account.[8]

In contrast, the sociological tradition has shown a constant preoccupation with how to conceptualize money while integrating it in a general account of the capitalist economy. For Marx ([1872] 2002, p. 103), money provided the material in which the expression of value was set in the world of commodities, and represented the value of the latter as qualitatively the same and as quantitatively comparable. Money has no price: in order for the other commodities to participate to this relatively unitary form of value, money had to be its own equivalent (Marx [1872] 2002, p. 104).[9] Money is the social embodiment of human labour and the standard measure of prices. These latter, in their turn, are the money name of the labour embodied in commodities (Marx [1872] 2002, p. 109). Prices, however, can deviate from the values of commodities (as consisting in social labour time), and will not automatically be the exact expression of the latter. Moreover, the price form contains what Marx calls a qualitative contradiction, in the sense that it can express not only value, but also entities which do not have value—that is, which do not incorporate any social labour time—such as honour or conscience. At the same time, the price form can conceal relationships derived from value (Marx ([1872] 2002, p. 110).

For Max Weber, money is not only a matter of prices, but also one of state monopoly and of the organization of capitalist enterprises. The state has the monopoly of printing money and of regulating its circulation (or order, as Weber writes, [1921] 1972, p. 97). While the monopoly of emitting money is not present everywhere, the regulation of money circulation appears as more important, being tied to forms of taxation applied by the state to its subjects, and also to payments made by the state (for instance, state debts). The state regulates these forms of exchange by establishing which monies are valid within certain spaces and for specific kinds of payments. Moreover, the state accumulates, manages, and distributes money, in the form of taxes, pensions, or debt payments, among others. In addition to this formal validity of money, the latter has material validity, established within circuits of commodity exchanges, as well as by individuals who evaluate the utilities of their incomes (Weber [1921] 1972, p. 99).[10]

The state's regulatory interventions as a factor of monetary economies (and hence of markets) points to at least two aspects: first, money has to be a material technology, because the state needs to keep track of taxes and payments. Second, technologies of accounting are related to legal technologies, enabling regulatory measures. Standardization (of money) goes hand in hand with territorial monopolies, with administrative and legal technologies. Economic accounting, powered by this standardization, appears thus as a technology of government; it creates responsibility, in the sense of economic actors having to respond in specific fashions to the requests of the state (Miller 2001, p. 380). This responsibility emerges not only at the level of the state, but at that of the enterprise as well, where the calculation of capital is tied to organizational discipline (Weber [1921] 1972, p. 58). Money appears thus as a tool and technology of capitalist calculation within organizations; at the same time, these organizations encounter each other on the market, where they compete. This competition takes place primarily through prices, expressed in money. In addition to being an accounting and calculation tool, money appears then as a means of competition, or struggle as well.

The standardizing aspect of money means that it can be reduced to quantities, and as such is used not only in economic exchanges, but also to express social relationships situated outside the economic sphere (Simmel [1901] 1989, pp. 484, 488). It thus becomes possible to set monetary relationships for activities, events, and entities seen as pertaining in the first place to reciprocal moral obligations; blood money is an instance of this, noticed by Georg Simmel, but we can also find more recent examples such as intimate relationships (Zelizer 2005*a*) or organ donation (Healy 2006). While this could be seen as commodification[11]—that is, as the transfer into the market sphere of entities which were previously ascribed to other spheres and defined by means of moral obligations—it enables the institutional regulation and control over the circulation of such entities (Healy 2006, p. 121).

Seen from the perspective of individual lives, the use of money as a standardizer may encourage individual freedoms, while at the same time increasing the individual's economic and social dependence on others (Simmel [1901] 1989, pp. 395, 397). Money separates being from having; if for Marx being was defined by ownership of certain objects (means of production), with the expansion of monetary exchanges social identities are linked mainly to money as a universal technology of expressing relationships. Universality, however, is undermined by the material character of this technology; if money can express various forms of social relationships, it can do so only based on its material shape. This opens up the possibility of differentiating among various shapes for expressing and classifying various kinds of relationships; moreover, it opens up the possibility of using special kinds of monies as opposed to standard currencies.

One of the social-structural forms discussed in Chapter 2 was the circuits of commerce, some of which are based on special tokens or local monies, seen as an alternative to standard currency and to the commercial exchanges associated with it (see also Maurer [2005, pp. 42–7]). Money can be physically earmarked for certain uses, or it can be segregated spatially; it can be deemed as suitable only for certain uses, according to how its provenience is judged, or it can be made part of allocation systems shaped by ethical considerations and by reciprocal obligations (Zelizer 1997, p. 209). What is more, money can be subjected to controversies and political struggles related to the definition of what constitutes proper money (Carruthers and Babb 1996, p. 1580). These definitions, in their turn, serve not only to justify a given economic order, but also to relate it to society at large in specific ways.

It follows from the above arguments that money can be seen as a material technology (a standardizer)[12] which not only makes possible the universal circulation of commodities (Marx ([1872] 2002, p. 122), but also allows setting these latter in relationship to each other (and to other entities). Money expresses thus social relationships which go beyond the sphere of market transactions. Conversely, money can contribute to transforming entities and relationships into economic ones. Since money circulates, it means that it transfers representations of relationships (what would be called then values) across different settings. As such, money is informative; it confronts transaction partners within dispersed settings with representations of social relationships which are taken as a starting point for further actions.

Since these (according to Marx, not always accurate) representations are contained in prices,[13] the latter become a medium of information. But prices as a medium of information, as we shall see below, cannot be separated from the technology which makes them visible to market participants. A price can be made visible by a couple of banknotes changing hands over the store counter, and also on the display of a credit card handheld terminal, on a receipt, or on a trading screen.[14] This indicates that the materiality of money (and of prices) should be sought not only in technologies of display, but also in those of recording, storing, and circulating transactions. Moreover, it indicates that the materiality of money is not neutral with respect to how this latter is perceived and used, to the actions and categories associated with it.

At the same time, the materiality of money as an expression of social relationships implies that its production, circulation, distribution, and uses is a matter of various social jurisdictions; these can be exercised by social institutions such as governmental bodies and regulators and also, on a smaller scale, by families, groups of friends, or religious groups. Jurisdictions can be expressed through (spatial and temporal) boundaries, and also through rules of emission, circulation, and use, or of membership in certain groups entitled to use certain monies.

If we take money to be informative, and if prices appear as a medium of information (about relationships, but not only), then in market contexts prices constitute a crucial piece of information. This information, as argued above, cannot be separated from the technology which generates it. Technology appears to be relevant not only with respect to how jurisdictions are created and maintained, but also to how various bits of information are lumped together or separated, how they are selected, perceived, and used by market actors. All these aspects—classifications, selections, jurisdictions, and the like—have to be made visible to market participants. Money and prices, as well as other data, have to be shown to them in specific, technology-induced forms.

In the same way in which the technologies of earmarking analysed by Viviana Zelizer (1997) make visible the categories to which monies belong and the uses they can be put to in the household, in markets prices and other relevant data are shown in specific forms, with specific technologies. Before anything else, they appear to observers and market participants alike as displayed data. Irrespective of whether on a price tag, on a supermarket label, on a handwritten note, or on a computer screen, these data provide the starting point and the fodder for further action. Indeed, if we look around, at least some markets seem to be heavily reliant on data display technologies—financial markets are a case in point here. At the same time, market data have continuously increased their presence in the public sphere—witness the display of stock prices on screens in public spaces, for instance. It is necessary, therefore, to examine closely how data displaying technologies work in the context of markets, and how they relate to the actions of market actors.

Data Technologies, Information, and Markets

Until now, market-relevant technologies have been approached as standard-izers, jurisdiction-makers, and generators, in relationship to how they transform the organization and entities implicated in market exchanges. But, as argued above, there is a special class of technologies, implicated not only in standardizing entities and circulating them, but also, above all, in displaying to market participants action-relevant data about these entities. The starting point for their analysis is provided by Bruce Carruthers and Arthur Stinch-combe's (2001, pp. 104–5) argument that standardization increases liquidity— that is, the readiness to transact in a given class of entities (for a different definition of the problem, see Aspers [2007, p. 435]). This readiness comes from the certainty of actors in a specific market that no one knows better the consensus price for an entity transacted within that market than the people who are buying and selling. Knowing that all participants are dealing in the same standardized entities contributes to their certainty. Consequently, Carruthers and Stinchcombe (2001, p. 104) call for a 'sociology of knowledge that represents buyers' and sellers' own epistemology of the market'.

Taking this call seriously, we should note, however, that there is more to the actors' ways of knowing than the awareness about the standardized character of, say, a specific class of securities like bonds. The ways of knowing in the market start with basic cognitive activities, such as observations of price displays and of price variations; if we want to see whether a market is liquid, we should observe how often entities are traded (and, if possible, by whom, for how much, and so on). This requires not only specific skills and techniques, but also specific technologies which make data about transactions visible to market participants. To use one of Carruthers and Stinchcombe's examples, an extra bunch of carrots bought by mistake in a supermarket cannot be quickly resold for a price near the one advertised by the supermarket. Supermarkets are illiquid market arrangements, in the sense that they do not offer customers the possibility of observing the frequency of other people's buying carrots, the quantities they buy, and the like.[15] This would require a cumbersome observational arrangement, such as somebody standing next to the vegetables and taking notes, risking thus to be asked to leave the store etc. Then, the notes about the frequency of buying carrot bunches should be made somehow available to all those interested in reselling carrots they have bought by mistake in supermarkets, and to those interested in buying carrots previously bought by mistake etc. Then the timing of this availability would have somehow to be set, which raises the question, by whom etc.

This example, however, shows that there is more to creating a (liquid) market than standardizing the objects being traded (after all, carrots are a standardized commodity). Markets work not only with prices and quantities, but also with price and quantity data. In fact, it could be argued that markets cannot work with prices and quantities if they do not work with data. Investigating the epistemology of market participants requires investigating how data are displayed for observation, by whom, where, under which circumstances, when, and so on. A market needs technologies for displaying data to several participants at once, and for controlling access to these data. Technologies for data display in markets are involved not only in issues of jurisdiction but are consequential for how market participants perceive, evaluate, and project future courses of action.

Data displaying technologies can change the temporal rhythms in which market participants get access to data and, therefore, the rhythms of their reactions to these data. Such technologies can also work as coordinating devices for market actors who are spatially dispersed. As argued above, they can both concentrate in specific spaces (e.g. trading rooms of banks, stock exchanges) and bring places which are far apart on the same temporal plane. What is more, data displaying technologies can integrate with action technologies, providing the opportunity of bringing the actors into a common action-response system: that is, a system of structural reflexivity (Goffman 1981, p. 117) where the market participants reciprocally align their actions based on common observations of data. An example in this sense, which will be discussed in more detail below, comes from financial markets, where trading screens integrate data observation and action (i.e. transactions). Also, data displaying technologies can shift the space of market transactions from physical enclosures to electronic networks and platforms, increasing the spatial mobility of participants to transactions. This is what actually happens in financial markets, for instance, where since the late 1990s the physical enclosure of the trading floor has been replaced by networks and electronic platforms (see Muniesa [2005]).

At the same time, by modifying the rhythms in which data are displayed and by making them available to interconnected, yet dispersed participants, technologies change the character of these data and with that the understanding of information on which market actors operate. In financial markets, the most important information—namely, price variations—was made available to participants on a continuous basis only in the late nineteenth century, when the stock ticker was introduced on the New York Stock Exchange (see Preda [2006]; Knorr Cetina and Preda [2007]). Until then, price variations did not constitute commonly available information to market participants, in the sense that they could not jointly observe changes in prices. These latter, however, constitute relevant information; they provide the surprises—the uncertainties—which drive the participants' further actions. Until the ticker was introduced in 1867, the prices from individual transactions were recorded on paper slips and sent by courier boys to brokerage houses. The prices published in newspapers did not reflect all transactions and depended on who furnished them to the journalists.

The introduction of the stock ticker—a version of the electric telegraph which could print letters, numbers, and symbols instead of Morse code— changed the situation, in the sense that it brought together dispersed price data into a flow, which was recorded on a paper strip, and could be observed in different brokerage offices at the same time. This technology made price variations into information relevant to market actors; by observing the printed prices from different subsequent transactions in the same security, market participants witnessed surprises—that is, uncertainties in price movements which provided the basis for further actions. These uncertainties did not mean, of course, that some market actors did not expect that the price of some particular security would go up and down: while such expectations existed, the exact, continuous price variations represented genuine surprises, new action-supporting events.

This reminds us of the aspect discussed in the introduction of this chapter, namely that market technologies are not only standardizers, but also generators which open up possibilities for new actions. By creating a new kind of surprise—price variations—to be jointly observed by market participants—a technology like the stock ticker opened up action possibilities which were not there before its introduction; for instance, the possibility of manipulating the flow of prices on the ticker tape.

Another instance of data display technologies which change the nature of information comes from financial markets too, but this time nearer to our days. It is highlighted in the work of Juan Pablo Pardo-Guerra (2010) and concerns the introduction of computers displaying price and volume data on the London Stock Exchange. In the 1970s, traders on the floor of the London Stock Exchange traded with each other at prices which were shaped by factors such as perceived trustworthiness, closeness of relationship, private knowledge about the counterpart's situation and position, and so on. Additionally, there were precise rituals about how an opening should be made or a question should be asked between potential trading partners. One and the same security could be offered at different prices to different people. While observers situated outside the stock exchange could observe price data on (primitive) monitors, they did not know who traded with whom at what price on the floor of the exchange, because such transactions were not observable. The prices displayed in offices came from (median) prices displayed on whiteboards on the floor of the exchange, but these were not always accurate—sometimes they were written there as a means of manipulation. Price data displayed in offices didn't come from a single provider, but from competing services—dispersed observers could not jointly see the same price variations.

In the late 1970s, a team of software engineers working for the London Stock Exchange—many of whom had previous experience in the defence industry—introduced a computer system which allowed the colour display of more price data. It became thus possible to colour-code price variations, making them more easily observable. In the 1980s, new regulations forced market makers to keep continuous quotations in securities, which they could feed now into the computer system (initially called TOPIC, afterwards SEAQ). With that, price data changed from approximate indications of what was going on to real-time price variations, which could be now observed on terminals installed in various offices. Subsequent innovations, like the introduction of the FTSE 100 Index in 1984 and the flashing of price data in red (down) or blue (up) contributed to transforming price variations into informational surprises—that is, into generators of uncertainty able to orient not only individual actions, but to coordinate these as well.

Episodes such as these highlight jurisdictional issues related to the phenomenon of connectivity discussed in the previous chapters, namely, that expert groups with jurisdiction over a particular body of knowledge (in this case, technological) can link in with market status groups and bring epistemic objects into market transactions, which in their turn require more expertise, not only technological, but also interpretive. New types of information (like price variations) generate a need for expert processing, in the form of analyses, tables, forecasts, models, and the like. Connectivity can also lead to jurisdictional challenges and, in some cases, to shifts in jurisdiction. In the above case, as Pardo-Guerra (2009) shows, tensions arose between the management of the London Stock Exchange, on the one hand, and the software engineers, on the other, who were seen as overstepping their perceived support attributions. In contemporary automated financial markets, many electronic trading platforms are operated by software engineers turned brokers rather than by traditional broker types.

It would be wrong, however, to think that display technologies work as generators of uncertainties only in financial markets. We need to look no further than to the strawberry market discussed in the previous chapter (Garcia-Parpet [1986] 2007, pp. 23–5) to see how the spatial reorganization of strawberry auctions, together with the introduction of computer technologies, introduced informational elements which were not there before. Buyers and sellers of strawberries were spatially separated by a wall, but could both see the lot prices displayed on an electronic panel by the auctioneer, who sat in a cabin. Buyers had to react to the price displays indicating willingness to buy a given lot at that price; sellers had to react by hand signs, indicating whether they agree with the sale or not. The displays started with the highest price, and the decrements were calculated by a software program, so that there was no room left for individual negotiations.

Thus, both sides (buyers and sellers) had to concentrate awareness on the same object (the electronic price panel), without being able to observe each other. The panel generated another type of information for each side: for buyers, it was given by a specific display and input about the seller's reaction to that particular display (agreement or disagreement). For sellers, it was the action triggered (or not) by a particular price display (a specific batch found willing buyers or not). This shows that information cannot be reduced to data displays or signals: in themselves, they are meaningless. They must be made sense of (i.e. judged upon), among others by relating them to the reactions (judgements) of other market players; judgements, actions, and reactions, however, fundamentally depend on showing mutual awareness of other players' presence. This mutual awareness[16] cannot be achieved but by shared observational activities, made possible and mediated by the data display technology.

Technology, Observational Systems, and Markets

This aspect of action coordination by means of shared cognitive activities, such as technology-mediated observations, has been more recently captured by the notion of markets as scopic systems and flow (Knorr Cetina 2003, 2005; Knorr Cetina and Preda 2007). The argument is that a conceptualization of markets as networks of personal relationships (be they strong or weak ties) does not seem to fit situations where market transactions take place within electronic mediums, and where information is not generated in personal, face-to-face interactions (of the kind supposed by networks),[17] but in new interaction formats (see also Chapter 1). Within electronic media, the situational resources used by market participants are different from those of face-to-face interactions. A new basic type of situation, analysed by Karin Knorr Cetina (2009), is the synthetic one, characterized by specific modes in which (market) actors become aware of each other's presence (this latter being a fundamental condition of action).

Whereas in face-to-face situations actors face each other, in synthetic situations they face technologically supported data displays. These displays can be situated in different geographical locations, so that from the viewpoint of participants what counts is using the display (the screen) as a means of temporal coordination. This is the case, for instance, in currency markets (see also Knorr Cetina and Bruegger [2002]), where traders are located mainly in

London, Zurich, New York, and Tokyo. When the medium of data display also acts as the medium of trading (i.e. when observation and reaction are integrated), traders become aware of each other's actions by observing the screen. From the perspective of individual market players, then, observing the screen means observing an aggregate of transaction events (which cannot be directly witnessed) and reacting to them. The reaction does not necessarily have to be a transaction; reactions can take the form of interpretations or judgements upon observations. This aggregate of events is perceived based on observations of data, which are taken as proof and representation of action.

In such electronic environments, traders relate to each other's presence as an on-screen presence, shown by numbers flashing up on screen. This relationship appears as necessary; in order to produce observations, traders have to ascribe intentions to the numbers they see flashing, and intentions cannot be ascribed but by assuming human actors (other traders) as the unseen origin of flashing numbers. The ascription of intentions and actions as the cause of what is seen on the screen allows traders to develop and use formats of social relationships (such as the on-screen conversations discussed in Chapter 1) in order to stabilize observations and produce informational surprises, which will serve as the basis of their actions. Hence, data displaying technologies act here as scopic systems, in the sense of them being a lens through which market actors see 'the market' and 'the world'. Without such lenses, action (i.e. transactions) would not be possible. Action, however, requires interacting with other market actors, which is made possible by cognitive activities such as observation.

In international debt management, data display technologies provide actors with a lens through which the world can be continuously observed as well. A key aspect of these relationships is the debt incurred by developing countries to global creditor institutions, such as the International Monetary Fund (IMF) and the World Bank, an issue investigated by Barbara Grimpe (2009). During the 1990s, the international financial system went through some serious crises when large debtor countries defaulted on their payments (see for instance Blustein [2001, 2005]). Even before that, though, creditor organizations and countries had realized the difficulties of keeping track of debts and payments which, within debtor countries, were managed by different institutions at different levels, without always communicating with each other. This often created a situation where nobody knew for sure how much a country owed to which creditor. Complications arose from the introduction of new loan types, where debtor countries could take loans in combinations of currencies, and could shift payment slices among these currencies.

In the 1980s, the IMF and a group of developed creditor countries (the Paris Club) initiated the creation and implementation of a computer system, integrated in one of the programmes of the United Nations Conference on Trade and Development (UNCTAD).[18] Going through a technological evolution over decades, in its current version the software allows managers of the IMF and of the UNCTAD (as well as officials of the debtor countries) to call up and manage detailed data about the debt level, its structure, its up-to-date payment, on local and aggregate levels, and to make forecasts about the evolution of each country's debt (see also Knorr Cetina and Grimpe [2008, p. 167]). From a quantity which could be evaluated only with some difficulty, debt became something concrete, to be called up with a couple of keystrokes on the computer screen. The implementation and development of this data display system also changed the relationship between country officials and the managers of international creditor organizations, with the latter becoming more and more involved in the monitoring and management of national debts. It also changed the array of possibilities for handling the entity called debt: by giving this latter an informational composition, displayed on screens, it became possible to rearrange it, in the sense of modifying its structure across relevant currencies, reshuffling payment schedules across currencies, and the like. It also became possible to react to events such as changes in the exchange rate between the debtor's national currency, on the one hand, and the currencies in which the debt was made, on the other.

From an entity which was dealt with at regular (payment) intervals, national debt became the object of continuous observation and management. In the same way in which traders in financial markets monitor the screen every day, day after day, debt managers in international creditor institutions do the same with debt data on their screens. This continuity of observation and action required by data display technologies has been captured in the notion of flow (Knorr Cetina 2003; Knorr Cetina and Preda 2007); data display technologies deal with ever changing data, requiring continuity of awareness, observation, and action. Since every participant has to react to the actions of other participants, actions which can be observed only in the changes they induce on screens, at the interaction level this creates a self-supporting dynamic centred upon technology as a coordinating device.

Scopic systems do at least the following: (*a*) they provide market actors with the resources for entering interactional transactions. Interactions, however, do not necessarily overlap with ties. As discussed in Chapter 1, interactions can be fleeting; they can be staged; they can be unique or repetitive. (*b*) Scopic systems provide participants with the resources for generating representations of the world and of markets as systems of competitive transactions. These representations do not overlap with the geographical world, or with the totality of transactions. They act as resources for further interpretations and analyses—that is, for the production of epistemic objects by relevant expert groups. Interpretations and analyses—many of which are generated within scopic systems[19]—can serve as orientation and props for further actions, triggering the production of new data which are displayed on screens. (*c*) Scopic systems provide participants with occasions and tools for intervention—that is, for transactions which will then become observable data, for their author and for other participants as well.

The notion of scopic systems does not mean that all kinds of markets work as observational arrangements in the same way, or that all market types should be understood as fitting this notion to the same degree. On an empirical level, it is meant to highlight that there are instances where the network concept does not capture adequately the interaction arrangements and the practical activities underlying market transactions. On a theoretical level, the notion of scopic systems opens up a programme of investigations focused on the cognitive activities supporting decision-making and transactions (observation being the key one here, but also calculation), and on the specific interaction formats supported by data technologies. On the same level, the notion discussed above opens up possibilities for investigating interaction-generated forms of expertise and the uses of epistemic objects (discussed in the previous chapter) in action. It thus complements the performativity programme, centred (at least until now) on the creation and implementation of such objects.

Markets from Scopic Systems

One of the key questions examined in Chapter 2 was that of the relationship between markets—understood as systems of competitive exchanges—and networks. Instead of asking how markets emerge from networks, we can ask how markets emerge from scopic systems. This question sends us back to the Bruce Carruthers and Arthur Stinchcombe example, discussed earlier: a market in carrots bought by mistake in supermarkets cannot emerge, because there is no liquidity—that is, no readiness to buy and sell such carrots. The absence of liquidity is tied to the potential participants' lack of knowledge—that is, to lack of procedures for displaying and observing, in a joint manner for participants, data about the price, volume, and quality categories of carrots, about how often they are bought and sold by other actors, etc.

The markets for legal services discussed in Chapter 2, for instance, lack possibilities for displaying and observing prices in a joint manner. In order to find out the price for a certain legal service, one would have to call or visit various law offices. In the same chapter, the market in plastic figurines from chocolate surprise eggs was set in place, among others, by the production of scopic systems (admittedly, of lower technological sophistication). The cataloguing of plastic figurines and its distribution through the internet, among others, brought together in a classificatory system objects which until then were treated as disparate. Comparisons were made possible, and also knowledge about which figurines were rare, about their colour variations, as well as about series of figurines. This catalogue was (and is) in constant change, being completed with new series. The catalogue created entities such as series, which previously could not be observed prior to their completion. Now it became possible to observe and identify gaps and variations—that is, informational surprises which worked as action opportunities. The observability of adjacent series in the catalogue made possible their comparison, as well as their ranking—or evaluations of their comparative desirability (see also Espeland [2001]; Espeland and Sauder [2007, p. 16]). Accidents (like the wrong colour on a figurine) became desirable collection pieces. Thus, seen as a scopic system, the catalogue of figurines contributed to creating a market in objects which—taken in isolation—would be seen by adults probably as less interesting than a bunch of carrots.

More sophisticated examples of how scopic systems contribute to market emergence are provided by Charles Smith in his investigation of how advertising spots on websites are priced in relationship to search engines. The notion that a search word or phrase can have a price may seem strange, but it has indeed in the world of internet advertising (Smith 2007, pp. 7–8). Words are auctioned to advertising firms, and the higher the frequency of a search word tied to a firm's ad, the higher the price will be. A price is put upon the observability of a firm's ads on the web (how prominent its ads will be displayed and on which websites, in relationship to which content, how often). This price, however, depends among others on technologies (i.e. algorithms) for making observability into a measurable material entity. This is tied to calculating the frequency of particular word searches, and the frequency of clicks, and has led to a redefinition of words as observable entities which can be bought and sold (Smith 2007, p. 16). This redefinition depends on a technology of data observability: while in the case of search engine providers words are not continuously bought and sold, they are nevertheless auctioned. Auctioning words is based on their newly acquired property, as observable, quantifiable, comparable data.

The above arguments also highlight the relevance of a research programme centred on various forms of scopic systems; while the concept has been developed mainly in relationship to financial markets, it does not mean that other market arrangements cannot be seen as scopic systems too; only the entities observed, the technologies and forms of observation, their particular arrangements, and the specific combinations of observation, calculation, and memorization differ. Such a research programme would have to investigate access to observation, issues of jurisdiction over observation and calculation, and matters of authoritative observations and calculations, among others. It would also have to investigate how the relationship between the object of observation, observers, and the public is constituted in various arrangements, and the effects of this relationship upon transactions, pricing, and possibilities for external intervention. To come back to the example which opened the first chapter, street transactions in fake designer handbags imply forms of observation, calculation, and memorization different from those of electronic financial transactions. This has consequences for the possibilities and forms of external intervention (regulatory intervention in financial transactions is different from that in handbag transactions), for the forms and effects of expertise (handbag experts differ from financial ones), as well as for how informational surprises are generated, and for the properties of these surprises.

An additional matter is provided by the forms of charisma present in scopic systems; while cognitive operations have been seen all too often as distinct from and opposed to emotions, I have argued in Chapters 1 and 2 that emotion and cognition do not exclude each other, and that charisma plays an important role in jurisdictional issues, respectively. Cognitive operations in market transactions, together with the technologies supporting them, are endowed with charismatic features. Therefore, the investigation of markets as scopic systems does not exclude, but requires the investigation of charismatic features as well.

Technology and Market Memory

As exemplified above, data display technologies do not necessarily have to be sophisticated software programs; a catalogue or a list can do as well. If we were to extend Wendy Espeland and Michael Sauder's arguments (2007, p. 16), data display technologies work not only as devices for organizing, integrating, and making information authoritative; they also work as memory devices.

In organizations, documents, among others, serve as memory stores for work processes, responsibilities, problems, or solutions. Artefacts such as memos serve not only as definitions of and alerts to problems, for instance, or as recordings of past interactions (meetings etc.), but also as a memory of organizational processes. They are circulated, retrieved, referred to, and stored, performing not only internal and external legitimating functions, but also constituting communicational paths (for an analysis of how such an organizational memory works, see Vaughan [1996, pp. 254–6]; also Yates [1989a]). In his study of how documents are produced and used at the International Monetary Fund, Richard Harper (1998, pp. 43, 281) saw them as technologies creating paths of organizational action which impose their own temporal structures. In banks, documents such as newsletters are regularly distributed to employees not necessarily because they contain the latest news about organization-internal and external events. In fact, for many bank employees (if not for a majority), these are old news. Relevant events get known much quicker through channels such as gossip at the water fountain. Newsletters are distributed and regarded as important by employees because they represent a collective memory of the competencies and knowledge available within the organization: who knows what, who works on which project, and so on (Preda 2002, p. 221; Spinuzzi 2008, p. 151). Being distributed regularly, newsletters act as a rich, live memory, in opposition to, say, a phone directory which gets updated once a year and does not show the knowledge of the persons listed in it. Other corporate documents, such as annual calendars and managerial protocols, work as tools for allocating decision rights between the board of directors, on the one hand, and managers, on the other (Useem and Zelleke 2006).

An additional technology for creating organizational memory is provided by the account books, which record both data and justificatory narratives for them, retracing and reinterpreting past actions. In their investigation of the rhetoric of account books, Bruce Carruthers and Wendy Espeland (1991) highlight how the merchants' account books reframe and record their actions as endowed with a specific rationality; expenditure and income, for instance, are defined and memorized within the rhetorical frame of rationality.

Forms can be also a technology for organizational memory, recording problems, diagnoses, responsibilities, and actions. Forms can accompany artefacts as they circulate through and between organizations: an example in this sense is provided by repair forms accompanying defective devices (see Orr [1996]). Artefacts, organizational and private, individual and collective can belong to the collective memory of an organization as well: witness here the private objects organizational workers collect and display in the workplace, and which, among others, serve as a reminder of their trajectories and careers within the organization. Official documents attesting professional qualifications also can serve not only as a visible assertion of jurisdiction and expertise, but also as a memory of the organizational members' trajectories. Data sheets, statistics, reports, also belong to the organizational memory. The integration of memos, forms, and data into organizational memory implies a technology-based organizational division of labour, exemplified in the creation of departments specialized in data recording and storage.

Historical investigations of organizational communication show that, at the turn of the twentieth century, the mechanization of communication (through the invention of the typewriter) and the mass duplication of documents (through the carbon copy, the Schapirograph, and photocopying, among others) went hand in hand with innovations in the storage and filing systems used by organizations. Whereas earlier commercial and manufacturing organizations used mostly ledgers and letter books, storage systems like vertical filing, together with classification schemes (like the Dewey Decimal Classification), led to the standardization and homogenization of organizational memories, among others, in the sense that a single storing and filing technology could integrate various types of documents (see Yates [1989*b*, pp. 50, 54, 58]). The increased role played by material memory in organizations, in its turn, led to an increase in internal correspondence and a formalization of communication processes within businesses (Yates 1989*b*, p. 62). Similarly, it can be argued that the spread of electronic technologies of communication and storage (e-mail is a case in point here) leads not only to an adaptation and increase of internal communication to the new technologies, but also to changes in communication genres, in what constitutes organizational memory, and its uses as well.

An example is provided by some of the differences between organizational letters and organizational e-mails. While organizational letters have a formal character, organizational e-mails mix formal and informal aspects, and can also mix private and public narratives and judgements. Statements and expressions which would never find their way in organizational, formal letters (being regarded as private), can be encountered in organizational e-mails. The same goes for visual communication modes, such as video statements posted on organizational websites, statements intended to 'put a human face' on organizational actors. Being embedded in organizational frameworks, however, such private communication can be judged as organizational, especially in instances where it is represented as breaching organizational codes, or as jeopardizing the organization. A case in point here is the scandal (and subsequent judiciary action) provoked by analysts' e-mails circulated within investment banks during the dotcom boom, e-mails which contained judgements opposite to the analysts' public recommendations (Gasparino 2005, p. 119; Swedberg 2005). The e-mails were used as evidence by the prosecution in the lawsuits following the implosion of the dotcom bubble.

This shows that data and statements from the past, stored in organizational memories, can be made into surprises—that is, they can be retrieved, reprocessed, and judged upon in ways which are relevant for the present state of an organization and for the organization's engagement in market transactions. Judgements upon past data or past statements can be made about their producers, or about their audiences, and not necessarily about the entities represented by data or statements. Such a shift of focus contributes to making organizational memory into a generator of potential informational surprises. In the financial analysts' scandals of 2000, the private judgements about the value of securities, made by analysts in e-mails, were seen by the prosecution as informative not because they were more accurate than the analysts' public recommendations, but because they told something about the character and professional ethics of their authors. The issue was one of dishonesty, not one of accuracy.

Organizational and market memories can also provide a basis for regulatory interventions, and can be mandated by regulators precisely because they offer possibilities for monitoring and intervention. Well into the twentieth century, for instance, stock exchanges did not keep records of transactions. In fact, in the state of New York, stock brokers were required by law to keep accounts only in 1909, and obliged to open them to inspection of the state comptroller only in 1913 (Preda 2009*b*, p. 62). This legal requirement arose also out of the relatively frequent lawsuits around specific orders having been put by clients with their brokers or not. Mandatory account keeping created a memory of the transactions done by each stock broker, a memory which was open to official scrutiny.

Since accounts were kept in ledgers, retrieving the information took time and clerical work. Moreover, since each broker kept his own accounts, there was no overall market memory, but only a memory of transactions done by individual agents on the stock exchange. Later technological advances made possible the computerized recording of continuous price data, and thus the creation of a unified, standardized market memory comprising all the transactions done on the exchange, with all the data about price and volume. Before 1960, the majority of investors on stock exchanges were individuals, not institutions. The US financial regulator, the Securities and Exchange Commission, commissioned a study of securities markets, with the aim, among others, to identify counter-measures to market manipulation by individuals. The final report, over seven thousand pages long and sent to the US Congress in 1963, recommended market automation as a means of surveillance; the use of computerized trading, with the automated recording of all trading data, created a market memory which made possible further regulation and investigation (see Preda [2009*b*, pp. 238–9]).

Moreover, uninterrupted data recording created databases which could be used in further research, contributing thus to the expansion of financial and economic expertise. Econometric research on financial markets, for instance, would be impossible without databases containing the price and volume of transactions. Not only that: art markets, or commodities markets operate with market memories as well. They collect and store data about past prices and artists (in the case of art markets), data which can influence the bidding at an art auction, as well as valuation by experts, for instance.

Databases—that is, market memories—can become the object of transactions too, contributing to the emergence of additional markets. Firms like Bloomberg (which sell subscriptions to databases of historical price and volume data) are an example here. Market memories can generate informational surprises in relationship to expertise; the significance and value of particular historical data can be contested among experts, a contestation which resonates in judgements about the relevance and usefulness of valuation tools used in market transactions. For example, since the early 1990s, an essential tool used by investment banks and hedge funds for evaluating value has been provided by the value-at-risk (VAR) models: these are mathematical models (embedded in software programs), with the help of which trading institutions calculate their exposure to risk (see Power [2005]). In order for these models to produce a numerical result about risk exposure, data need to be fed into them; this means not only data about current trades, but also about the past prices of financial securities. VAR models are widely being blamed for the financial crisis which started in late 2008, and their usefulness appears to be hotly debated among economists and market practitioners. It is argued that these models led practitioners to miscalculate risks; their use contributed to the huge losses incurred by investment banks and hedge funds. One point of contention appears to be the range of historical data used in the model (Nocera 2009). Because VAR models were mostly used with data over a few weeks and rarely over more than two years, they are considered by some as a skewed measure of risk exposure. In this case, what academics and market practitioners dispute is which kind of data constitute proper information, able to make the model work. The relevance of the model, while contested, is tied to the relevance of historical data: which kind of data constitutes a proper representation of the financial past? Such debates presuppose the existence of automated market memories capable of recording and storing standardized data, which can be then processed into informational surprises about the past.

In these cases, technology-supported market memories seem to work as scopic systems as well; they allow the observation of the past as existing in the present, for the actual purposes of market participants. This observation of the past from the vantage point of present actions and situations implies not only re-evaluations (judgements about relevance) and selections (which past is actually relevant for the present situation); it also opens up unforeseen paths of future action, as in the case of revised risk models. While the observation of the past raises issues of jurisdiction (who is entitled to this activity, who can do valid observations), it also allows external interventions and monitoring of activities (for instance, by regulators).

One of the key arguments formulated in the preceding chapters is that market transactions are bounded, and that these boundaries have a social and symbolic character (also expressed in some cases in their legal codification). This enables non-economic groups to take positions with respect to market transactions and to intervene in them, or to make market transactions into an object of non-economic activities (regulation, for example). This is the case of political or religious groups, or of communities. Oftentimes, such groups are crystallized around social institutions, understood as sets of rules and forms of social organization: political parties, governing and administrative bodies, churches, family organizations, schools, and the like. The boundaries of transactions imply then connectivity at the institutional level as well, where market institutions meet and respond to other kinds of social institutions. It is this level which I examine in the next chapter.

☐ **NOTES**

1. This sends us back to Émile Durkheim's division of social labour, which includes not only industrial processes, but also extends to knowledge production. The division of social labour is a source of organic solidarity in industrial sectors as well as within the professions (Durkheim [1893] 1984, pp. 137–8).

2. An example here is provided by the standardization of currency. In the eighteenth century for instance, after the American War of Independence, a variety of local currencies existed in the newly created United States, being circulated among villages and towns in particular regions. Some of these currencies were state debt, some were the British currency, and some were local state money and debt certificates. Banking reforms (i.e. the creation of the first chartered US banks), the creation of the US Mint, and the emergence of networks of merchants who bought up local debt contributed among others to the slow emergence of a standardized currency.

3. Objects, tools, and technologies can bring together groups with different interests and fields of expertise, allowing thus communication across professional and disciplinary boundaries (see Star and Griesemer [1989]).

4. The growing role of technology both as the scaffolding of markets and as an object of transactions can be illustrated with the example of the energy consumption of the City of London—that is, of London's financial district. In 2008, the City's power demand was 1,000 MW and expected to grow by 80 per cent over the next few years (Warren 2008). The New York Stock Exchange (NYSE) defines technology as 'the single most important asset and the core enabler in our market' (NYSE 2008).

5. One should also notice here that the urban spaces in which financial markets emerge in the eighteenth century are not necessarily the most reputable. In London, Paris, and New York, financial transactions took place in streets of bad reputation and in cafes. It is only in the early nineteenth century that stock exchange buildings were erected, among others as symbols of power and respectability (see also Preda [2009*b*, chapter 2]). While during the nineteenth century respectable financial transactions moved indoors, and access to them was controlled, less reputable transactions continued to be conducted in the street. On the official stock exchange, the daily intervals during which transactions were allowed were strictly regulated. In the street, transactions were not subjected to time regulations. This system continued until the Second World War, showing one more time how control of space and time can become a means of establishing jurisdiction. It also shows how less reputable markets can establish themselves as spatially adjacent to reputable ones.

6. The role of technologies for standardizing time has been a somewhat neglected issue in the sociology of markets. One has to take into account that, generally speaking, the standardization of time happens only in the late nineteenth century, and it requires particular technologies, among other the construction of special clocks and telegraphs (see Galison [2003, pp. 93–5]; also Zerubavel [1981]).

7. This version has been modified by increasingly introducing game-theoretical assumptions about the strategies of participants in transactions, strategies based on the actors' expectations, and the information available to them. Note, however, that this does not solve the problem of introducing money into the general equilibrium theory. This is somehow replicated in contemporary economic sociology, where accounts of markets (especially social-structural ones) do not treat money as a primitive variable.

8. This does not mean, however, that monetary theories do not play a prominent role in the contemporary landscape of economics. The quantity theory of money, as a theory of the demand for money (Friedman 1956, p. 4) has been very influential at least since the 1960s. It just means that money does not occupy a special place in the theory of general equilibrium, although attempts have been made to introduce it as a device for the intertemporal reallocation of consumption, as part of the utility function, or as a prerequisite of consumption (see Lewis and Mizen [2000, pp. 93–5]).

9. Marx hesitates between seeing money as material—that is, as embodying human labour—and seeing it as something ideal or conceptual, hesitations which have marked the subsequent sociological discussions. If money is seen as material and as embodying human labour, while being at the same time the general equivalent of value, how can a specific form of labour be the equivalent of all others? This led Marx to see gold and silver as two commodities different from money. At the same time, he saw prices as depending on the 'real money material' (Marx ([1872] 2002, p. 105).

10. Weber appears to be influenced here by theories of marginal utility, and considers economic actors as calculative actors. It should be stressed, however, that Weber does not see the actors' calculation and rationality as given, but as the product of specific institutional dynamics.

11. It should be stressed here that commodification does not depend solely on money as a standardized technology of expressing relationships, but also on more complex technological underpinnings, supported by institutional structures. In the case of organ donations, for instance, their commodification depends among others on adequate technologies for preservation and transport.

12. Marx's difficulties with conceiving money as having material character are resonated in some contemporary arguments against 'money-stuff'—that is, against seeing money as tied to a material support (Ingham 2004, p. 33). In seeking the conceptual filiations of money, Geoffrey Ingham (2004, p. 71) argues that it can be traced to its unit of account function, and to the state's tax levying activities. This, however, does not make money less material, since account-keeping cannot be separated from a host of material technologies related to writing (see also Goody [1986]).

13. The economics argument that prices are informative overlaps thus with the Marxian position on monetary prices as representations of value and hence of social relationships.

14. The fact that money and prices cannot be separated from the material technologies displaying them and recording transactions indicates that the arguments about the 'dematerialization of money' with the advent of electronic money, arguments which were popular at some point in the 1990s, are actually moot. In fact, money has become more and more material, in the sense of depending more and more on complex technologies for displaying, recording, and transmitting transaction data.

15. It should be noted that there are other examples of illiquid commodities or services as well: legal or medical services cannot be resold by those who have hired a lawyer or have made a

dentist appointment. If I want to cancel a dentist appointment, it will be difficult to resell the appointment slot to somebody else, not least because the dentist's office will claim jurisdiction over that slot. At the same time, taking a slot in a queue for somebody else, making appointments for somebody else, etc. can be the object of transactions. In the example of the supermarket carrots discussed here, it doesn't mean that data about one supermarket's sales of carrot bunches do not exist; it just means that they are not made available to customers. Supermarkets, however, reciprocally observe their data, both as statistical aggregates and individually. These reciprocal observations form the basis of 'price wars'. Moreover, internet comparison sites now make it possible to compare observations compiled from different supermarket chains. Also, internet sites allow for the emergence of markets in 'unwanted bunches of carrots'. Examples here are not only eBay and Amazon (for books), but also sites selling high fashion remainders. Such markets are made possible not only by bringing together and making entities comparable, but also by providing technologies for observing them.

16. While Heath et al. (2002) define awareness as event-related (something is taking place), in markets awareness is also related to the presence of other participants, and hence actor-related.

17. I have argued in Chapter 2 that the conceptualization of markets as networks and status groups does not pay much attention to the qualitative differences of various interaction media and formats, and operates with the face-to-face format as the basic generator of market information. With many markets moving nowadays to electronic formats, with a minimum of face-to-face interactions (or none at all), the notion of networks does not provide much explanatory capacity with respect to information and decision-making.

18. The programme's name is DMFAS, or Debt Management Financial and Analysis System.

19. In financial markets, for instance, trading software includes links to providers of expertise, which can be displayed on screen. Thus, financial data and the expert interpretation of this data become simultaneously available; in many instances, this is real time availability as well.

5 Markets, Firms, and Institutions

Firms v. Markets

While markets are connected to and make an impact upon many social institutions (witness here family life, local communities, or government, among others), the modern institution[1] to which markets are connected (and sometimes opposed to) comes from the economic domain as well: the firm. Firms and corporations are nothing new, their role and influence in economic and social life having already been noticed by classical sociologists; in his analysis of capital, Karl Marx ([1872] 2002, p. 706) argued that the accumulation of capital required not only the socialization of work (through increased division of labour) but also the concentration of the means of production, meaning, among others, changes in the size of enterprises and in their ownership structure. Building on this, Max Weber ([1921] 1972, p. 127) stressed the fact that capitalist rationalization, going hand in hand with the spread of calculative practices (like accounting, or the calculation of costs and benefits) led to the emergence of specific groups not only in the public and state administration but in private enterprises as well: bureaucrats. The phenomenon of bureaucracy is accompanied by another set of features characteristic for economic modernization, namely, the growing irrelevance of the family as the main site of economic production, the separation of economic production from family and kinship, increased economic individualization, and the transfer of economic functions to a different form of rational socialization, namely, the enterprise (Weber [1921] 1972, pp. 213, 227).

In advanced capitalism, bureaucrats can be encountered in state administration, churches, political parties, economic corporations, interest groups, charities, and the like (Weber [1921] 1972, p. 128). They embody the pure type of legal domination (Weber [1921] 1972, p. 126), characterized through hierarchy of office and of competencies, selected (in principle) on the basis of competencies, with specific factual and procedural knowledge,[2] and with office duties separated from personal lives. Bureaucrats act on the basis of rules and adhere to internal codes of discipline. Since bureaucrats are present in economic organizations (and especially large ones), embodying structures of (legal) domination, and since, according to Marx, capitalist accumulation leads to large size economic organizations, it follows that structures of domination are at work in economic corporations. At first sight, their widespread presence challenges the notion that markets as systems of competitive transactions are central to the economic order of capitalism (competition and legal domination cannot be reconciled easily).

A second aspect is that the major role bureaucrats play in economic enterprises requires a separation between ownership and management; the owners of businesses are not necessarily involved in their management, but entrust this to bureaucrats (see also Veblen [1923]), who in time have evolved into a professional managerial class. Such a class, however, has little interest in entering competitive exchanges in the market (see also Useem [1984] 2001, p. 225); it would rather tend to cultivate business ties within a restricted circle and reach less than competitive deals. Additionally, the presence of managerial bureaucracy, together with its separation from ownership, raises questions related to the control of its activities, to the authority it has, the rules it obeys, and the contracts it enters into. All these aspects require investigating a basic institution of capitalist economic life—the firm—and positioning it conceptually in relationship to markets.

In economic theory, the problem of the firm was rediscovered in the 1970s by neoinstitutional economics, with recourse to the work done in the 1930s by Ronald Coase. Coase's starting point was the question of why do firms exist as alternatives to markets (Ménard 2005, p. 303). This formulation implies acknowledging that corporations (sometimes) prefer circumventing competitive exchanges, for instance, by manufacturing components in-house instead of buying them on the market, or by working with small networks of suppliers, on a cost-plus basis. Coase (2005, p. 33) had noticed that in capitalism firms employ most economic resources, and that the use of these resources depended in the first place on administrative decisions made by the management, and not on market transactions. Translated in sociological terms, this means that business bureaucracies establish jurisdiction over resources and allocate them according to criteria pertaining less to efficiency than to the reproduction of the organization—internal interests, group dynamics, or power relationships, among others. (This spanned a whole branch of research in the sociology of organizations, discussed below.)

Firms and markets appear thus as opposed concepts: the former are primarily understood in terms of cooperation, groups, and hierarchies, while the latter are understood in terms of competition and atomization (see also Ménard [2005, p. 302]; Williamson [1985, pp. 4, 9]). This does not mean an absolute opposition between organizational hierarchies and competing individuals; indeed, I have argued in Chapter 2 that the social structural approach understands markets as hierarchies of groups involved in competitive exchanges. Neither does it mean that there is no competition within firms. Quite the contrary: hierarchically organized groups can compete against each other, both on the same organizational level and across levels.

From the economics point of view, the (relatively contrived) opposition[3] between the two modes of doing business (firms v. markets) becomes relevant when we take into account that each mode is related to a specific set of transaction costs. Entering competitive transactions implies a series of costs related to obtaining and evaluating stories about the trustworthiness of transaction partners, quality of products, delivery schedules, and the like. These costs may be significantly lower if, say, a spare part is manufactured within the firm which integrates it into the final product. Manufacturing processes can be supervised better, participant groups can be controlled—overall, there can be more authority and control over the entire process, when compared with buying the same spare part on the market. With that, transaction costs may be lower when the transaction is kept within the firm than when it is done in a competitive form (also Stinchcombe [1990, p. 348]).

This highlights the following elements:

1. The costs (of information) are not entirely expressed in monetary terms, but in social ones as well.

2. These costs are associated with social issues like authority and control (Williamson 1985, pp. 18–19), which are necessary in order to keep in check the opportunistic behaviour of economic actors, who will follow in the first place their personal gain. Since actors are opportunistic, they will search for ways to circumvent the institutional constraints put on their actions (see for instance Abolafia [1996, pp. 105, 109–13]). Not only individual actors but also whole organizational departments can attempt (and, at least for a while, succeed) at circumventing institutional constraints, for instance, by increasing their influence and control over the business organization. An example in this sense is provided by the financial scandals of the 1980s, where the high yield bond department at the Drexel Burnham Lambert investment bank had a disproportionate influence over the bank's decisions. This influence was justified by referring to the profits brought in by the department, profits which in the end turned into disastrous losses leading to the death of the bank (Zey 1993, p. 234).

3. Transactions, which are seen as the basic economic unit (Williamson 2005, p. 43), do not imply only competition but also cooperation. Moreover, they imply rules; the most important set of rules is given by the legal frame defining the responsibilities and obligations, as well as the rights of parties entering a transaction, or a contract. The most important of these are property rights, which need to be codified, socially as well as legally. This latter means that individuals and groups involved in transactions as contracts will have some common understanding of the (transfer of rights) implied by the transaction. The firm provides a governance structure which can deal with all aspects essential for economic processes—that is, with transaction costs, with rules, with contracts, and with control.

The notion of transaction, as understood in neoinstitutional economics (and, by extension, neoinstitutionalist sociology) does not overlap with the interaction-based notion examined in Chapter 1, but is rather understood as an abstract, yet iterable relationship, legally codifiable, conducted according to rules, and submitted to (formal and informal) control mechanisms. The notion of transaction qua relationship which has to be governed or controlled immediately raises the problem of trust, answered at the levels of procedural and personal trust, as well as at that of authority (see Chapter 2 for a more detailed discussion). Such an understanding is confronted with a series of relevant issues; for instance, how do we make the transition from observable interaction to relationship, or what do we do with these transactions—the handbag peddlers from Venice discussed in Chapter 1—which do not seem codifiable at all, are ephemeral, yet take place all the time?

The view on firms as social institutions opened up a sociological research programme which processes questions of pricing and allocation with sociological tools. This research programme has at least three main components: (*a*) a focus on the firm, (*b*) the relationships between firms and other social institutions (mainly political ones), and (*c*) the relationships between political institutions and markets. Before examining them, it should be recalled here how information is treated in this context.

Information within the firm is seen as codification and standardization, or as signals (Ménard 2005, p. 293). Sociologically speaking, codification and standardization mean in the first place the production and circulation of documents which present statements, descriptions, instructions, evaluations, and judgements in the same form to all recipients. As discussed in the previous chapter, these technologies allow the creation of organizational memories, the formal definition of organizational roles and responsibilities, as well as of processes and paths of organizational action. Formalization through documents allows legal codifications as well, and makes economic organizations able to connect with non-economic institutions. In a legal dispute between two businesses, for instance, such documents can play a key role. An example is provided by the legal disputes of October 2008 between Citibank and Wells Fargo concerning the acquisition of the Wachovia Bank. While Wachovia had initially agreed to being sold to Citibank, after only four days it accepted a merger offer with Wells Fargo (see Sorkin [2008]). An issue in the ensuing dispute was whether the initial merger agreement between Citibank and Wachovia was legally binding or not. But the agreement had to be approved by the boards of directors; this didn't happen before Wells Fargo stepped in with a counter-offer. This illustrates the role of formal procedures of codification (and of formal documents) in the creation of contracts among firms.

Formalization and standardization are seen as consolidating trust, and as contributing to the formation of routines, including legal ones (see Stinchcombe [2001, p. 81]). Signals, in turn, are external inputs coming into the firm;

they are understood as (a broad array of) documents produced by other organizations (economic or not), stories, data, visualizations, and the like. Standardization and codification enable the processing of such signals, that is, they offer templates with the help of which organizational actors make sense of them. At the same time, since firms are hierarchically organized, with different levels of status, knowledge, and skills, codification and standardization do not preclude different interpretations of the same signals at different levels. From the economics viewpoint, this can increase the transaction costs of the firm (Ménard 2005, p. 293). From a sociological viewpoint, this points to the possibility of firms generating internal informational surprises, and thus of an internal informational dynamics which might affect their transactions.

The Firm as Myth and Symbol

The fact that the hierarchical organization of the firm does not preclude internal competitions and conflicts is compounded by the fact that a firm's primary goal is that of maintaining and reproducing its existence. This requires activities which legitimate the firm internally and externally. Legitimating the firm implies legitimating its authority and prestige, including those of the upper organizational levels. This sends us back to the issue of charismatic authority, discussed in Chapter 2, an authority which is achieved, among others, with symbolic and ritual means, and implies addressing different publics and convincing them of the legitimacy of the firm. These publics can be internal (their own employees), other institutions (political or regulatory bodies, for instance), or the media, among others. Addressing such heterogeneous publics implies using specific technologies of representation (both material and discursive), as well as enacting rituals of authority. Examples in this sense are not difficult to find: public statements of earnings, profits, and losses are technologies of representing the firm as efficient; public declarations of social and environmental engagement; public presentations of new products at trade shows; and internal (formal and informal) rituals such as meetings, or end-of-year parties, and many more.

The public self-presentation of businesses makes use, among others, of categories and classifications which position the said businesses in relationship to other similar firms (competitors), and also to organizations which are perceived as different. More recent research suggests that public positioning (achieved with the help of classifications) is relevant for firms launching new product categories (Kennedy 2008, p. 289). These firms can establish themselves more easily if they appear to the public as part of an already existing category.

This, in turn, requires mentioning competing firms in press releases. The self-presentation of the firm as part of a competitive field is helpful in the incipient stages of a new product category, but less so at later stages.

The existence of symbolic representations and rituals, addressing various publics, raises the issue of the relationship between representations, on the one hand, and the stated goals of the firm (efficient, effective transactions) on the other. The argument put forth by John Meyer and Brian Rowan (1977, pp. 343–4), which triggered a whole research programme in the sociology of organizations, is that 'the myths generating formal organizational structure . . . are rationalized and impersonal prescriptions that identify various social purposes as technical ones and specify in a rule-like way the appropriate means to pursue these technical purposes rationally. Secondly, they are highly institutionalized and thus in some measure beyond the discretion of any individual participant or organization'. It follows from this argument that firms translate social goals (such as self-maintenance) into technical ones (efficiency and rationality), and specify the means to pursue these goals in an appropriate manner (Hirsch and Lounsbury 1997, p. 408). The implementation of technical purposes, in their turn, changes the organization along broader social lines, which cannot be entirely controlled. Social goals are then objectified (represented as technical issues) and tied to formal procedures meant, among others, to ensure a degree of trust in them. Therefore, we can investigate this process of translation in particular instances and see how specific organizational elements are legitimating the firm. Research on interlocking corporate boards and networks (especially the work of Gerald Davis, Edward Zajac, and James Wetsphal, discussed in Chapter 2) has highlighted their role in legitimating networks of relationships and existing structures of authority, while contributing little to the efficiency of firms.

At the same time, firms observe each other; they develop isomorphic features as a way of dealing with legitimacy-related issues, and also with the standardization of knowledge, or with the division of labour. Isomorphism means that firms will adapt to or follow changes imposed by political actors, or initiated by economic agents perceived as particularly successful. Paul DiMaggio and Walter Powell (1991, p. 67) distinguish among coercive, mimetic, and normative isomorphism. While the first kind is adaptation to external pressures (e.g. to politically imposed pollution standards), the second kind is imitation of particularly successful agents (e.g. adoption of Japanese production models). The third kind of isomorphism is triggered by professionalization (e.g. hiring managers with an MBA degree). Isomorphism, though, is geared towards producing representations of legitimacy and compliance, presenting the firm to observers as a regular, efficient, and competent one.

The role of symbolic representations and rituals of the firm cannot be separated from the ways in which they are used with regard to different audiences. These ways imply an element of power, or authority; the authors of particular representations of the firm have the power and prestige to address publics in certain ways, and to present these publics not only with descriptions but also with prescriptions for action. As argued above, publics are not only external but also firm-internal. The managerial levels themselves constitute specific publics, which are addressed not only descriptively but also normatively—for instance, with prescriptions of what firms should be, or of how they should create value. Such prescriptions can come from consultants (there is an entire industry specialized in 'turning around' firms), from analysts, or from leading managers, who are considered by their peers as particularly successful. In other words, there are at least two authoritative sources of prescriptive representations: expertise and charisma. These sources can create informational surprises, in the sense of periodically launching new prescriptions about what the successful firm should be and what sort of value it should pursue. This happens against the background of established, routine representations about what a successful business is.

Take shareholder value here as the most important value corporations should pursue. Shareholder value, understood as the rise in share prices, is not an immediate and natural candidate for the top spot in the declared hierarchy of values of publicly held corporations. It excludes, for instance, workers and employees, as well as customers from this spot. While today it appears as the dominant value orienting the activity of publicly held corporations, it was not always so. Neil Fligstein (1990; Fligstein and Shin 2004, p. 7) argues that shareholder value is not merely an abstract notion: being prescriptive, it has consequences for how business is conducted, for managerial decisions, for the firm's operations, and for its relationships with regulators, the public, and the owners, among others. In other words, shareholder value is a conception of organizational control. In the 1970s, when US businesses were in crisis, and as a reaction to this, the shareholder value conception became dominant. Its origins were in the agency theory of the firm, a branch of financial economics from the 1970s, which conceived managers as agents acting on behalf of shareholding principals (Fligstein and Shin 2004, p. 8). The turn to the shareholder value as the dominant conception of control led to wide changes in corporations, including mergers and computer investments, which were not necessarily and immediately related to rises in productivity or efficiency (Fligstein and Shin 2004, p. 25).

Other, internal instruments of control seem to follow a similar logic. For instance, organizations encounter the unexpected on a rather regular basis: incidents, internal frictions, and the like. In order to be able to cope with this information (i.e. with the surprises generated by their activities), since the early 1990s businesses have increasingly introduced tools of risk management: value-at-risk (VAR) models, much discussed during the financial crisis of 2008–9, are a case in point here. While such models do not foresee or eliminate surprises, they are used in organizational rituals of compliance (Vaughan 2005, pp. 57, 61; Power 2007, p. 113)—that is, in rituals allowing organizations to ascribe responsibility internally and to make it visible to other involved institutions. According to reports (Nocera 2009), mathematical models of value-at-risk, widely used by banks to estimate their exposure, initially used a normal distribution curve, thus excluding any exceptional events from risk estimates. But this is exactly what happened in the crisis of 2008–9; an exceptional event (correlated financial failures) occurred, which was not included in the VAR models used by banks. When the blaming started, VAR models were pointed at as responsible, although some critics drew attention to the fact that responsibility must be ascribed to human actors, not to technology. This indicates that tools of control perform ritual roles as well, and that these roles can change, from compliance to scapegoating, in this case.

Not only managerial models emphasizing the internal organization of the firm (hierarchical or not) but the orientation to markets as well can be seen as an instance of control (Boltanski and Chiapello 1999, p. 128). Because competitive exchanges lack the element of internal control provided by hierarchies, managerial discourses emphasizing the former also have to stress trust and self-control as compensatory mechanisms. They stress the informal aspects of contracts more than the formal ones, together with networks as alternatives to hierarchical control (Boltanski and Chiapello 1999, p. 131). According to this logic, the emphasis put on networks (including the one coming from economic sociology) cannot be simply seen as a better model, but as part and parcel of the shift to a newer model of control within the firm. It is part of a struggle which took place in the 1990s to replace organizational models regarded as valid in the previous period (Boltanski and Chiapello 1999, p. 133). The new model legitimates the insecurities triggered by globalization and the associated processes (e.g. outsourcing), redefines organizational work as project-oriented (by definition limited and insecure)[4], and incorporates self-critique (and hence change) as part of the managerial model itself.

The research discussed above (and similar investigations such as Zorn et al. 2005) shows that symbolic representations are endowed with authority, and that they intervene in the organizational structure of firms. It shows, moreover, that they have relative stability—that is, there is competition among various authoritative voices and groups producing symbolic representations. In this competition, informational surprises arise—new prescriptive representations about value, control, governance, and the like, which strive for dominance, or carve themselves niches within organizations. If we are to follow the arguments of Luc Boltanski and Eve Chiapello, discussed above, the incorporation of self-criticism into the new managerial model provides a source of continuous surprises; the model presents itself as only temporary, and can change in unforeseen ways.

Since symbolic representations appear to have their roots at least in part in academic theories (and certainly in various forms of expertise), this brings us back to the issue of performativity discussed in Chapter 3. In that case, the use of models changed the character and result of transactions. The use of managerial models (which can be seen as analogous to models from economics) change economic organizations. They produce normative views of what it means to be an efficient manager, a well managed organization, and the like. While the notion of performativity mainly stresses calculative aspects, the processes discussed here emphasize symbolic and ritual aspects. It should not be deduced from this, however, that the use of formal models (from financial economics, for instance) cannot have symbolic and ritual dimensions. The role of VAR models in the ongoing financial crisis points to the ritual uses and invocations of formal models as well.

The fact that organizational models are endowed with authority, that they compete for dominance, and that they are used in rituals of compliance raises the question of power, not only within businesses but also among firms, as well as between firms and political institutions. This opens the way for investigating the role of these latter in the regulation of inter-firm relationships and the creation of markets.

Firms, Markets, and Politics

Political institutions shape inter-firm relationships in the first place by providing the legal frame (including regulatory measures) within which reciprocal rights and obligations are defined. Issues of ownership rights and of formal contracts play a central role here. In both cases, the state, through the legal system, sets the possibilities and constraints for transactions. For instance, the legal system defines what can constitute property, what can be bought and sold, under which circumstances, the nature of contracts, the rights and obligations defined by them, the nature of proofs, the witnesses required by a valid contract, and so on. In addition to this, the legal system establishes the taxation of economic activities, the exceptions to this, or the institutions which enforce contracts and taxation, among others. These formal definitions and requirements, embodied in state institutions, can overlap with informal distinctions between what can be gifted and what can be sold, or with informal understandings of ownership and rights (see also Carruthers and Ariovich [2004] for an overview). Moreover, informal understandings of these issues can be supported by traditional institutions and differ substantially from the legal definitions contained in the formal legal system. A case in point here is provided by the property rights of women in developing countries, where formal and traditional rights clash.

Market transactions can emerge from (and partly replace) traditional systems of exchange as a consequence of changes in property rights, labour contracts, taxation, and other forms of state intervention, as in the case of the Orma population of Kenya, investigated by Jean Ensminger (1992). Up to the 1970s, the Orma, a pastoralist population of Kenya, lived within an economic system predominantly based on reciprocal obligations along kinship lines (a 'moral economy'), although they also practised cattle trade over longer distances. In part, this was determined by the need for cash required to pay taxes introduced by the colonial administration. At the same time, the dominance of Islam provided the ideological framework in which property rights and contracts could work in the absence of a state supported legal system. Additional forms of trade included small shopkeeping based on selling items like sugar and tea (also made popular by the colonial administration). The labour force required by cattle rearing was provided within a clientele-based system, working along kinship lines as well. Cattle was raised on the collectively owned land of the tribe, but remained individually owned. This ownership system supported the Orma's semi-nomadic lifestyle.

After Kenya's independence, the government began nationalizing land which was held by the tribe in the absence of any written legal proofs of ownership (theirs being an oral system of property rights). With the encouragement of the government, the tribe became sedentary and split into villages, which now began asserting rights over surrounding pastures, and prevented non-villagers from using them. In time, the land which was off limits to nomads grew more and more, and the basis of nomad livelihood narrowed. The new villages, anchored in property rights different from those of the semi-nomad tribe, were encouraged to raise cattle for sale, a trend also supported by increased prices. This new market orientation was accompanied by internal differentiation, with new job types made necessary by sedentary village life (carpenters, teachers, nurses, etc.) and with an increased reliance on commercial exchanges for covering the needs of everyday life. At the same time, the labour system did not change to a salaried one, but continued to be clientele-based. This hybrid of market transactions and personal indenture increased social and economic differentiation among families, and amplified the power and influence of the local rich. In this case, the multi-level intervention of the state, through nationalization, the introduction of new property rights, and cattle-raising programmes, among others, led to the transition from a moral economy oriented mainly towards subsistence to a hybrid market economy, which combined traditional reciprocal obligations with commercial transactions conducted over long distances.

While in this case the intervention of the state through economic policy programmes and legal definitions of ownership and contracts contributed to the emergence of market transactions, in other cases new firms enter market transactions by symbolic imitation; they mimic businesses already present in the market, without entirely adapting their internal structure to efficiency criteria, or modifying their political ties. Chinese businesses, for instance, have symbolically copied the practices of Western business organizations, without changing their internal modus operandi or modifying their deep links with political structures (Guthrie 1999, p. 204). Symbolic mimicry means here that when encountering Western businesses, Chinese firms will adopt a discourse of flexibility and efficiency as a way of attracting foreign orders and investment, of getting access to technology and capital, and of appearing as legitimate and knowledgeable in public (see also Bandelj [2009] for Eastern Europe). At the same time, internal production processes follow less a pattern of efficiency than one of maintaining longstanding ties with political organizations and of creating patronage systems towards the employees. Concomitantly, external interventions in the organization of firms (through joint ventures, for instance) put pressure on firms to rationalize their production and to adopt formal codes of procedure (Guthrie 1999, p. 213).

Lucia Siu's work (2008, p. 110) on the emergence of commodities exchanges in China also emphasizes the role played by the state; while the legal status of these exchanges is that of autonomous institutions, they have in fact dual properties, as part of the market and of the state structure, respectively. This is reflected, among others, in the appointment of exchange managers by the state. In their turn, these latter have a double position, reflecting that of the exchange itself: they are both managers of market firms, and state and party cadres (Siu 2008, p. 98). Within the exchange building, state managers and traders are physically and symbolically separated, not only by the colour of their jackets but also by having distinct canteens, among others (Siu 2008, p. 83).

That the transition from a socialist, state-controlled economy to a capitalist, market-oriented one does not mean radical, overnight change has also been highlighted in the work done by David Stark and Balasz Vedres, as well as by Nina Bandelj (Stark 1996, 2001; Stark and Vedres 2006; Bandelj 2008) on Eastern European firms. Confronted with the collapse of the socialist economy and with multinational corporations becoming a direct competition in national markets, Hungarian firms, for instance, used ties they had previously formed with each other within the socialist, state-controlled economy, in order to develop inter-firm ownership networks. These networks were not geared in the first place towards increasing profitability, but the firms' chances of survival. Inter-firm ownership allowed business organizations to socialize liabilities and to offload debts onto taxpayers. In this process, firms used their existing ties as a resource for coping with the uncertainties of the restructuring process and for taking advantage of specific economic policies.

In still other instances, politics intervenes in market creations by promoting state, group, and party interests. An example here is provided by the emergence of the first financial markets in the eighteenth century, in relationship to the fiscal activities of France and England. Financial markets are an interesting case study, because until the turn of the twentieth century there was no legal framework regulating the ownership and transfer of financial securities on the stock exchange, the contracts between brokers and clients, or the character of securities as commodities. Stock exchanges in London and New York, among others, worked largely as private associations, based on (more or less respected) internal regulations. The emergence of a financial market in London, as well as in Paris, was tied to increased state expenditure related to wars (Neal 1990; Carruthers 1996). Economic institutions such as the Bank of England, the South Sea Company, or the Compagnie du Mississippi were created with state support, mainly as lenders to the state. In principle, ownership in these companies meant having a say in politics (since they were creditors to the state), but it was dispersed across the whole territory. One way of centralizing ownership, control, and hence of gaining more political influence was to take control over the said companies. This, in turn, meant acquiring shares from dispersed shareholders. The best way of doing this was creating a market where these shares were bought and sold. In addition to the economic advantages provided by gaining control, there were clear political advantages. The struggle for control over shares in the main British companies involved the Whigs and the Tories, who saw this as a means of extending their political influence (Carruthers 1996, p. 19). Thus, economic action (trading shares in the market, in the absence of a legal frame regulating transactions) appears in this case as a means for achieving political goals, and as an element in the struggle for political control.

The cases discussed above highlight different, complementary mechanisms through which, under the influence of political institutions, economic entities adapt to competitive systems of transactions: hybridization and mimicry. Both occur as a result of external pressures and as a response to the need for legitimacy. Competitive market transactions also appear as an instrument of political control, and as a constraint to which firms adapt. In this process of adaptation, symbolic elements relevant for the participants' identity and legitimacy are transferred within the system of competitive transactions, so that this latter necessarily cannot work along pure lines of rationality and efficiency. While these studies can be seen as a critique of economic models of rational competition, a critique which they also explicitly formulate, they highlight an important element for the sociology of markets: competitive transactions do take place, involving not only the allocation of material resources (money, or cattle, or shares) but also symbolic elements, which seem to play an important role with respect to allocation processes.

Markets, Institutions, and Culture

While political groups may instrumentalize market exchanges for their goals, do they also try to impose a vision on transactions as well? This rather general question can be translated as follows: do economic policies regulating market exchanges incorporate a unitary (and unique) vision of capitalism, or do they rather reflect particular political relationships and struggles which have less to do with such a vision than with politics? If a vision truly exists, then we are back to Max Weber's spirit of capitalism. If not, the relationship between markets and political institutions might be more complicated than initially thought.

Existing research on economic policies has tended to answer the question about the vision of capitalism[5] in the negative, replacing it with specific economic (or industry) cultures and with specific, locally determined policy paradigms. While the latter are determined by the specific constellation of relationships among the state, political groups, parties, and their constituencies, the former are principles of economic organization and behaviour (Dobbin 1994, p. 18). When examining industrial policy in the railway age in the United States, Britain, and France, Frank Dobbin (1994, pp. 23–5) distinguishes, for instance, among an industrial culture of collective self-rule (the United States), as opposed to one of state intervention (France), or individualism (Britain), respectively. This encouraged private financing of railway enterprises in Britain, as opposed to active state planning and supervision in France, or to local involvement in planning and financing in the United States.

In the same vein of the argument, Monica Prasad (2006) also rejects 'spirit' or 'ideology' as an explanatory factor of economic policies, opting instead for various political cultures which shape the relationships among players involved in economic policy making. In addressing the question whether the neoliberal ideology was indeed influential across various countries in economic policy making in the 1980s, she answers in the negative. Instead, specific political cultures played a major role in how economic policy issues were addressed (Prasad 2006, pp. 23–4); while in the United States a culture of political entrepreneurship dominated, France was characterized by a technocratic one, Britain by class confrontation, and Germany by compromise and cooperation between employers and employees. These different cultures led to different 'free market' policies, which may appear as surprising given the clichés about the political left–right divide, but which are fully explicable against the background of the local political culture.

What Frank Dobbin and Monica Prasad call culture (i.e. local principles of economic and political organization) is a dimension of fields[6] in Neil Fligstein's work (2001, p. 29). These principles provide actors with 'cognitive maps'[7] (see also DiMaggio [1997]) which help them make sense of their situations. In addition to such principles, fields include routines (which actors perform in their everyday relationships) and the social relationships themselves. Stable markets are characterized by structured exchanges (in opposition to infrequent exchanges, which are unstructured); they are fields, in the sense that the products being exchanged are regarded as legitimate by customers, and that there is a status hierarchy among suppliers (Fligstein 2001, p. 31). But such fields presuppose modes of governance (competition has to be contained), as well as an organization for the production of goods. The modes of governance (see also Fligstein 1996, p. 657), which are in essence those discussed in the opening sections of this chapter (property rights, governance structures, rules of exchange, and conceptions of control), necessarily involve non-economic social institutions (mainly the political institutions of the state).

Political institutions can be regarded as being empirically prior with respect to markets; we can find many examples where competitive systems of exchange are set in place by and operate under the supervision of political institutions. But, again, we can find many examples where this is not the case; the stock exchanges of the nineteenth and early twentieth century are a case in point here. At the same time, political institutions can be regarded as being conceptually prior as well; we need first conceptions of control, rules, governance, and property rights in order to keep in check competition, and in order to regulate the organizations producing goods. In this sense, firms must also be conceptually prior to markets. If we take political institutions in a restricted sense (as the state, political parties, and the like), there are situations where property rights, controls, rules, and the governance defined by them do not necessarily extend to all systems and objects of transactions. If we take institutions in a broader sense, as shared understandings of ownership in relationship to transactions, of differences between gift and commercial exchanges, then it can be argued that (conceptually) they are prerequisites of market exchanges, be they stable or not. At the same time, the issue would be to see how these understandings are enacted in transactional interactions and to what consequences.

Irrespective of this, however, in principle markets as politics can be understood in at least the following ways: first, as systems of competitive transactions constrained, enabled, and shaped by shared understandings. Their maintenance and reproduction implies rituals and symbols, as well as elements of authority such as charisma. Second, they can be understood as systems of competitive exchanges constrained by tools of political intervention and by the relationships among political actors. These constraints include those put upon firms as market players.

These two understandings, which are not always analytically separated, can lead to several different approaches. A first approach continues the investigation of local political institutions in relationship to specific systems of competitive transactions. This is the 'varieties of capitalism' approach.[8] A second approach investigates the links between political institutions and markets not as locally determined, but as being shaped on a much larger scale. This is the globalization approach. A third avenue continues the investigation of culture as a principle of societal organization, trying to specify the links (and differences) between economic cultures and other types of institutions. It stresses not so much the differences among local modes of organization than those among different types of institutions. This is the economy of conventions approach. In the following, I will discuss them one by one.

Markets, Varieties of Capitalism, and Globalization

The view of markets as being shaped by local, historically grown political forces and institutions implies that they will not conform to a single template, not even to a unique model of 'Western capitalism'. What we get instead are several versions of capitalist markets, in the Western hemisphere, as well as in newly developed and developing countries. Rights, rules, and control are not only constraints for firms but also resources they use in their actions. The ways in which these resources are used cannot be determined by a pre-existing 'market template', but depend of local constellations of political forces and interests (see Dobbin [2005]). This, among others, is why we do not see transitions to pure forms of markets in developing or in former socialist countries, but rather hybridizations—that is, elements of traditional, or state controlled economic activities combined with market-oriented, competitive ones. David Stark (1996) calls this hybridization process 'recombinant capitalism'. The view on markets as depending on local political configurations resonates with voices from heterodox economics (see Mirowski [2007]) arguing that there is no single, dominant market template. Nevertheless, while these latter emphasize the possibility of conceiving market transactions as algorithms (i.e. as rule formalization susceptible of automation), neoinstitutionalism stresses not only the formal aspects of rules and control but also their symbolic character, meant to confer legitimacy upon transactions. This runs counter to the notion that markets are amenable to complete formalization.

Some authors consider that several styles of capitalism can be distinguished, depending on how the state is configured, on intra-state political styles (understood as the relationships among political parties, unions, local communities, and central government), and on the trust put by citizens in these styles. Accordingly, Volker Bornschier (2005, pp. 211–12) distinguishes among five varieties of capitalism, going from the Anglo-Saxon model to the Latin-Mediterranean and East-Asian styles, with stopovers at the Northern-Scandinavian and Middle-West European styles. While these classes or styles are meant to help understand how specific relationships between businesses and the state emerge, they can also be indicative of the direction taken by larger political-economic entities which incorporate several market styles. An example of this would be the European Union which incorporates all styles except the East-Asian one. Another example would be NAFTA, the North American Free Trade Agreement, which could be seen as incorporating the Anglo-Saxon and the Latin-Mediterranean models (if one takes the Mexican economy as a version of the latter). However, postulating transnational styles of capitalism does not entirely harmonize with the principle of local action, according to which markets are configured by the local interplay of specific political and social forces.

More important than this, perhaps, is the investigation of a set of processes which seem to run counter to local styles of markets, by creating all-encompassing systems of exchange: globalization. While lacking a precise definition, economic globalization has been understood as implying (*a*) growing economic interdependencies among countries and their firms, resulting, among others, in the emergence of transnational networks of firms; (*b*) the emergence of transnational corporations which are not bound to the regime of control of any single state; and (*c*) the emergence of trans- and supranational forms of governance (see also Gereffi [2005, pp. 164, 168]). Processes of economic globalization can be supported by changes within the structure and practices of corporations, such as the growing importance of financial activities as an independent centre of profit, which encourages transnational capital flows (see also Krippner [2005, p. 202]). At the same time, economic globalization is not necessarily something new; the period before the First World War is regarded by economic historians as one of market integration and globalization, even perhaps to a greater extent than today (see O'Rourke and Williamson [1999, 2000, 2001]).

In this perspective, economic globalization is not taken to mean the emergence of a unique and unitary economic system at planetary level, but accommodates different economic 'styles' and control arrangements. What it means is rather the expansion and consolidation of firms or networks of firms which, because they go beyond specific state boundaries, are not subjected exclusively to control mechanisms set up by a particular state. This raises the issue of trans- and supranational institutions as effective control arrangements. Institutions like the World Trade Organization (WTO), the International Monetary Fund (IMF), or the World Bank, to name but a few, became more and more prominent during the 1990s, as economic globalization accelerated its pace. Other institutions, such as the Organization of Petroleum Exporting Countries (OPEC) had already achieved notoriety in the 1970s.

While the emergence of transnational corporations and international economic integration can correspond to patterns also encountered in the case of national firms—i.e. the emergence of networks of firms, procedural standardization combined with local adaptations, or setting up rituals and symbols of legitimacy—transnational regulatory bodies, such as the International Monetary Fund or the World Bank pose more interesting problems. First, the existence of these bodies indicates that modes of governance at state level cannot always adequately confront the challenges posed by economic globalization. Therefore, the question arises about the emergence of global modes of governance different in nature from state-based ones. Second, how does the relationship between national and transnational institutions affect governance modes? This relationship cannot be automatically regarded as one of cooperation or subordination (of national to transnational institutions). Moreover, if we take a look at financial markets we can see that national institutions, such as the Securities and Exchange Commission (SEC) in the United States or the Financial Services Authority (FSA) in the United Kingdom, enjoy an influence going well beyond national borders, in the sense that their regulatory measures are often regarded as setting standards. Third, since even economic globalization is not a homogeneous process, but implies several aspects (e.g. flows of capital, but also international migration of the workforce), can we find core aspects of economic globalization affecting the ways in which transnational institutions work?

Recent sociological work attempts to answer all three questions, albeit with different implications. On the one hand, organizations such as the WTO, which arbitrates trade disputes between states and suprastatal organizations (such as those between the United States and the EU, for instance), have led to (*a*) the judicialization of the economic relationships between states (in the sense of creating legal mechanisms for settling disputes), (*b*) a rescaling of state authority (the ultimate authority being the WTO), as well as to (*c*) the international reorientation of the state (with international trade becoming much more important). On the level of trade policies, the authority of the state was restricted (protectionist practices became more difficult), while market-oriented policies were encouraged (Chorev 2005, p. 347). While setting up transnational economic institutions was a political project which could not have been possible without support at state level (Chorev 2007), once these institutions were created they changed the character of international economic relations.

On the other hand, transnational economic institutions are organizations and, therefore, the features encountered in firms at state level will be encountered here as well: legitimacy and survival as overarching goals supported by rituals and symbols, a preoccupation with internal controls and hierarchies, as well as internal inter-group competitions. Therefore, as in any organization, the policies adopted by the management can be both inertial and symbolic, that is, they are maintained long after the conditions for which they were designed have changed, and they are maintained not necessarily for their effectiveness, but because they legitimate the institution. Take the lending policies practised in the late 1990s by the IMF; these policies, which required from borrowing states that they adopt strict balance of payments adjustments and painful budget cuts, had been devised in the 1950s, when exchange rates were fixed (Babb 2007, p. 158). Under a fixed rate regime, it made sense to pay close attention to budget spending and the balance of payments. While the regime of fixed rates was abolished in the 1970s, the IMF maintained its policy of conditioning lending upon budgetary cuts and balance adjustment, although these conditions made little sense under a regime of free currency exchange. However, inertia combined with the need to legitimate the institution as rigorously applying the same conditions to all borrowers led to maintaining these lending policies.

While most students of economic globalization relate it to institutional factors, and not least to the creation of trans-and supranational instruments of governance, other scholars have pointed out that the material arrangements used by these institutions matter at least as much as the formal, legal definitions of rights and obligations, contracts, and rules. A key aspect here is that governance requires data, which in its turn requires specific technologies of standardization, collection, and storage. At the same time, technology is required not only by regulatory projects but by global transactions as well. While technology-based transactions offer opportunities for data collection and monitoring, they pose challenges with respect to regulation and control. For instance, technologies supporting market transactions have led to the emergence of global exchange forms which are not subjected to immediate controls, or where controls seem to fail in important instances. An example in this sense is provided by the global currency markets studied by Karin Knorr Cetina and Urs Bruegger (2002), the daily functioning of which does not seem to be subjected to tight controls via property rights regulated by the state or by supranational institutions. (We can, of course, find counter-examples here, when a state decides to impose currency controls.) At least as relevant, perhaps, is the rise of real time electronic transaction platforms, which integrate trading in various commodities and financial securities. Transactions conducted on them cannot be subjected to the same kind of governance mechanisms to which, say, exporting bananas is subjected. Moreover, the regulatory regimes of electronic transactions (among others) can be seen not only as a constraint but also a resource in the competition for attracting business. Economic globalization, then, implies not only the creation of a set of supranational institutions (such as the regulatory agencies of the European Union, or the International Monetary Fund) but also competition among national regulatory bodies with a supranational influence. Examples in this sense are the Securities and Exchange Commission (discussed in the preceding chapter) and the Financial Services Authority, respectively.

Technology can also serve in creating regimes of control based on data standardization and monitoring, regimes which do not necessarily prevent, but rather favour market exchanges. The example of debt databases set up by IMF and World Bank agencies, discussed in the previous chapter, is a case in point here. These databases are used in order to manage the debt of borrowing countries not by simply imposing policy rules, but by allowing the debtors to adapt and react to market conditions (Grimpe 2009, chapter 3.4.1). Since the debt is held in various currencies and can be continuously restructured by buying and selling currency options, it needs to be permanently managed. Imposing rigid policy rules about the balance of payments and budgetary deficits helps less with this management than a monitoring system allowing borrowing countries to react to changing market conditions.

This indicates that institutional controls do not serve only to constrain and limit market exchanges but also to enable them in specific formats. Markets and (transnational) institutions appear not as opposed to each other; the latter set up the format for specific competitions and act as referees (WTO is an example here), while encouraging tools which allow new forms of market participation. Again, these tools appear not only as assemblages of rules and policy measures constrained upon participating actors but also as technological platforms which simultaneously allow governance and market participation.

Markets and Values

While debates about economic globalization focus mainly on the links between political institutions, firms, and markets, with an emphasis on their historical dynamics, systems of competitive transactions also have to relate to institutions other than the state: family life, the arts, education, and the like. Since, as neoinstitutionalism argues, each institution sets up systems of symbols and rituals meant to ensure its legitimacy, and which provide the basis for its continuity, what place do market rituals and symbols occupy vis-à-vis those of other institutions? This question concerns not only lived rituals but also the symbolic representations and explanatory modes which legitimate markets. These modes involve reflection and the elaboration of specific discourses which situate markets within society at large, and also in relationship to other institutions. One way of doing this is identifying a central feature, or value, of markets as social institutions, which places them in relationship to key features of other social institutions. This notion of value is different from value (or valuation) as the price achieved during a transaction. Yet, 'value' as in 'the social value of market transactions' must be linked to and able to justify transactions, by situating them within the landscape of social institutions.

At the same time, the notion of discourse implied by the justification of value includes theoretical rationalizations of routine activities (why do people do that?), and also debates and clashes in the public sphere about events, phenomena, or institutions. Such debates do not necessarily take the form of direct confrontations; they can run as parallel or tangential streams of justificatory explanations, contained in newspaper articles, interviews, and the like.

Discourses of value can act as a mediator between concrete transactions and larger social institutions; they help subjects situate and explain their transactions, relate them to other, non-economic domains of action, and justify them in the broader context of social life. And, since we are talking about subjects, a concept which implies ethical norms of behaviour, it means that discourses of value influence not only distinctions between what is right and what is wrong in transactions, and what is the rightful way of conducting them, but also situate such distinctions in the broader landscape of institutions-specific justifications of right and wrong actions.[9] Acting both as mediators among social institutions and as constraining orientations, values appear to be central to the fabric of social life.

Institutional values are not mutually exclusive, but coexist and can combine in different ways. Thus, the values of monetary transactions and of family life, respectively, need not preclude each other; rather, they can combine in particular ways, so that intimate relationships, for instance, characteristic for family life, are expressed in monetary transactions. This is one of the arguments brought forth by Viviana Zelizer's critique (2006, pp. 20–1, 29) of the 'hostile worlds' view: institutional values do not exclude each other (i.e. market transactions are not necessarily opposed and hostile to intimate relationships), but rather intermingle. This approach opens the way for investigating how institutional arrangements overlap (what Zelizer calls dual relationships) and how monetary transactions serve to express social relationships without necessarily alienating them (paying a teenage family member to mow the lawn does not necessarily alienate kinship). At the same time, it draws attention to the fact that there is no unique economic 'value', but institutional values which constantly intermingle (see also Beunza and Stark [2004, p. 369]; Wherry [2008]). These values designate (at least in Zelizer's work) sets of routines, as well as discourses which legitimate these routines and which, in their turn, can become (legally) codified. To go back to the previous example, paying a family member to mow the lawn is a set of routines, which can be repeatedly encountered in the life of various families. These practices are at the same time coupled with discursive rationalizations, which argue why it is ethical to do so, why these practices instil values, a work ethic, and the like. While the practices can be seen as having an economic side (families save money by not hiring a gardening service), they are justified with respect to other social values; it is good to do so not because of the financial savings, but because of the work ethic. This doesn't preclude that one and the same activity can be negotiated by the same participants in a situation as paid work, and in another situation as a mutual obligation. Neither does it preclude tensions within such negotiations, related to conflicting rationalizations. Rationalizing discourses appear in this perspective as contributing to translate non-economic relationships into monetary ones, and also as connecting non-economic institutions to economic ones.

Assuming that value has a discursive character, consisting in the reflexive modes and explanatory strategies used to legitimate and connect different domains of social action (institutions) to each other, Luc Boltanski and Laurent Thévenot[10] (1991, pp. 96, 107) distinguish several domains, which they call cities, or forms of civic life. Each of these forms has its own central justificatory principle. Thus, there is the inspired city, including the religious institutions; the domestic city, modelled after the hierarchical character of traditional family life; the city of opinions, where public renown plays a key role; the civic city, characterized by public order and by legitimate political relationships (such as those of representation in political bodies); and the industrious city, where the crucial element is the place occupied in the division of labour by social groups. The order of the industrious city is neither the political nor the divine, but that of mundane activities which reproduce social life by transforming nature. In this order, rules of rational calculation dominate, because the reproduction of mundane life implies managing resources, allocating money, budgeting, and the like (Boltanski and Thévenot 1991, p. 155).

These cities, or forms of accepted discourse,[11] can combine and overlap, forming 'common worlds' (Boltanski and Thévenot 1991, p. 165), which include both agreements and disagreements about what is appropriate. Agreement or disagreement can concern the fundamental principles, the actors, the objects, relationships among them, the evidence for actions and events having taken place. Keeping within the terminology of Boltanski and Thévenot, we can illustrate this by going back to the previous example, that of a teenage family member being asked to mow the lawn. At least two cities meet here: the domestic and the industrious one. The value of the practice can be constituted through agreement with respect to a fundamental principle, or to actors, to the object of action, and so on. One can say that it is good to mow the lawn because work teaches you the value of money (principles), because the kid needs to spend more time in fresh air anyway (actor), because the new lawnmower should be tested (object), and so on. Or we can have disagreement with respect to principle (I won't obey your orders, I'm not a slave here), action (I did it last week), actor (I need to do homework), and the like.

In such a case, the value of an action (i.e. its desirability from the viewpoint of various participating actors) is contested or agreed upon by means of discursive rationalizations invoking different cities with their principles, actors, objects, relationships. At the same time, the relationship between action and its discursive rationalization is not a simple one; one and the same action can be justified in multiple ways, and the justification is not necessarily determined by the intrinsic properties of the practical action. (There is nothing intrinsic in lawn mowing which ascribes it exclusively to the domestic city, or to the industrious one.) In these rationalizations, the principles, actors, and objects specific for a certain type of city are continuously redefined in terms of the overlapping cities at the intersection of which common worlds are constituted; in the above case, the actors and objects of the domestic city are redefined in terms of the industrious one and vice versa. Thus, institutional values are not mutually exclusive, but rather positioned into a web of dynamic relationships, allowing their continuous reconfiguration according to the necessities of the moment. This brings us away from a reified notion of value as something immutable and hidden in the actors' subconscious, to the investigation of the discursive dynamics through which actions are justified.

Methodologically speaking, this requires investigating discursive rationalizations in their relationship to, and not as isolated from, interactions. Moreover, discursive rationalizations are not only retrospective but unfold within the action itself. A family argument about who is going to mow the lawn does not necessarily have to take place as separated from the action, but can unfold within the action itself; we can easily find situations where complaints about 'why is it always me who has to do this?' are formulated while the lawn is mowed. This sends us back to the interaction order discussed in the first chapter: values (understood as discursive rationalizations) are not separated from, but are part of the interaction order. The investigation of their properties cannot thus be separated from the investigation of the interaction order.

We can now move close up to how the world of markets works. First of all, argue Boltanski and Thévenot (1991, pp. 241–4), this world is neither identical with the industrious city nor reducible to pure competition. While competition is indeed the leading principle, this world is constituted at the intersection of the civic, domestic, and opinion cities; as such, it is marked by the regulatory principles of hierarchy and prestige. These principles shape competition, in the sense that (*a*) market actors are not justified as atomized individuals, but as positions in a social hierarchy. At the same time, within transactions, they appear as independent from each other, and hence as atomized (Boltanski and Thévenot 1991, p. 248). (*b*) Transactions are ordered along hierarchies of prestige and authority. What is at stake in transactions is the dignity of actors (Boltanski and Thévenot 1991, p. 246). Yet, this dignity, while designating the capacity to participate to the common good, is related exclusively to the individual. (*c*) The said transactions are not aims in themselves, but a medium through which individuals relate their desires to those of other actors (Boltanski and Thévenot 1991, p. 250)—in other words, a medium for creating social relations. The notion of dignity sends us back to the concept of gameworthiness discussed in previous chapters, while indicating that the socially relevant attributes at stake in a transaction cannot be separated from attributes considered as relevant in other situations. In other words, if market transactions are about dignity—that is, about achieving valuation on socially relevant attributes—then these transaction-specific attributes cannot be kept in isolation from those relevant in other activities.

In this perspective, the justificatory discourse of market values appears not as a relentless celebration of competition, but rather as rife with contradictions. This discourse cannot exist in isolation from other values; it is in fact constituted at the intersection of several 'cities', to use Boltanski and Thévenot's notion. Because of this, the rationalization of market competition has to acknowledge and integrate the governing principles of these cities—such as those of civic life, or of public opinion, albeit in a modified fashion. Even 'neoliberal' rationalizations of market competition have to justify this latter as serving not egoistic goals of enrichment, but the common good. Participants to market transactions are represented in a contradictory fashion, as social actors responding to collective obligations, and also as atomized and opportunistic. Such forms of discursive rationalization leave room for ethical norms as intrinsic to transactions, offering thus possibilities for intervention and control (Zelizer 2007, p. 15). With that, the discourses around market values can intervene as instruments of control and as tools of valuation (see also White [2008, p. 223]); they provide opportunities for introducing issues of reciprocal obligations, of moral responsibilities, or of civic engagement which, in their turn, can affect the public perception and the justification of actions in the marketplace.

A concrete example here is provided by recent research into how in the 1990s a secondary market in life insurance policies evolved from scattered practices (Quinn 2008). While the practice of selling one's life insurance policy was deemed legal since the early 1900s, it still confronted moral ambivalence, an ambivalence which has been present since life insurance was established in the nineteenth century (Zelizer 1979). Life insurance sprang out of the practical necessities of urban families with a sole male breadwinner, but the idea of insuring life was not immediately accepted as legitimated. This revealed the contradictions raised by definitions of life pertaining to different cities, or domains of activity. However, the creation of a system of transactions in life insurance policies raised additional ethical questions, related to the notion of exploiting personal difficulties for commercial gains. At the same time, the argument was made that life insurance policies are nothing more than a specific investment asset, which should be used when circumstances demand it. Moreover, according to a third argument, selling one's life insurance policy helps to avoid debt and allows people to die with dignity (Quinn 2008, p. 755). These different definitions are formulated according to different principles, each pertaining to a different city, to use again Boltanski and Thévenot's terminology. There is personal dignity (the domestic city), and also a personal investment at stake (the industrious city), and a public dignity (the opinion city). The practice of reselling life insurance policies gains its legitimacy at the interface of the debates and rationalizations which follow these different principles. At the same time, these discourses act as instances of control, containing the practice within certain limits of social acceptability.

Another example in this respect is the recent prominence of issues such as the corporate social responsibility (CSR), which defines firms not only in terms of profit and transaction efficiency but in terms of social obligations as well. While it may be argued that that CSR is only a tool used for managing public relations, the incorporation of this issue in justificatory discourses (we need corporations because they are good citizens) creates a mechanism of control for evaluating practical actions against justifications (good corporate citizenship is exemplified by actions). This, of course, does not change the nature of the corporation, but opens up additional ways of public intervention and scrutiny. For instance, when it was revealed that US corporations, which had received bail-out money in the financial crisis of 2008–9, spent considerable sums on bonuses, spa treatments, and lavish office refurnishings, the public outcry put pressure on managers, and led to calls for tighter controls. This would not have been possible without the justification of corporations as civic actors, and as having a responsibility towards the taxpayers who bailed them out. At the same time, we can notice here how controversies and clashes develop rather quickly around justifications; while the issue of public responsibility was seen as justifying a (partial) return of the paid bonuses, voices argued that by paying them, corporations will keep control of individuals who might leave with inside knowledge and trade against their former employers (Sorkin 2009). Still, others pointed out that this is like 'giving bonuses to the arsonists who started a fire because they alone knew what kind of accelerants they used to start it' (Dowd 2009).

All in all, then, understanding market values from the viewpoint of justification, and also from that of control, opens the way for investigating inter-institutional dynamics on a cultural level, which complements the framing of institutions in terms of rights and contracts. It also enlarges the understanding of the social mechanisms of control and intervention in market transactions, revealing how these go beyond regulatory supervision. At the same time, this approach is perfectly compatible with the neoinstitutionalist emphasis on symbolic representation and rituals: justificatory discourses include symbolic elements and are used in organizational rituals.

Institutions and Information

Up to this point, the discussion of markets as social institutions has emphasized how constraints and forms of control limit and regulate competitive market exchanges. Such forms of control cover a wide spectrum, going from legal to cultural features, from explicit rules and regulations of exchange to discursive clashes and debates about values. At the same time, institutions are about routines, about organizational rituals, symbolic representations, and routinized forms of behaviour geared towards maintaining and reproducing organizational structures. Yet, since a major focus of this book has been the relationship between competitive transactions and information, where does this latter stand with respect to institutions?

Market information, I have argued in the previous chapters, is not simply signals about routines, but the production and management of uncertainties (what I have called informational surprises). At the first sight, if we adopt this perspective, apparently institutions do not have much to do with information. Nevertheless, the production and management of uncertainties as encountered in market exchanges is characterized by relational, technological, and epistemic boundaries. After having discussed the links between markets and institutions, we can add institutional boundaries as a further way in which market information is shaped. These institutional boundaries contribute to setting up the conditions and parameters within which surprises can be produced; conditions which can take the form of legal constraints, of political interventions, of means of control, or of value definitions, among others.

At the same time, institutional boundaries themselves can become a source of informational surprises in at least two situations. The first is when there is breach of boundaries (which has been discussed in Chapter 1 with respect to the interaction order), that is, when the mechanisms of control and governance already in place are revealed as malfunctioning or as ineffective. The second is when discursive debates about values take place, heightening rather than solving uncertainties, and opening up the field for new and unexpected discursive interventions.

Financial crises and swindles are examples of the first case; they are informational not only in uncovering the ineffectiveness of governance[12] but also the ways in which controls are circumvented. They produce uncertainties not only in the sense of disrupting routines but also in opening up avenues for further action. Crises and swindles require setting in place new modes of calculation and control which are not known beforehand, but require judgement and decision (Miller and Power 1995, p. 54). Take the swindle perpetrated over decades by Bernard Madoff, the money manager who lost his clients about $65 billion. This swindle revealed not only the inadequacy of the SEC controls but, at least as important, its investigation is expected to reveal how

Madoff circumvented them (see Creswell and Thomas [2009]). This informational surprise is liable to have an impact on further institutional actions—that is, on the revision of control and disclosure mechanisms.

Public discourses about crises and values, too, can be a source of informational surprises because the dynamic of the debates, their arguments, the order in which they are formulated, and the opportunities for new, unexpected interventions cannot be foreseen in advance. This sends us back to the properties of social action discussed in Chapter 1, namely, sequentiality and polythetic character. Taking the financial crisis of 2008–9 as a background, one of the issues subjected to public debates was that of the value of short selling.[13] 'Value' meant here not only profitability but social value too—value to the community. The debate was informational not only in that it brought an apparently obscure issue into the public spotlight, transforming it from a technicality into a matter of public concern, but also because the character of the arguments was only partly foreseeable. While some of the positions against short selling expectedly treated it as gambling, defenders said that short selling was doing a service to the community, as giving a voice to those who believed that specific firms were hiding losses.

From the viewpoint of information, then, it is relevant to investigate crisis situations—big and small—which reveal how institutional controls, as well as justifications, become problematic, and how their problematic character affects market transactions. In other words, what happens when limits are revealed as ineffective, or as insecure? While there is little sociological research on the issue of crises, this is one of the most promising avenues for future investigations, especially when taken in combination with crises of technology or of epistemic authority, as in the counterperformativity case discussed in Chapter 3.

☐ **NOTES**

1. The term ' institution' is reputedly fuzzy; while the more general understanding is that of sets of rules regulating specific domains of social action (Mohr and Friedland 2008, p. 424), a different take on institutions is that of 'different types of interlocking networks ... that link actors together in various social relations and role systems' (Mohr and White 2008, p. 488). This opens the way for combining the neoinstitutionalist approach with the social structural one in the conceptualization of markets, taking the notion of social relationships as the key element.
2. Weber ([1921] 1972, p. 127) notices that in economic corporations (as well as in government) the top positions (the CEO, for instance) are not necessarily occupied by bureaucrats with specific procedural and factual knowledge. The CEO of a supermarket chain, for instance, could have worked previously in the chemical industry. But such a CEO will have a staff with specific knowledge of marketing, suppliers, etc. Because of this interchangeability, Weber sees the top positions in the economic bureaucracy as pure positions of domination.

3. Neoinstitutional economists are aware of the artificial and rather instrumental character of this opposition, used to highlight the firm as a sui generis entity. They have suggested the notion of network (discussed in Chapter 2) as a hybrid meant to avoid conceptual problems, and as a way of overcoming the artificial opposition between firms as hierarchies and markets as competitions (see also Powell [2001, pp. 58–9]). Moreover, competitions among firms do take place, as illustrated by investment banks or brokerage houses competing with each other on financial markets.

4. For an instance of this view, see Powell 2001, pp. 55–8.

5. Authors like Luc Boltanski and Eve Chiapello (1999), who will be discussed in more detail in the following, tend to understand the spirit of capitalism as 'discourse', as exemplified by the managerial discourses which act as instruments of control. While the notion of discourse is not much clearer than that of spirit, it points to systems of symbolic representations which, by the prestige of their authors, gain normative power within businesses.

6. Fligstein takes over and adapts Pierre Bourdieu's (1980) concept of field as a system of differences among social groups, organized along routines.

7. 'Cognitive maps' refer here to shared understandings, and not to specific cognitive actions, as discussed in the previous chapters. While this notion may evoke a mentalist understanding of cognition, the issue here is that any reference to shared understandings will have to take interaction into account. An understanding of market transactions as relationships, not as interactions makes this difficult.

8. The notion 'varieties of capitalism' initially designated various welfare regimes adopted in advanced Western economies (see Esping-Andersen [1990]; Hicks and Kenworthy [2003]). Meanwhile, it has come to designate various combinations of control instruments which shape the role and influence of market exchanges within national economies.

9. Ethical norms and distinctions between right and wrong can differ from institution to institution; for instance, it is right for a family to ask a teenager to mow the lawn without remuneration, but it would be wrong to ask a hired employee to do so. Family life can be framed by reciprocal obligations (the moral economy), with specific normative expectations, in ways different from marketplace transactions. Therefore, the issue of value boils down to tacit normative expectations *and* justificatory discourses (more or less loosely) related to these expectations.

10. While Boltanski and Thévenot' original subtitle is 'the economies of greatness', the translation published by Princeton University Press in 2006 bears the subtitle 'economies of worth' (Boltanski and Thévenot 2006). 'Greatness' here refers both to values and to common social life (things which are greater than the individual), a classic Durkheimian theme.

11. If one wonders, for instance, where the place of aesthetic values is in these cities, or domains, they can be located within the divine city; the contemplation of beauty is taken, for instance, to establish a relationship between the observer and a transcendent domain.

12. Institutional mechanisms of control reveal their informational potential not only in moments of big crises but in organizational daily life as well, when routines are disrupted, or when little crises occur. Think of situations where organizational rules do not cover unforeseen situations, when they cannot act as indicators for further action, or when an employee does something unexpected (aka 'does not play by the rules').

13. Short selling is the practice of selling financial securities without owning them, in the expectation that they will decline in price. The seller then buys them back at a lower price and pockets the difference.

Conclusion
The Sociology of Markets and Its Research Agendas

This book has opened with the metaphor of playing a soccer game, which illustrated the links between information, on the one hand, and market transactions, on the other. Each chapter has examined a specific aspect of the play: the players' interactions in the field; the teams; the comments which are an intrinsic part of the play; the technologies providing the game's scaffolding; the institutions which integrate the sport into civic life. Each aspect of the play metaphor has been discussed based on the corresponding research programmes, in relationship to their main theoretical notions, and to their empirical results. Markets have been characterized as systems of competitive transactions—a view on which classic and contemporary sociology agree—but they have also been discussed from the perspective of hierarchies of groups and networks, of the scopic systems, and of the expertise which shape them. In the same way in which the empirical examples discussed throughout this book illustrate the variety of market forms, the perspectives presented here highlight the multifaceted character of markets, which can be investigated using complementary theoretical toolboxes, according to the aspect of the play providing the focus of theoretical attention.

Each of the domains I have discussed has developed specific research programmes: the study of the interaction orders of markets, for instance, investigates among others the sequential character of transactions and the crystallization of 'decisions' within such sequences. Or, take the links between cognition and emotions, the investigation of which is relatively recent, but yielding great potential. While emotions have been so often seen as manifestations of irrationality which negatively affect the calculations and strategies of market players, in situ studies of the interaction order indicate the opposite. Another line of investigation concerns the cognitive activities of market actors, such as observation, classification, calculation, and memorization, understood not as mental operations or as abstract templates, but as interactional achievements.

The structural research programmes, in their turn, stress the role of various types of relationships with respect to market transactions, and to the ways in which relevant elements, such as prices, are constituted. Other significant areas of research here have been the role of status (including its symbolic features) in market segmentation, as well as the forms of community-specific transactions. The emphasis put on the role played by symbolic elements in the constitution and legitimacy of market groups has brought the social structural investigation of markets closer to neoinstitutionalist approaches, so that a hybridization or synthesis between the two is now advocated by scholars.

The investigation of forms of market expertise and technologies, which is a more recent development, includes various directions of research, the performativity programme being one of them. The emphasis here lies on examining models as tools used in market transactions, as well as on reconceptualizing the role played by technology, and on the jurisdictional shifts related to the technologization of transactions.

In its turn, the neoinstitutionalist agenda includes several areas of research, among which the relationships between states and markets play, not unexpectedly, a prominent role. However, more recently the focus of attention has shifted to the institutions promoting economic globalization, to the policies supporting these processes, and to the symbolic factors influencing their adoption and implementation. Yet, another major direction of research which can be located here is the study of values—including the links between market transactions and ethical values. As discussed in Chapter 5, the study of values departs from their conceptualization as abstract, mental entities, emphasizing instead the role of discourse, understood as justificatory mechanisms which support the connections between markets, on the one hand, and the institutions of social life, on the other.

These research programmes have employed a variety of investigative methods, including quantitative historical studies, analytical reconstructions of the processes through which markets emerge, quantitative studies of networks, organizational ethnographies, and studies of the interaction order using naturally occurring data. Practically, the sociology of markets makes use of a very broad spectrum of analytical methods and techniques, and has been at the forefront of methodological innovation, both on the quantitative and on the qualitative side.

This, however, does not mean that the contemporary sociology of markets is a more or less loose collection of concepts, definitions, methods, and techniques. By now, I have hopefully persuaded readers that the themes and the research programmes presented here open up a series of interfaces to each other (see Figure C.1), and pursue a series of common themes, albeit from different angles and with different conceptual understandings. Now, it is time to bring together the themes and concepts discussed throughout the chapters and sketch these interfaces, tentatively identifying the agendas for future research which can be located here. In a non-exhaustive manner, I will start with re-examining three of the main themes and concepts which provide the leitmotivs of this book: market transactions, pricing, and valuations, in their relationship to information.

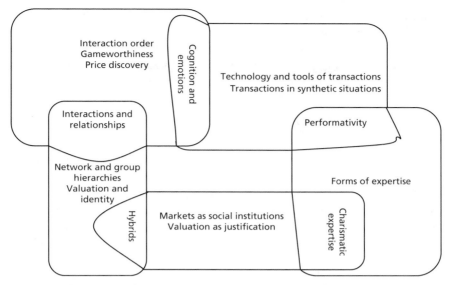

Figure C.1 Research programmes in the sociology of markets and their interfaces

The overall thrust of the book has been that market information should not be seen as routines which reduce uncertainty. Rather, routines provide the background against which information—understood as surprises, as unexpected action elements—is generated in transactions. This understanding of market information allows approaching transactions as dynamic competitive interactions, with the analytical potential of a tool for analyzing both 'normal' and crisis situations in markets, and of integrating the investigation of issues such as market valuation, relationships, and interaction.

Transactions as Interactions and as Relationships

While various research programmes—from the study of market interaction orders to neoinstitutionalism, going through social structural approaches— agree that the basic analytical unit of the sociology of markets is the transaction, this concept does not have the same meaning in these programmes. Based on the preceding discussion, at least two understandings can be identified: the transaction as a social interaction, and the transaction as a social relationship. While related, these two understandings do not overlap: market transactions as social interactions pertain to research programmes stressing the role of the interaction order, while market transactions as relationships pertain to structural and neoinstitutionalist programmes. These differences have not only theoretical, but also methodological consequences: the toolbox used in the analysis of market interactions is not the same as that used in the analysis of market relationships, if these latter are seen as distinct from interactions. If we think of the ways in which market cognition and information are approached based on each of these understandings, the gap widens. Interaction-oriented research programmes have emphasized cognition as intrinsic to interactions and as irreducible to mental processes. Moreover, cognition—understood as observation, classification, calculation, and memorization activities—is distinct from, yet related to skills and knowledge. Interaction-oriented agendas have more recently begun to investigate the links between cognitive operations, on the one hand, and emotions, on the other, in the conduct of market transactions. These investigations highlight the role of emotional arousal—as an interaction-based accomplishment—in dealing with surprises and in shaping not only cognitive activities, but also decision-making. A rich research agenda opens up here, one which has the potential of going beyond the usual postulates of rationality v. irrationality, by investigating in depth, using naturally occurring data, how decisions are made with respect to information. Research programmes focusing on transactions as relationships mainly emphasize classifications, as well as routines and rules with respect to market information.

One way for opening up an interface among these research programmes is related to bridging the differences between the seemingly different notions of interaction and relationship, respectively. In Chapter 1, I have argued that social relationships have to be made visible in interactions, or tagged—that is, their existence and character must be recognized by transaction partners and the public alike. Or, again, the exclusion of the public from witnessing the interaction tells as something about the character of the relationship. In connection to the main interaction forms discussed there, this opens the way for an interaction-oriented study of market relationships, a study which should specify their concrete forms and role with respect to how information is produced and handled. A second area of investigation here would be the interaction-oriented study of forms of authority in market relationships: how, for instance, is charismatic authority generated in interactions? This opens up the research interface for contributions coming from the study of market technologies: since a considerable number of transactions are synthetic, and not face to face, how is (charismatic) authority produced in synthetic situations?

Insisting for a moment on the role played by transaction technologies, it cannot be emphasized enough here that the advancing computerization of market transactions has multiplied the situations where transaction partners do not necessarily entertain social relationships, or even do not know each other. The growing integration of trading platforms is bound to increase the relevance of online, anonymous transactions. Examples here are provided by day traders, who transact with each other without knowing each other. This, however, does not mean that they do not interact with each other, and that interactions do not lead to relationships specific to the synthetic situations of trading online. The problem of anonymity in market transactions—which also provides a basic assumption for economic models of transactions—can be reformulated sociologically as that of the specific relationships brought about by interactions in synthetic market situations. Thus, interactions and relationships need neither be opposed to each other, nor treated as two separate notions. Bringing them together sensitizes research for new forms of market transactions, relevant for issues concerning valuation and pricing, as well as authority and expertise in online anonymous markets.

Pricing as Discovery and as Agreement

Pricing, which appears as a key issue in the sociology of markets, can be seen as partly overlapping with the notion of valuation discussed in this book. While there is agreement in the sociology of markets about the social elements which flow into the constitution of prices—in the sense that these latter are not simply determined by abstract demand and supply mechanisms—the ways in which pricing is understood differs among research programmes. One understanding of pricing, highlighted mainly in Chapters 1 and 4, is that of price discovery, seen as an interactional achievement of transaction partners. Another understanding of pricing, discussed in Chapters 2 and 5, is that of social agreements controlled by rules and shaped by social relationships. Discovery and agreement are not the same, albeit both are the object of sociological enquiry. The notion of price discovery sends us to the inter- actions through which relevant cognitive activities, such as observation, calculation, and memorization are performed, operations without which the price as an element intrinsic to lived transactions cannot be achieved. In this perspective, the price itself appears less as an already existing, natural entity, waiting to be discovered (in the way in which we might discover a coin under a rock, for instance), and more as an element intrinsic to transactional sequences. It should also be emphasized here that this approach pays more attention to price data, as elements without which transaction-relevant cog- nitive operations cannot unfold. This creates an interface with research programmes investigating the technologies which allow operations such as price observation, and which endow data with specific social characteristics.

If we take into account that technologies of observation, of calculation, and of trading are more and more integrated on the same platform, as in the case of electronic anonymous markets, the issue of price discovery as a feature of market interactions gains in relevance. It is intrinsic to investigating how market forms evolve, in relationship to changes in the interaction formats supported by technology. The relevance of price data comes to the fore in relationship to issues of expertise as well, as illustrated by the performativity programme: data-generating tools are used in transactions, acting both as observational lenses and as intervention instruments, with the help of which new discoveries are made. This brings us to the issue of online forms of expertise, and the ways in which they integrate data-generating tools with conducting transactions. The issue of pricing, then, depends on investigating the double character of expertise—as a lens and as a tool—in online market environments.

This does not mean that issues related to forms of control and constraints—emphasized by the understanding of pricing as a social agreement—disappear from the agenda. The research interface opened here needs to investigate the forms of control specific to online market environments: the greater emphasis put on data disclosure as a tool of control in electronic financial transactions, together with the resistances to it, are a case in point here. Not only that: following the neoinstitutionalist argument about multiple levels of formal and informal control, levels which do not always harmonize with each other, the question arises about the informal controls present in anonymous electronic markets, where one would expect that personal ties will not work so well.

But even if we were to leave out computerized markets, the two understandings of pricing discussed above need not be opposed to each other. Pricing as a set of activities determined by social agreements, routines, and rules does not exclude that prices have to be made visible as data, that prices have to be made observable to specific audiences, and in specific formats. This raises the issue of boundaries discussed throughout the book. If we were to go back to the example of Venetian peddlers discussed in Chapter 1, the visibility or invisibility of prices, their written character as data or their orality, their stability or malleability, respectively, are intrinsic to how transactions are constituted within specific boundaries. They are also intrinsic to the status elements of the actors involved in these transactions, and to the ways in which apparently opposed transaction types can coexist in space and time. Research into how social agreements influence pricing activities can benefit from paying attention to prices as data.

Valuation as Gameworthiness, as Identity, and as Justification

Valuation is another issue which has featured prominently in the more recent sociology of markets, while its roots are deeply anchored in classic sociology.

Yet, if we were to look closer at how valuation is understood, based on the previous chapters, we can see that various research programmes operate with different understandings of the term. Among these understandings, we can distinguish at least three major ones: valuation as gameworthiness, as identity, and as justification. All these understandings depart from the standard view that what market transactions value is the object, or the commodity. They emphasize instead—and this is the truly sociological element here—that in market transactions players value themselves in relationship to their partners/opponents, and in relationship to society. Moreover, all these understandings reposition the accent away from value as an intrinsic, given property of an entity to valuation—that is, to the relationships achieved in market transactions. With that, valuation as a sociological concept does not entirely overlap with that of pricing: while interlinked, they are kept apart in the analytical arsenal of the sociologist.

Valuation as gameworthiness is present in the first place in the study of the interaction orders of markets. Building upon the concept introduced by Erving Goffman for the analysis of strategic actions in games, the notion of gameworthiness highlights the ways in which participants in transactions compete on socially relevant attributes, such as cunning or endurance, and how these competitions actually contribute to shaping the outcome of transactions. In this perspective, it becomes possible to study and establish market typologies based on gameworthiness, where transaction forms which are apparently disconnected can be assigned to the same class of socially relevant attributes. In the same way in which we can classify together car racing and boxing as valuing endurance as a social attribute, we can examine the relevant attributes of gameworthiness present in market exchanges and order transaction types according to them. Moreover, we can then compare these transaction types with other valuation principles specific to other social activities, in order to understand better the role played by transactions with regard to other action forms. I wrote in the introduction that modern societies apparently include competitions in all domains of social life and at all levels, going from jam contests at village fairs to professional sports competitions attracting the public in the millions. The valuation principles, as well as the interaction formats of various kinds of competitions can be compared with those of market transactions, in order to gain insights into the role and place of competitive market transactions among the many forms of social competitions displayed by modern societies. Such an investigation would help us understand better the features of modern societies, and hence confer to the sociological study of markets a relevance going well beyond the realm of economic life. This can—and should—become a central part of an interaction-oriented programme of research on markets, which in its turn could then be seen as part of a larger investigative agenda on competitions.

The second understanding of valuation comes mainly from the structural approach, as discussed in Chapter 2. It concerns the positions market competitors take with respect to each other, positions which require in the first place establishing one's identity within a specific segment, or group. In its turn, this identity is related to factors such as the volume and quality which competitors choose to produce. Volume and quality, however, do not appear as ends in themselves, but rather as instruments of valuation—that is, of achieving the participants' specific identities within the competition. Again, returning to the arguments presented earlier in this conclusion, this understanding of valuation emphasizes relationships rather than interactions.

The third understanding of valuation, discussed mainly in Chapter 5, refers to the justifications of market transactions with respect to other forms of social life. These justifications need not be anchored exclusively in consensus, but include agonistic elements as well. They also include renegotiations of definitions, dealing with ambivalences, or confronting issues like permissibility or desirability. These aspects come to the fore especially in situations where entities, processes, or actors are transferred and reconfigured within the sphere of market transactions, or when they should be excluded from it. It could be said that this understanding of valuation emphasizes the constant reformulations—accompanied by contestations—of the legitimacy of markets towards other social institutions. Perhaps nowhere are these struggles and repositioning more visible than in moments of crisis, when (more or less tacitly) accepted formulations of legitimacy are suspended or invalidated.

Valuation as justification does not stand in opposition with the other two understandings. In fact, we can well imagine—and should call for—a research agenda geared towards investigating justifications not as disconnected from, but as connected to gameworthiness. This would imply investigating how legitimating strategies are produced and used in market transactions, and how they relate to what actors perceive as socially relevant attributes in these transactions. A recent example can make this clearer. In the financial crisis of 2008–9, on both sides of the Atlantic, a public outcry arose against executive compensation packages and bonuses, which were perceived as excessive and unjustified, especially for those corporations which had been bailed out by taxpayers. We encounter here an example of how executive compensation, formerly accepted as legitimate by the public (albeit more or less tacitly), were contested as unjustified and even as immoral. Yet, in many cases, these contestations came after the compensation and bonuses had been formally agreed and approved upon by the corporations' boards, as part of a negotiation process which can often include competitive components (of the kind who receives how much, or why should X receive less than Y). On the part of the corporations' executives, compensation was often justified with the argument that, were they not paid, valuable (i.e. gameworthy) managers would go elsewhere. The task, therefore, would be to investigate not only contestations of legitimacy, but also the justificatory elements present in such negotiations, together with the competitions of gameworthiness possibly unfolding within them.

A Research Agenda on Economic Crises

The above examination of conceptual foci and research agendas does not aim at being exhaustive: additional research programmes can be identified, both within each of the above fields, as well as at their interfaces. Nevertheless, there is one agenda which I believe has remained largely underexplored within the sociology of markets: the investigation of economic crises. Of course, it could be well argued that such an agenda is motivated by the ongoing economic events of 2008–9. Beyond this motivation, however, it is hard not to notice the regularity with which crises occur, as well as the lack of a systematic investigation within the domains discussed in this book. Of course, concepts such as counterperformativity have made a beginning here, but my argument is that we need to go beyond this and develop more sustained, systematic research programmes at the interfaces of the domains presented here.

For instance, we still know very little about the interaction formats of crises: what does it mean to be in a crisis from the perspective of transactions qua interactions? Do crisis situations affect these interaction formats or not? Does the dynamic of emotions and cognitive activities change here? Can we distinguish different crisis forms in face-to-face and synthetic situations, respectively? To say that crises represent a breakdown of trust is not a satisfactory answer to the problem, as long as we haven't investigated the interaction order of economic crises. If we were to go back to Harold Garfinkel's classic article on trust (1963), a true breakdown of trust is not even possible at the interaction level, since participants in the situation will make every effort to restore it. A true breakdown of trust would overlap with a breakdown of the interaction order, a notion which is very problematic in itself.

In the introduction of this book, as well as throughout its chapters, various forms of trust have been discussed: procedural but also relational, institutional as well as technology-related trust. They have been examined in relationship to the routines and rules against which information is produced. This latter, I have argued, is provided by non-routine elements which have to be dealt with in transactions, based on the available tools and resources. In this perspective, a sociological research programme on market crises would start investigating how the links between information and forms of trust, between surprises and routines are reshaped during crises, how forms of authority are affected here, and how valuation processes change, or seem to be suspended.

To say that economic crises imply irrational elements—aka emotions—taking over rational ones—aka calculation—is not very satisfactory either, since, as I have discussed in Chapter 1, emotions and cognition within transactions cannot be opposed to each other. What we need here is an investigation into the forms and role of information in crisis situations, in relation not only to technology, but also to possible changes in relationships. That information plays an important role here is indicated by the surprises, revelations, and unexpected turns which seem to accompany crises. In situations of crisis, relationships can be changed, in the sense of possible suspensions, or redefinitions. Authority can be contested, or suspended as well. Institutional rules and controls can be interpreted in ways different from those of 'normal' transactions, and the legitimation of actions can be affected as well. All in all, and without being able to go into much detail, I would argue that the study of market crises from multiple angles, going from the interaction order to the institutional frames, should be placed at the core of future research agendas in the sociology of markets.

At this point, it is time to ask again, and not entirely in a rhetorical fashion: Why a sociology of markets? Hopefully, by now I may have persuaded readers that markets, as fundamental institutions of modern societies, deserve full sociological attention. We may be critical towards them, or we may accept them to various degrees: irrespective of this, however, an appropriate understanding of social life is not possible without studying them. To use a notion from the introduction of this book, markets are polythetic, dynamic, evolving forms of social order. Looking back at the sociological classics discussed in this book—Marx, Weber, and Simmel, among others—what strikes one is that, in spite of their considerable differences, they agree on competitive transactions as a basic form of sociality, the study of which should be put at the core of the sociological enterprise. If we take to heart the first sociological commandment, that of studying forms of social order, then we cannot do without the investigation of market orders.

⬚ REFERENCES

Abbott, Andrew. 1988. *The System of Professions. An Essay on the Division of Expert Labor*. Chicago: University of Chicago Press.

Abolafia, Mitchel. 1996. *Making Markets. Opportunism and Restraint on Wall Street*. Cambridge MA: Harvard University Press.

Akerlof, George. 1970. 'The Market for "Lemons". Quality Uncertainty and the Market Mechanism'. *Quarterly Journal of Economics* 84/3: 488–500.

—— 2002. 'Behavioral Macroeconomics and Macroeconomic Behavior'. *American Economic Review* 92/3: 411–33.

Alborn, Timothy L. 1994. 'Economic Man, Economic Machine: Images of Circulation in the Victorian Money Market'. In Philip Mirowski (ed.), *Natural Images in Economic Thought. 'Markets Read in Tooth and Claw'*, pp. 173–95, Cambridge: Cambridge University Press.

Aspers, Patrik. 2006. *Markets in Fashion. A Phenomenological Approach*. London: Routledge.

—— 2007. 'Wissen und Bewertung auf Märkten'. *Berliner Journal für Soziologie* 17/4: 431–49.

Austin, John Langshaw. 1962. *How To Do Things with Words*. Oxford: Clarendon.

Babb, Sarah. 2001. *Managing Mexico. Economists from Nationalism to Neoliberalism*. Princeton NJ: Princeton University Press.

—— 2007. 'Embeddedness, Inflation, and International Regimes. The IMF in the Early Postwar Period'. *American Journal of Sociology* 113/1: 128–64.

Baker, Wayne. 1984. 'The Social Structure of a National Securities Market'. *American Journal of Sociology* 89/4: 775–811.

Bandelj, Nina. 2008. *From Communists to Foreign Capitalists. The Social Foundations of Foreign Direct Investment in Postsocialist Europe*. Princeton NJ: Princeton University Press.

—— 2009. 'The Global Economy as an Instituted Process. The Case of Central and Eastern Europe'. *American Sociological Review* 74: 128–49.

Barley, Stephen. 1986. 'Technology as an Occasion for Structuring. Evidence from Observation of CT Scanners and the Social Order of Radiology Departments'. *Administration Science Quarterly* 31/1: 78–108.

—— 1996. 'Technicians in the Workplace. Ethnographic Evidence for Bringing Work into Organizational Studies'. *Administration Science Quarterly* 41/3: 404–41.

Bearman, Peter. 2005. *Doormen*. Chicago: University of Chicago Press.

Bechky, Beth. 2003. 'Object Lessons. Workplace Artifacts as Representations of Occupational Jurisdiction'. *American Journal of Sociology* 109/3: 720–52.

Beckert, Jens. 1996. 'What is Sociological about Economic Sociology? Uncertainty and the Embeddedness of Economic Action'. *Theory and Society* 25/6: 803–40.

—— 2007. *The Great Transformation of Embeddedness. Karl Polanyi and the New Economic Sociology*. MPIfG discussion paper 07/1. Cologne: MPIfG.

Berezin, Mabel. 2005. 'Emotions and the Economy'. In Neil Smelser and Richard Swedberg (eds.), *Handbook of Economic Sociology*, 2nd edn, pp. 109–27, Princeton and New York: Princeton University Press and the Russell Sage Foundation.

Bertinotti, Dominique. 1985. 'Carrières féminines et carrières masculines dans l'administration des postes et télégraphes à la fin du XIXe siècle'. *Annales ESC* 3: 625–40.

Beunza, Daniel and David Stark. 2004. 'Tools of the Trade. The Socio-technology of Arbitrage in a Wall Street Trading Room'. *Industrial and Corporate Change* 13/2: 369–400.

—— —— 2005. 'How to Recognize Opportunities. Heterarchical Search in a Trading Room'. In Karin Knorr Cetina and Alex Preda (eds.), *The Sociology of Financial Markets*, pp. 84–101, Oxford: Oxford University Press.

Biggart, Nicole Woolsey. 1989. *Charismatic Capitalism. Direct Selling Organizations in America*. Chicago: University of Chicago Press.

Bijker, Wiebe E., Thomas P. Hughes, and Trevor Pinch (eds.). 1987. *The Social Construction of Technological Systems*. Cambridge MA: MIT Press.

Birchler, Urs and Monika Bütler. 2007. *Information Economics*. London: Routledge.

Blau, Peter, Cecilia McHugh Falbe, William McKinley, and Tracy Phelps. 1976. 'Technology and Organization in Manufacturing'. *Administration Science Quarterly* 21/1: 20–40.

Blustein, Paul. 2001. *The Chastening: Inside the Crisis that Rocked the Global Financial System and Humbled the IMF*. Oxford: Public Affairs.

—— 2005. *And the Money Kept Rolling In (and Out): Wall Street, the IMF, and the Bankrupting of Argentina*. New York: Public Affairs.

Boczkowski, Pablo. 2004. *Digitizing the News. Innovation in Online Newspapers*. Cambridge MA: MIT Press.

Boehm, Stephan. 1994. 'Hayek on Knowledge: Some Question Marks'. In M. Colonna and H. Hagemann (eds.), *The Economics of F. A. Hayek*. Vol. 2, *Capitalism, Socialism and Knowledge*, pp. 160–77, Aldershot: Elgar.

Bogdan, Radu. 1994. *Grounds for Cognition. How Goal-Guided Behavior Shapes the Mind*. Totowa NJ: Lawrence Erlbaum.

Boltanski, Luc and Eve Chiapello. 1999. *Le nouvel esprit du capitalisme*. Paris: Gallimard.

—— and Laurent Thévenot. 1991. *De la justification. Les économies de la grandeur*. Paris: Gallimard.

—— —— 2006. *On Justification. Economies of Worth*, trans. Catherine Porter. Princeton NJ: Princeton University Press.

Bolton, Gary, Ben Greiner, and Axel Ockenfels. 2008. 'Engineering Trust. Reciprocity and Strategic Timing in the Production of Reputation Information'. Paper presented at the NSF-DFG Conference Contextualizing Economic Behavior, New York City, August 2008.

—— Elena Katok, and Axel Ockenfels. 2005. 'How Effective are Online Reputation Mechanisms? An Experimental Study'. *Management Science* 50/11: 1587–602.

Bornschier, Volker. 2005. *Culture and Politics in Economic Development*. London: Routledge.

Bourdieu, Pierre. 1979. *La distinction. Critique sociale du jugement*. Paris: Minuit.

—— 1980. *Le sens pratique*. Paris: Minuit.

—— 1992. *Les règles de l'art. Genèse et structure du champ littéraire*. Paris: Seuil.

—— 1994. *Raisons pratiques. Sur la théorie de l'action*. Paris: Seuil.

Bowker, Geoffrey C. 1994. *Science on the Run. Information Management and Industrial Geophysics at Schlumberger, 1920–1940*. Cambridge MA: MIT Press.

Breslau, Daniel 2003. 'Economics Invents the Economy: Mathematics, Statistics, and Models in the Work of Irving Fisher and Wesley Mitchell'. *Theory and Society* 32: 379–411.

—— 2007. 'The Everyday Platonism of Market Designers. Economics and the Restructuring of Markets for a Reliable Power Supply'. *Paper presented at the conference Making, Evaluating, and Using Social Scientific Knowledge. The Underground of Practice. December 2007, New York: Russell Sage Foundation.*

—— and Yuval Yonay. 1999. 'Beyond Metaphor. Mathematical Models in Economics as Empirical Research'. *Science in Context* 12/2: 317–32.

Breton, Yves. 1992. 'L'économie politique et les mathématiques en France 1800–1940'. *Histoire et mesure* 7/1–2: 25–52.

Bruce, Brian. 2002. 'Stock Analysts: Experts on Whose Behalf?' *Journal of Psychology and Financial Markets* 3/4: 198–201.

Bruegger, Urs. 1999. 'Wie handeln Devisenhändler? Eine ethnographische Studie über Akteure in einem globalen Markt'. PhD dissertation, University of Sankt Gallen.

Buffett, Warren. 2008. 'Buy American. I Am'. *New York Times,* 17 October 2008. Downloaded at http://www.nytimes.com/2008/10/17/opinion/17buffett.html?_r=1&scp=1&sq=buy%20american.%20i%20am&st=cse.

Burt, Roland. 2001. 'Bandwidth and Echo. Trust, Information, and Gossip in Social Networks'. In James E. Rauch and Alessandra Casella (eds.), *Networks and Markets*, pp. 30–74, New York: Russell Sage Foundation.

—— 2005. *Brokerage and Closure. An Introduction to Social Capital.* Oxford: Oxford University Press.

Buskens, Vincent and Arnout van de Rijt. 2008. 'Dynamics of Networks if Everyone Strives for Structural Holes'. *American Journal of Sociology* 114/2: 371–407.

Button, Graham. 2008. 'Against "Distributed Cognition"'. *Theory, Culture & Society* 25/2: 87–104.

Callon, Michel. 1998. 'Introduction'. In Michel Callon (ed.), *Laws of Markets*, pp. 1–51, Oxford: Blackwell.

—— 2007*a*. 'What Does It Mean to Say That Economics Is Performative?' In Donald MacKenzie, Fabian Muniesa, and Lucia Siu (eds.), *Do Economists Make Markets? On The Performativity of Economics*, pp. 311–57, Princeton NJ: Princeton University Press.

—— 2007*b*. 'An Essay on the Growing Contribution of Economic Markets to the Proliferation of the Social'. *Theory, Culture & Society* 24/7–8: 139–63.

—— and John Law. 2003. *On Qualculation, Agency and Otherness.* Published by the Centre for Science Studies, Lancaster University, at http://www.comp.lancs.ac.uk/sociology/papers/Callon-Law-Qualculation-Agency-Otherness.pdf.

—— and Fabian Muniesa. 2005. 'Economic Markets as Calculative Collective Devices'. *Organization Studies* 26/8: 1229–250.

Capurro, Rafael and Bjorn Hjørland. 2003. 'The Concept of Information'. *Annual Review of Information Science and Technology* 56/1: 343–411.

Carrier, James. 1996. 'Exchange'. In Alan Barnard and Jonathan Spencer (eds.), *Encyclopedia of Social and Cultural Anthropology*, pp. 218–21, London: Routledge.

Carruthers, Bruce. 1996. *City of Capital. Politics and Markets in the English Financial Revolution.* Princeton NJ: Princeton University Press.

—— and Laura Ariovich. 2004. 'The Sociology of Property Rights'. *Annual Review of Sociology* 30: 23–46.

Carruthers, Bruce and Sarah L. Babb. 1996. 'The Color of Money and the Nature of Value. Greenbacks and Gold in Postbellum America'. *American Journal of Sociology* 101/6: 1556–91.

—— —— 2000. *Economy/Society. Markets, Meanings, and Social Structure*. Thousand Oaks CA: Pine Forge Press.

—— and Wendy Nelson Espeland. 1991. 'Accounting for Rationality. Double-Entry Bookkeeping and the Rhetoric of Economic Rationality'. *American Journal of Sociology* 97/1: 31–69.

—— and Arthur L. Stinchcombe. 2001. 'The Social Structure of Liquidity. Flexibility in Markets, States, and Organizations'. In Arthur L. Stinchcombe, *When Formality Works. Authority and Abstraction in Law and Organizations*, pp. 100–39, Chicago: University of Chicago Press.

Chen, Yan and Robert Gazzale. 2004. 'When Does Learning in Games Generate Convergence to Nash Equilibrium? The Role of Supermodularity in an Experimental Setting'. *American Economic Review* 94/5: 1505–35.

Chorev, Nitsan. 2005. 'The Institutional Project of Neo-Liberal Globalism. The Case of the WTO'. *Theory and Society* 34: 317–55.

—— 2007. *Remaking US Trade Policy. From Protectionism to Globalization*. Ithaca NY: Cornell University Press.

Clark, Colin and Trevor J. Pinch. 1995. *The Hard Sell. The Art of Street-Wise Selling*. New York: Harper Collins.

Coase, Ronald. 2005. 'The Institutional Structure of Production'. In Claude Ménard and Mary M. Shirley (eds.), *Handbook of New Institutional Economics*, pp. 31–9, Berlin: Springer.

Cohen, Lizbeth. 2003. *A Consumer's Republic. The Politics of Mass Consumption in Postwar America*. New York: Vintage.

Collins, Harry and Robert Evans. 2002. 'The Third Wave of Science Studies: Studies of Expertise and Experience'. *Social Studies of Science* 32/2: 235–96.

Collins, Randall. 2004. *Interaction Ritual Chains*. Princeton NJ: Princeton University Press.

Cook, Karen S., Russell Hardin, and Margaret Levi. 2005. *Cooperation without Trust?* New York: Russell Sage Foundation.

Cootner, Paul (ed.). 1964. *The Random Character of Stock Market Prices*. Cambridge MA: MIT Press.

Coslor, Erica. 2009. 'Hostile Worlds. Questionable Speculation and Contests of Meaning. Three Types of Conflict around Art'. Paper presented in the Sociology Department, University of Edinburgh, 28 January 2009.

Coulter, Jeff. 1995. 'The Informed Neuron. Issues in the Use of Information Theory in the Behavioral Sciences'. *Minds and Machines* 5/4: 583–596.

—— 1999. 'Discourse and Mind'. *Human Studies* 22: 163–81.

Creswell, Julie and Landon Thomas. 2009. 'The Talented Mr. Madoff. *New York Times*, 25 January 2009. Downloaded at http://www.nytimes.com/2009/01/25/business/25bernie.html?scp=1&sq=the%20talented%20mr.%20madoff&st=cse.

Cronon, William. 1991. *Nature's Metropolis. Chicago and the Great West*. New York: W.W. Norton.

Dash, Eric and Andrew Ross Sorkin. 2008. 'Citicorp Buys Banking Operations of Wachovia'. *New York Times*, 30 September 2008. Downloaded at http://www.nytimes.com/2008/09/30/business/30bank.html?scp=1&sq=Citicorp%20buys%20banking%20operations%20of%20wachovia&st=cse.

Davis, Gerald F. 2005. 'New Directions in Corporate Governance'. *Annual Review of Sociology* 31: 143–62.

—— and Gregory Robbins. 2005. 'Nothing but Net? Networks and Status in Corporate Governance'. In Karin Knorr Cetina and Alex Preda (eds.), *The Sociology of Financial Markets*, pp. 290–311, Oxford: Oxford University Press.

Desrosières, Alain. 1998. *The Politics of Large Numbers. A History of Statistical Reasoning.* Cambridge MA: Harvard University Press.

Didier, Emmanuel. 2007. 'Do Statistics "Perform" the Economy?' In Donald MacKenzie, Fabian Muniesa, and Lucia Siu (eds.), *Do Economists Make Markets? On the Performativity of Economics*, pp. 276–310, Princeton NJ: Princeton University Press.

DiMaggio, Paul. 1997. 'Culture and Cognition'. *Annual Review of Sociology* 23: 263–87.

—— and Walter W. Powell. 1991. 'The Iron Cage Revisited. Institutional Isomorphism and Collective Rationality in Organization Fields'. In Walter W. Powell and Paul J. DiMaggio (eds.), *The New Institutionalism in Organizational Analysis*, pp. 63–82, Chicago: University of Chicago Press.

Dimson, Elroy and Massoud Mussavian. 1998. 'A Brief History of Market Efficiency'. *European Financial Management* 4/1: 91–103.

Dobbin, Frank. 1994. *Forging Industrial Policy. The United States, Britain, and France in the Railway Age.* Cambridge: Cambridge University Press.

—— 2005. 'Comparative and Historical Approaches to Economic Sociology'. In Neil Smelser and Richard Swedberg (eds.), *The Handbook of Economic Sociology*, 2nd edn, pp. 26–48, Princeton NJ and New York: Princeton University Press and the Russell Sage Foundation.

Dowd, Maureen. 2009. 'No Boiled Carrots'. *New York Times*, 17 March 2009. Downloaded at http://nytimes.com/2009/03/18/opinion.18dowd.html.

Downey, Gregory J. 2000. 'Running Somewhere between Men and Women: Gender in the Construction of the Telegraph Messenger Boy'. *Knowledge and Society* 12: 129–52.

—— 2002. *Telegraph Messenger Boys. Labor, Technology, and Geography 1850–1950.* New York: Routledge.

Duneier, Mitchell. 1999. *Sidewalk.* New York: Farrar, Straus, and Giroux.

Durkheim, Émile. [1893] 1984. *The Division of Labor in Society.* New York: The Free Press.

—— [1915] 1965. *The Elementary Forms of Religious Life.* New York: The Free Press.

Eckel, Catherine C. and Rick Wilson. 2007. 'Social Learning in Coordination Games. Does Status Matter?' *Experimental Economics* 10/3: 317–29.

England, Paula. 1993. 'The Separate Self. Androcentric Bias in Neoclassical Assumptions'. In Marianne A. Ferber and Julie A. Nelson (eds.), *Beyond Economic Man. Feminist Theory and Economics*, pp. 36–53, Chicago: University of Chicago Press.

Ensminger, Jean. 1992. *Making a Market. The Institutional Transformation of an African Society.* Cambridge: Cambridge University Press.

Espeland, Wendy. 2001. 'Commensuration and Cognition'. In Karen Cerulo (ed.), *Cognition in Mind*, pp. 63–88, New York: Routledge.

—— and Michael Sauder. 2007. 'Rankings and Reactivity. How Public Measures Recreate Social Worlds'. *American Journal of Sociology* 113/1: 1–40.

—— and Mitchell Stevens. 1998. 'Commensuration as a Social Process'. *Annual Review of Sociology* 24: 313–43.

Esping-Andersen, Gøsta. 1990. *The Three Worlds of Welfare Capitalism.* Princeton NJ: Princeton University Press.

Evans, Robert. 2005. 'Introduction. Demarcation Socialized. Constructing Boundaries and Recognizing Differences'. *Science, Technology, & Human Values* 30/1: 3–16.

—— 2007. 'Social Networks and Private Spaces in Economic Forecasting'. *Studies in History and Philosophy of Science* 38: 686–97.

Feiger, George. 1976. 'What Is Speculation?' *The Quarterly Journal of Economics* 90/4: 677–87.

Finlay, William and James E. Coverdill. 2002. *Headhunters. Matchmaking in the Labor Market.* Ithaca NY: Cornell University Press.

Flam, Helena. 2002. 'Corporate Emotions and Emotions in Corporations'. In Jack Barbalet (ed.), *Emotions and Sociology*, pp. 90–112, Oxford: Blackwell.

Fleck, Christian. 2007. *Transatlantische Bereicherungen. Die Erfindung der empirischen Sozialforschung.* Frankfurt: Suhrkamp.

Flichy, Patrice. 1995. *Dynamics of Modern Communication: The Shaping and Impact of New Communication Technologies.* London: Sage Publications.

Fligstein, Neil. 1990. *The Transformation of Corporate Control.* Cambridge MA: Harvard University Press.

—— 1996. 'Markets as Politics. A Political-Cultural Approach to Market Institutions'. *American Sociological Review* 61/4: 656–73.

—— 2001. *The Architecture of Markets. An Economic Sociology of Twenty-First Capitalist Societies.* Princeton NJ: Princeton University Press.

—— 2002. 'Agreements, Disagreements, and Opportunities in the "New Sociology of Markets"'. In Mauro F. Guillén et al. (eds.), *The New Economic Sociology. Developments in an Emerging Field*, pp. 61–78, New York: Russell Sage Foundation.

—— and Luke Dauter. 2007. 'The Sociology of Markets'. *Annual Review of Sociology* 33: 105–28.

—— and Taekjin Shin. 2004. 'The Transformation of the American Economy, 1984–2001'. Department of Sociology, UCLA, paper #16.

Fogarty, Timothy J. and Rodney K. Rogers. 2005. 'Financial Analysts' Reports. An Extended Institutional Theory Evaluation'. *Accounting, Organizations and Society* 30: 331–56.

Fourcade, Marion. 2006. 'The Construction of a Global Profession: The Transnationalization of Economics'. *American Journal of Sociology* 112/1: 145–94.

—— 2007. 'Theories of Markets and Theories of Society'. *American Behavioral Scientist* 50/8: 1015–34.

—— and Kieran Healy. 2007. 'Moral Views of Market Society'. *Annual Review of Sociology* 33: 285–311.

François, Pierre. 2008. *Sociologie des marchés.* Paris: Armand Colin.

Friedman, Daniel and Shyam Sunder. 1994. *Experimental Methods. A Primer for Economists.* Cambridge: Cambridge University Press.

Friedman, Milton. 1956. 'The Quantity Theory of Money—A Restatement'. In Milton Friedman (ed.), *Studies in the Quantity Theory of Money*, pp. 3–24, Chicago: University of Chicago Press.

Galison, Peter. 2003. *Einstein's Clocks, Poincaré's Maps. Empires of Time.* London: Hodder and Stoughton.

Gambetta, Diego. 1993. *The Sicilian Mafia. The Business of Private Protection.* Cambridge MA: Harvard University Press.

Garcia-Parpet, Marie-France. [1986] 2007. 'The Social Construction of a Perfect Market. The Strawberry Auction at Fontaines-en-Sologne'. In Donald MacKenzie, Fabian Muniesa, and Lucia Siu (eds.), *Do Economists Make Markets? On the Performativity of Economics*, pp. 20–53, Princeton NJ: Princeton University Press.

Garfinkel, Harold. 1963. 'A Conception of, and Experiments with "Trust" as a Condition of Stable Concerted Actions'. In O. J. Harvey (ed.), *Motivation and Social Interaction. Cognitive Determinants*, pp. 187–238, New York: The Ronald Press Co.

—— 1967. *Studies in Ethnomethodology*. Englewood Cliffs NJ: Prentice Hall.

—— 2008. *Toward a Sociological Theory of Information*. Ed. Anne Warfield Rawls. Boulder CO: Paradigm Publishers.

—— and Harvey Sacks. [1970] 1990. 'On Formal Structures of Practical Actions'. In Jeff Coulter (ed.), *Ethnomethodological Sociology*, pp. 55–84, Brookfield VT: Edward Elgar.

Gasparino, Charles. 2005. *Blood on the Street. The Sensational Inside Story of How Wall Street Analysts Duped a Generation of Investors*. New York: The Free Press.

Geertz, Clifford, Hildred Geertz, and Lawrence Rosen. 1979. *Meaning and Order in the Moroccan Society. Three Essays in Cultural Analysis*. Cambridge: Cambridge University Press.

Gereffi, Gary. 2005. 'The Global Economy. Organization, Governance, and Development'. In Neil Smelser and Richard Swedberg (eds.), *The Handbook of Economic Sociology*, 2nd edn, pp. 160–82, Princeton NJ and New York: Princeton University Press and the Russell Sage Foundation.

Gertner, Jon. 2008. 'Capitalism to the Rescue'. *New York Times Magazine*, 5 October 2008. Downloaded at http://www.nytimes.com/2008/10/05/magazine.

Gintis, Herbert. 2000. *Game Theory Evolving. A Problem-Centered Introduction to Modeling Strategic Behavior*. Princeton NJ: Princeton University Press.

Godechot, Olivier. 2007. *Working rich. Salaires, bonus et appropriation du profit dans l'industrie financière*. Paris: La Découverte.

Goffman, Erving. 1959. *The Presentation of the Self in Everyday Life*. New York: Doubleday.

—— 1970. *Strategic Interaction*. Oxford: Basil Blackwell.

—— 1971. *Relations in Public. Microstudies of the Public Order*. London: Allen Lane.

—— 1972. *Encounters. Two Studies in the Sociology of Interaction*. Harmondsworth: Penguin.

—— 1974. *Frame Analysis*. New York: Harper Collins.

—— 1981. *Frames of Talk*. Philadelphia: University of Pennsylvania Press.

—— 1983. 'The Interaction Order'. *American Sociological Review* 48/1: 1–17.

Goody, Jack. 1986. *The Logic of Writing and the Organization of Society*. Cambridge: Cambridge University Press.

Granovetter, Mark. 1973. 'The Strength of Weak Ties'. *American Journal of Sociology* 78/6: 1360–80.

—— 1985. 'Economic Action and Social Structure. The Problem of Embeddedness'. *American Journal of Sociology* 91/3: 481–510.

Grimpe, Barbara. 2009. 'Nationaloekonomien sichtbar machen. Skopische Systeme und Monitoring-Kultur im transnationalen Schuldenmanagement'. PhD thesis, University of Konstanz.

Grint, Keith and Steve Woolgar. 1995. 'On Some Failures of Nerve in Constructivist and Feminist Analyses of Technology'. *Science, Technology & Human Values* 20/3: 286–310.

Guala, Francesco. 2001. 'Building Economic Machines. The FCC Auctions'. *Studies in History and Philosophy of Science* 32: 453–77.

Guala, Francesco. 2005. *The Methodology of Experimental Economics*. Cambridge; Cambridge University Press.

Guthrie, Doug. 1999. *Dragon in a Three-Piece Suit. The Emergence of Capitalism in China.* Princeton NJ: Princeton University Press.

Harper, Richard. 1998. *Inside the IMF. An Ethnography of Documents, Technology, and Organizational Action.* London: Academic Press.

Harrington, Brooke. 2008. *Pop Finance. Investment Clubs and the New Investor Populism.* Princeton NJ: Princeton University Press.

Harris, Lawrence. 2008. 'Reputation in Block Trading. Implications for Floor versus Automated Trading'. Paper presented at the NSF-DFG Conference Contextualizing Economic Behavior, New York City, August 2008.

Hasselström, Anna. 2003. 'On and Off the Trading Floor. An Inquiry into the Everyday Fashioning of Financial Market Knowledge'. PhD dissertation, Stockholm University.

Hayek, Friedrich von. 1976. *Individualism and Economic Order*. London: Routledge.

—— 1978. *New Studies in Philosophy, Politics, Economics, and the History of Ideas.* Chicago: University of Chicago Press.

Healy, Kieran. 2006. *Last Best Gifts. Altruism and the Market for Human Blood and Organs.* Chicago: University of Chicago Press.

Heath, Christian and Paul Luff. 2007. 'Ordering Competition. The Interactional Accomplishment of the Sale of Art and Antiques at Auction'. *British Journal of Sociology* 58/1: 63–85.

—— Marcus Sanchez Svensson, Jon Hindmarsh, Paul Luff, and Dirk von Lehn. 2002. 'Configuring Awareness'. *Computer Supported Cooperative Work* 11: 317–47.

Heidegger, Martin. [1926] 2001. *Sein und Zeit.* Tübingen: Max Niemeyer.

Henderson, Kathryn. 1998. *On Line and On Paper. Visual Representations, Visual Culture, and Computer Graphics in Design Engineering.* Cambridge MA: MIT Press.

Hicks, Alexander and Lane Kenworthy. 2003. 'Varieties of Welfare Capitalism'. *Socio-Economic Review* 1/1: 27–62.

Hirsch, Paul and Michael Lounsbury. 1997. 'Ending the Family Quarrel. Toward a Reconciliation of "Old" and "New" Institutionalisms'. *American Behavioral Scientist* 40/4: 406–18.

Hirshleifer, Jack. 1975. 'Speculation and Equilibrium. Information, Risk, and Markets'. *Quarterly Journal of Economics* 89/4: 519–42.

Holm, Peter and Kåre Nolde Nielsen. 2007. 'Framing Fish, Making Markets. The Construction of Individual Transferable Quotas (ITQ)'. In Michel Callon, Yuval Millo, and Fabian Muniesa (eds.), *Market Devices*, pp. 173–95, Oxford: Blackwell.

Hsu, Greta, Michael T. Hannan, and Özgecan Koçak. 2009. 'Multiple Category Memberships in Markets. An Integrative Theory and Two Empirical Tests'. *American Sociological Review* 74: 150–69.

Husserl, Edmund. 1995. *Cartesianische Meditationen.* Hamburg: Felix Meiner.

Hutchins, Edwin. 1995. *Cognition in the Wild.* Cambridge MA: MIT Press.

Ingham, Geoffrey. 2004. *The Nature of Money.* Cambridge: Polity.

Jovanovic, Franck. 2008. 'The Construction of the Canonical History of Financial Economics'. *History of Political Economy* 40/2: 213–42.

—— and Philippe Le Gall. 2001. 'Does God Practice a Random Walk? The "Financial Physics" of a Nineteenth-Century Forerunner, Jules Regnault'. *European Journal of the History of Economic Thought* 8/3: 332–62.

Kalthoff, Herbert. 2005. 'Practices of Calculation. Economic Representations and Risk Management'. *Theory, Culture & Society* 22/2: 69–97.

Keister, Lisa. 2001. 'Exchange Structures in Transition: Lending and Trade Relations in Chinese Business Groups'. *American Sociological Review* 66/3: 336–60.

Kennedy, Mark Thomas. 2008. 'Getting Counted. Markets, Media, and Reality'. *American Sociological Review* 73: 270–95.

Khurana, Rakesh. 2002. *Searching for a Corporate Savior. The Irrational Quest for Charismatic CEOs.* Princeton NJ: Princeton University Press.

—— 2007. *From Higher Aims to Hired Hands. The Social Transformation of American Business Schools and the Unfulfilled Promise of Management as a Profession.* Princeton NJ: Princeton University Press.

Kirman, Alan. 2001. 'Market Organization and Individual Behaviour. Evidence from Fish Markets'. In James E. Rauch and Alessandra Casella (eds.), *Networks and Markets*, pp. 155–95, New York: Russell Sage Foundation.

Kleipa, Sandra. 2004. 'Überraschungseier—mit Spannung, Spiel und Schokolade zur Wertanlage? Was den Wert einer Plastikfigur ausmacht'. [Surprise eggs—Playful investments? The value of a plastic toy]. Seminar report, Course on Econography, University of Konstanz, summer semester 2004.

Knorr Cetina, Karin. 1999. *Epistemic Cultures. How the Sciences Make Knowledge.* Cambridge MA: Harvard University Press.

—— 2003. 'From Pipes to Scopes. The Flow Architecture of Financial Markets'. *Distinktion* 7: 7–23.

—— 2005. 'How Are Global Markets Global? The Architecture of a Flow World'. In Karin Knorr Cetina and Alex Preda (eds.), *The Sociology of Financial Markets*, pp. 38–61, Oxford: Oxford University Press.

—— 2009. 'The Synthetic Situation. Interactionism for a Global World'. *Symbolic Interaction* 32/1: 61–87.

—— and Urs Bruegger. 2002. 'Global Microstructures. The Virtual Societies of Financial Markets'. *American Journal of Sociology* 107/4: 905–50.

—— and Barbara Grimpe. 2008. 'Global Financial Technologies. Scopic Systems That Raise the World'. In Trevor Pinch and Richard Swedberg (eds.), *Living in a Material World. Economic Sociology Meets Science and Technology Studies*, pp. 161–90, Cambridge MA: MIT Press.

—— and Martina Merz. 1997. 'Deconstruction in a "Thinking" Science: Theoretical Physicists at Work'. *Social Studies of Science* 27: 73–111.

—— and Alex Preda. 2007. 'The Temporalization of Financial Markets. From Network to Flow'. *Theory, Culture & Society* 24/7–8: 116–38.

Kollewe, Julia. 2008. 'How the HBOS Attack Unfolded'. *The Guardian*, 20 March 2008. Downloaded at http://www.guardian.co.uk/business/2008/mar/20/hbosbusiness.marketturmoil.

Krasa, Stefan and Nicholas C. Yannelis. 1994. 'The Value Allocation of an Economy with Differential Information'. *Econometrica* 62/4: 881–900.

Krippner, Greta. 2001. 'The Elusive Market. Embeddedness and the Paradigm of Economic Sociology'. *Theory and Society* 30: 775–810.

—— 2005. 'The Financialization of the American Economy'. *Socio-Economic Review* 3: 173–208.

Krippner, Greta. and Anthony S. Alvarez. 2007. 'Embeddedness and the Intellectual Projects of Economic Sociology'. *Annual Review of Sociology* 33: 219–40.

Krugman, Paul. 2009. 'Banking on the Brink'. *New York Times*, 23 February 2009. Downloaded at http://www.nytimes.com/2009/02/23/opinion/23krugman.html?scp=1&sq=banking%20on%20the%20brink&st=cse.

de La Pradelle, Michèle. 1996. *Les vendredis de Carpentras. Faire son marché en Provence ou ailleurs.* Paris: Fayard.

Lamont, Michèle and Virág Molnár. 2002. 'The Study of Boundaries in the Social Sciences'. *Annual Review of Sociology* 28: 167–95.

Langley, Paul. 2008. *The Everyday Life of Global Finance. Saving and Borrowing in Anglo-America.* Oxford: Oxford University Press.

Lash, Scott. 2002. *Critique of Information.* London: Sage.

Latour, Bruno. 2005. *Reassembling the Social. An Introduction to Actor-Network Theory.* Oxford: Oxford University Press.

Laube, Stefan. 2008*a*. 'The Sounds of the Market. How Brokers at the Electronic Exchange Keep the Pace with a "Silent" Market-on-screen'. Paper presented at the 38th World Congress of the IIS, Budapest, Hungary.

—— 2008*b*. ' "Scheiss-Markt!" Embodied Emotions als Beobachtungs- und Erkenntnisinstrumente im informationstechnologischen Finanzmarkt' ['Shit-Market!' Embodied Emotions as Observational and Epistemic Instruments in Technology-supported Financial Markets]. Paper presented in the research colloquium on markets and information, University of Konstanz, December 2008.

Layne, Linda. 2000. 'The Cultural Fix. An Anthropological Contribution to Science and Technology Studies'. *Science, Technology & Human Values* 25/4: 492–519.

LeRoy, Stephen. 1989. 'Efficient Capital Markets and Martingales'. *Journal of Economic Literature* XXVII: 1583–621.

Levin, Peter. 2001. 'Gendering the Market. Temporality, Work, and Gender on a National Futures Exchange'. *Work and Occupations* 28/1: 112–30.

Lewis, Mervyn K. and Paul D. Mizen. 2000. *Monetary Economics.* Oxford: Oxford University Press.

Lewis, Michael. 2009. 'Wall Street on the Tundra'. *Vanity Fair*, April 2009, Downloaded at http://www.vanityfair.com/politics/features/2009/04/iceland200904.

Livingston, Eric. 1999. 'Cultures of Proving'. *Social Studies of Science* 29/6: 867–88.

—— 2006. 'The Context of Proving'. *Social Studies of Science* 36/1: 39–68.

Llewellyn, Nick and Robin Burrow. 2008. 'Streetwise Sales and the Social Order of City Streets'. *British Journal of Sociology* 59/3: 561–83.

Lo, Andrew and Dmitri Repin. 2002. 'The Psychophysiology of Real Time Financial Risk Processing'. *Journal of Cognitive Neuroscience* 14: 323–39.

Lounsbury, Michael and Marc Ventresca. 2003. 'The New Structuralism in Organizational Theory'. *Organization* 10/3: 457–80.

Lowenstein, Roger. 2008. 'What's Really Wrong with the Price of Oil'. *New York Times Magazine*, 19 October 2008. Downloaded at http://www.nytimes.com/2008/10/19/magazine/19oil-t.html?scp=1&sq=what%27s%20really%20wrong%20with%20the%20price%20of%20oil&st=cse.

Luhmann, Niklas. 1990. *Essays on Self-Reference.* New York: Columbia University Press.

Lynch, Michael. 1992. 'Extending Wittgenstein. The Pivotal Move from Epistemology to the Sociology of Science'. In Andrew Pickering (ed.), *Science as Practice and Culture*, pp. 215–65, Chicago: University of Chicago Press.

Machlup, Fritz. 1984. *The Economics of Information and Human Capital*. Princeton NJ: Princeton University Press.

MacKenzie, Donald. 2005. 'How a Superportfolio Emerges: Long-Term Capital Management and the Sociology of Arbitrage'. In Karin Knorr Cetina and Alex Preda (eds.), *The Sociology of Financial Markets*, pp. 62–83, Oxford: Oxford University Press.

—— 2006. *An Engine, Not a Camera. How Financial Models Shape Markets*. Cambridge MA: MIT Press.

—— 2008. 'End-of-the-World Trade'. *London Review of Books* 30/9: 24–6.

—— 2009. *Material Markets. How Economic Agents Are Constructed*. Oxford: Oxford University Press.

—— and Judith Wajcman (eds.). 1985. *The Social Shaping of Technology*. Buckingham: Open University Press.

Malinowski, Bronislaw. 1922. *Argonauts of the Western Pacific. An Account of the Native Enterprise and Adventure in the Archipelagoes of Melanesian New Guinea*. London: G. Routledge and Sons.

Mankiw, N. Gregory. 1997. *Principles of Economics*. Forth Worth TX: The Dryden Press.

Mars, Frank. 1998. '"Wir sind alle Seher". Die Praxis der Aktienanalyse'. PhD dissertation, University of Bielefeld, Germany.

Martin, John Levi. 2009. *Social Structures*. Princeton NJ: Princeton University Press.

Marx, Karl. [1872] 2002. *Das Kapital*. 2nd edn. Köln: Parkland.

—— and Friedrich Engels. [1848] 2004. *Manifesto of the Communist Party*. Downloaded at http://www.marxists.org.

Maurer, Bill. 2005. *Mutual Life, Limited Islamic Banking, Alternative Currencies, Lateral Reason*. Princeton NJ: Princeton University Press.

Mauss, Marcel. [1950] 1999. *Sociologie et anthropologie*. Paris: Quadrige/PUF.

Mead, Rebecca. 2002. 'Tales Out of Preschool'. *The New Yorker*, 2 December 2002. Downloaded at http://www.newyorker.com/archive/2002/12/02/021202ta_talk_mead.

Ménard, Claude 1980. 'Three Forms of Resistance to Statistics: Say, Cournot, Walras'. *History of Political Economy* 12/4: 524–41.

—— 2005. 'A New Institutional Approach to Organization'. In Claude Ménard and Mary M. Shirley (eds.), *Handbook of New Institutional Economics*, pp. 281–318, Berlin: Springer.

Merton, Robert King. 1968. *Social Theory and Social Structure*. New York: The Free Press.

Meyer, John and Brian Rowan. 1977. 'Institutionalized Organization: Formal Structure as Myth and Ceremony'. *American Journal of Sociology* 83/2: 340–63.

Mihm, Stephen. 2008. 'Dr. Doom'. *New York Times Magazine*, 15 August, 2008. Downloaded at http://www.nytimes.com/2008/08/17/magazine/17pessimist-t.html?scp=1&sq=dr.%20doom&st=cse.

Milgate, Murray. 1989. 'Equilibrium: Development of the Concept'. In John Eatwell, Murray Milgate, and Peter Newman (eds.), *The Invisible Hand*, pp. 105–13, London: Macmillan.

Miller, Michael B. 1981. *The Bon Marché. Bourgeois Culture and the Department Store, 1869–1920*. Princeton NJ: Princeton University Press.

Miller, Peter. 2001. 'Governing by Numbers. Why Calculative Practices Matter'. *Social Research* 68/2: 379–96.

—— and Michael Power. 1995. 'Calculating Corporate Failure'. In Yves Dezelay and David Sugarman (eds.), *Professional Competition and Professional Power. Lawyers, Accountants, and the Social Construction of Markets*, pp. 51–76, London: Routledge.

Mirowski, Philip. 1989. *More Heat than Light. Economics as Social Physics, Physics as Nature's Economics*. Cambridge: Cambridge University Press.

—— (ed.). 1994. *Natural Images in Economic Thought. 'Markets Read in Tooth and Claw'*. Cambridge: Cambridge University Press.

—— 2002. *Machine Dreams. Economics Becomes a Cyborg Science*. Cambridge: Cambridge University Press.

—— 2005. 'How Positivism Made a Pact with the Postwar Social Sciences in the United States'. In George Steinmetz (ed.), *The Politics of Method in the Human Sciences. Positivism and Its Epistemological Others*, pp. 142–72, Durham NC: Duke University Press.

—— 2007. 'Markets Come to Bits: Evolution, Computation and Markomata in Economic Science'. *Journal of Economic Behavior & Organization* 63: 209–42.

—— and Edward Nik-Khah. 2007. 'Markets Made Flesh. Performativity, and a Problem in Science Studies, Augmented with Consideration of the FCC Auctions'. In Donald MacKenzie, Fabian Muniesa, and Lucia Siu (eds.), *Do Economists Make Markets? On the Performativity of Economics*, pp. 190–224, Princeton NJ: Princeton University Press.

Mohr, John C. and Roger Friedland. 2008. 'Theorizing the Institution. Foundations, Duality, and Data'. *Theory and Society* 37: 421–6.

—— and Harrison C. White. 2008. 'How to Model an Institution'. *Theory and Society* 37: 485–512.

Muniesa, Fabian. 2005. 'Containing the Market. The Transition from Open Outcry to Electronic Trading at the Paris Bourse'. *Sociologie du travail* 47: 485–501.

—— and Michel Callon. 2007. 'Economic Experiments and the Construction of Markets'. In Donald MacKenzie, Fabian Muniesa, and Lucia Siu (eds.), *Do Economists Make Markets? On the Performativity of Economics*, pp. 163–89, Princeton NJ: Princeton University Press.

Neal, Larry. 1990. *The Rise of Financial Capitalism. International Capital in the Age of Reason*. Cambridge: Cambridge University Press.

Nippert-Eng, Christena. 1995. *Home and Work. Negotiating Boundaries through Everyday Life*. Chicago: University of Chicago Press.

Nocera, Joseph. 2009. 'Risk Mismanagement'. *New York Times Magazine*, 4 January 2009. Downloaded at http://www.nytimes.com/2009/01/04/magazine/04risk-t.html?scp=1&sq=-risk%20mismanagement&st=cse.

NYSE. 2008. Technology. Downloaded at http://www.nyse.com/PDFs/Education-Technology.pdf. on 26 November 2008.

O'Rourke, Kevin and Jeffrey Williamson. 1999. *Globalization and History: The Evolution of a Nineteenth-Century Atlantic Economy*. Cambridge MA: MIT Press.

—— —— 2000. *When Did Globalization Begin?* Cambridge MA: NBER Working Paper #7632.

—— —— 2001. *Globalization and Inequality*. Cambridge MA: NBER Working Paper #2685.

Olson, Mancur. 1965. *The Logic of Collective Action. Public Goods and the Theory of Groups*. Cambridge MA: Cambridge University Press.

Orr, Jackie. 2006. *Panic Diaries. A Genealogy of Panic Disorder*. Durham NC: Duke University Press.

Orr, Julian. 1996. *Talking about Machines. An Ethnography of a Modern Job*. Ithaca NY: ILR Press.

Orr, Winnie W. F. 2007. 'The *Bargaining* Genre. A Study of Retail Encounters in Traditional Chinese Local Markets'. *Language in Society* 36: 73–103.

Pardo-Guerra, Juan Pablo. 'Creating Flows of Interpersonal Bits. The Automation of the London Stock Exchange, 1955–1990'. *Economy and Society* 39, forthcoming.

—— 2009. 'Computerizing Finance. The Automation of the London Stock Exchange 1965–1995'. PhD thesis, University of Edinburgh.

Pentland, Alex (with Tracy Heibeck). 2008. *Honest Signals. How They Shape Our World.* Cambridge MA: MIT Press.

Perrow, Charles. 1999. *Normal Accidents. Living with High Risk Technologies.* 2nd edn. Princeton NJ: Princeton University Press.

—— 2002. *Organizing America. Wealth, Power, and the Origins of Corporate Capitalism.* Princeton NJ: Princeton University Press.

Peterson, Richard L. 2007. 'Affect and Financial Decision-Making: How Neuroscience Can Inform Market Participants'. *Journal of Behavioral Finance* 8/2: 1–9.

Pinch, Trevor and Frank Trocco. 2002. *Analog Days. The Invention and Impact of the Moog Synthesizer.* Cambridge MA: Harvard University Press.

Pitluck, Aaron. 2008. 'Moral Behavior in Stock Markets: Islamic Finance and Socially Responsible Investment'. In K. E. Browne and B. Lynne Milgram (eds.), *Economics and Morality: Anthropological Approaches,* pp. 233–55, Lanham MD: AltaMira Press.

Pixley, Jocelyn. 2002. 'Emotions and Economics'. In Jack Barbalet (ed.), *Emotions and Sociology,* pp. 69–89, Oxford: Blackwell.

—— 2004. *Emotions in Finance. Distrust and Uncertainty in Global Markets.* Cambridge: Cambridge University Press.

Podolny, Joel. 1993. 'A Status-Based Model of Market Competition'. *American Journal of Sociology* 98/4: 829–72.

—— 2001. 'Networks as the Pipes and Prisms of the Market'. *American Journal of Sociology* 107/1: 33–60.

—— 2005. *Status Signals. A Sociological Study of Market Competition.* Princeton NJ: Princeton University Press.

Polanyi, Karl. 1945. *Origins of Our Time. The Great Tranformation.* London: Victor Gollancz.

Poon, Martha. 2007. 'Scorecards as Devices for Consumer Credit: The Case of Fair, Isaac & Company Incorporated'. In Michel Callon, Yuval Millo, and Fabian Muniesa (eds.), *Market Devices,* pp. 284–306, Oxford: Blackwell.

—— 2009. 'From New Deal Institutions to Capital Markets: Commercial Consumer Risk Scores and the Making of Subprime Mortgage Finance'. *Accounting, Organizations and Society* 34/5: 654–74.

Poovey, Mary. 1998. *A History of the Modern Fact. Problems of Knowledge in the Sciences of Wealth and Society.* Chicago: University of Chicago Press.

—— 2002. 'Writing about Finance in Victorian England. Disclosure and Secrecy in the Culture of Investment'. *Victorian Studies* 45/1: 17–41.

—— 2008. *Genres of the Credit Economy. Mediating Value in Eighteenth and Nineteenth-Century Britain.* Chicago: University of Chicago Press.

Porter, Theodore M. 1994. 'Information, Power, and the View from Nowhere'. In Lisa Bud-Frierman (ed.), *Information Acumen. The Understanding and Use of Knowledge in Modern Business,* pp. 217–29, London: Routledge.

—— 1995. *Trust in Numbers. The Pursuit of Objectivity in Science and Public Life.* Princeton NJ: Princeton University Press.

Portes, Alejandro and Margarita Mooney. 2002. 'Social Capital and Community Development'. In Mauro F. Guillén, Randall Collins, Paula England, and Marshall Meyer (eds.), *The New*

Economic Sociology. Developments in an Emerging Field, pp. 303–29, New York: Russell Sage Foundation.

Potts, Jason. 2001. 'Knowledge and Markets'. *Journal of Evolutionary Economics* 11: 413–31.

Powell, Walter. 1990. 'Neither Market Nor Hierarchy. Network Forms of Organization'. *Research in Organizational Behavior* 12: 295–336.

—— 2001. 'The Capitalist Firm in the Twenty-First Century. Emerging Patterns in Western Enterprise'. In Paul DiMaggio (ed.), *The Twenty-First-Century Firm. Changing Economic Organization in International Perspective*, pp. 33–68, Princeton NJ: Princeton University Press.

—— Kenneth Koput and Laurel Smith-Doerr. 1996. 'Interorganizational Collaboration and the Locus of Innovation. Networks of Learning in Biotechnology'. *Administrative Science Quarterly* 41: 116–45.

—— Douglas White, Kenneth Koput, and Jason Owen-Smith. 2005. 'Network Dynamics and Field Evolution. The Growth of Interorganizational Collaboration in the Life Sciences'. *American Journal of Sociology* 110/4: 1132–205.

Power, Michael. 2005. 'Enterprise Risk Management and the Organization of Uncertainty in Financial Institutions'. In Karin Knorr Cetina and Alex Preda (eds.), *The Sociology of Financial Markets*, pp. 250–68, Oxford: Oxford University Press.

—— 2007. *Organized Uncertainty. Designing a World of Risk Management.* Oxford: Oxford University Press.

Prasad, Monica. 2006. *The Politics of Free Markets. The Rise of Neoliberal Economic Policies in Britain, France, Germany, & the United States.* Chicago: University of Chicago Press.

Preda, Alex. 2002. 'Financial Knowledge, Documents, and the Structures of Financial Activities'. *Journal of Contemporary Ethnography* 31/2: 207–39.

—— 2004. 'Informative Prices, Rational Investors: The Emergence of the Random Walk Hypothesis and the Nineteenth Century "Science of Financial Investments"'. *History of Political Economy* 36/2: 351–86.

—— 2005. 'Legitimacy and Status Groups in Financial Markets'. *British Journal of Sociology* 56/3: 451–71.

—— 2006. 'Socio-Technical Agency in Financial Markets: The Case of the Stock Ticker'. *Social Studies of Science* 26/5: 753–82.

—— 2007. 'Where Do Analysts Come From? The Case of Financial Chartism'. In Michel Callon, Yuval Millo, and Fabian Muniesa (eds.), *Market Devices*, pp. 40–64, Oxford: Blackwell.

—— 2009*a*. 'Brief Encounters. Calculation and the Interaction Order of Anonymous Electronic Markets'. *Accounting, Organizations and Society* 34/5: 675–93.

—— 2009*b*. *Framing Finance. The Boundaries of Markets and Modern Capitalism.* Chicago: University of Chicago Press.

Quinn, Sarah. 2008. 'The Transformation of Morals in Markets. Death, Benefits, and the Exchange of Life Insurance Policies'. *American Journal of Sociology* 114/3: 738–80.

Rauch, James E. and Gary G. Hamilton. 2001. 'Networks and Markets. Concepts for Bridging Disciplines'. In James E. Rauch and Alessandra Casella (eds.), *Networks and Markets*, pp. 1–29, New York: Russell Sage Foundation.

Rawls, Ann Warfield. 2008*a*. 'Harold Garfinkel, Ethnomethodology, and Workplace Studies'. *Organization Studies* 29/5: 701–32.

—— 2008*b*. 'Editor's Introduction'. In Harold Garfinkel, *Toward a Sociological Theory of Information*, ed. Anne Warfield Rawls, pp. 1–100, Boulder CO: Paradigm Publishers.

Reichmann, Werner. 2006. 'Institutionen, Methoden, Karrieren. Österreichische Konjunktur-forschung im soziologischen Vergleich'. PhD dissertation, University of Graz.

Rheinberger, Hans-Jörg. 1997. *Toward a History of Epistemic Things. Synthesizing Proteins in the Test Tube.* Stanford CA: Stanford University Press.

Ricciardi, Victor. 2008. 'The Psychology of Risk: The Behavioral Finance Perspective'. In Frank J. Fabozzi (ed.), *Handbook of Finance*, Vol. 2. *Investment Management and Financial Management*, pp. 85–111, New York: Wiley.

Roberts, John. 1991. 'Perfectly and Imperfectly Competitive Markets'. In John Eatwell, Murray Milgate, and Peter Newman (eds.), *The World of Economics*, pp. 534–43, London: Macmillan.

Roeren, Cecilie. 2008. 'The Interaction Order of Conspicuous Consumption'. MA thesis, University of Edinburgh.

Rosselli, John. 1989. 'From Princely Service to the Open Market. Singers of Italian Opera and Their Patrons, 1600–1850'. *Cambridge Opera Journal* 1/1: 1–32.

Rothschild, Michael and Joesph Stiglitz. 1976. 'Equilibrium in Competitive Insurance Markets. An Essay on the Economics of Imperfect Information'. *Quarterly Journal of Economics* 90/4: 629–49.

Sacks, Harvey. 1995. *Lectures in Conversation*, Vol. 2. Oxford: Blackwell.

—— Emmanuel Schegloff, and Gail Jefferson. 1974. 'A Simplest Systematics for the Organization of Turn Taking for Conversation'. *Language* 50/4: 696–735.

Sahlins, Marshall. 1972. *Stone Age Economics.* Chicago: Aldine-Atherton.

—— 2000. *Culture in Practice. Selected Essays.* New York: Zone Books.

Sassen, Saskia. 2001. *The Global City. New York, London, Tokyo.* Princeton NJ: Princeton University Press.

—— 2005. 'The Embeddedness of Electronic Markets. The Case of Global Capital Markets'. In Karin Knorr Cetina and Alex Preda (eds.), *The Sociology of Financial Markets*, pp. 17–37, Oxford: Oxford University Press.

—— 2006. *Cities in a World Economy.* 3rd edn. Thousand Oaks CA: Pine Forge Press.

Saxenian, AnnaLee. 1994. *Regional Advantage. Culture and Competition in Silicon Valley and Route 128.* Cambridge MA: Harvard University Press.

Schabas, Margaret. 2005. *The Natural Origins of Economics.* Chicago: University of Chicago Press.

Schor, Juliet B. and Douglas B. Holt (eds). 2000. *The Consumer Society Reader.* New York: The New Press.

Schryer, Stephen. 2007. 'Fantasies of the New Class. The New Criticism, Harvard Sociology, and the Idea of the University'. *PMLA* 122/3: 663–78.

Schull, Natasha Dow. 2005. 'Digital Gambling. The Coincidence of Desire and Design'. *Annals of the American Academy of Political and Social Science* 597: 65–81.

—— 2006. 'Machines, Medication, Modulation: Circuits of Dependency and Self-Care in Vegas'. *Culture, Medicine and Psychiatry* 30: 223–47.

—— and Caitlin Zaloom. 2008. 'The Computational Subject of Neuroeconomics'. Paper presented at the conference Our Brains, Ourselves, Harvard University, May 2008.

Schumpeter, Joseph. 1943. *Capitalism, Socialism, and Democracy.* London: George Allen & Unwin.

—— [1954] 1994. *History of Economic Analysis.* New York: Oxford University Press.

Schütz, Alfred. 2003. *Theorie der Lebenswelt 1. Die pragmatische Schichtung der Lebenswelt*, ed. Martin Endress and Ilja Srubar. Konstanz: UVK.

Schütz, Alfred and Thomas Luckmann. 2003. *Strukturen der Lebenswelt*. Konstanz: UVK.

SEC. 2008. U.S. Securities and Exchange Commission Litigation Release No. 20537, 24 April, 2008. Downloaded at http://www.sec.gov/litigation/litreleases/2008/lr20537.htm.

Segre, Sandro. 2008. *A Weberian Analysis of Business Groups and Financial Markets*. Aldershot: Ashgate.

Shleifer, Andrei. 2000. *Inefficient Markets. An Introduction to Behavioral Finance*. Oxford: Oxford University Press.

Simmel, Georg. [1901] 1989. *Philosophie des Geldes*. Frankfurt: Suhrkamp.

—— 1908. *Soziologie. Untersuchungen über die Formen der Vergesellschaftung*. Leipzig: Duncker & Humblot.

Siu, Lucia Leung-Sea. 2008. 'Cadres, Gangs, and Prophets. The Commodity Futures Markets of China'. PhD thesis, University of Edinburgh.

Smith, Adam. [1776] 1991. *Wealth of Nations*. Amherst NY: Prometheus Books.

Smith, Charles W. 1989. *Auctions. The Social Construction of Value*. New York: The Free Press.

—— 2007. 'Markets as Definitional Practices'. *Canadian Journal of Sociology* 32/1: 1–39.

Smith, Vicki and Esther B. Neuwirth. 2008. *The Good Temp*. Ithaca NY: Cornell University Press.

Sorkin, Andrew Ross. 2008. 'Citi Blasts Wachovia-Wells Fargo Merger Plan'. *New York Times*, 3 October 2008. Downloaded at http://dealbook.blogs.nytimes.com/2008/10/03/citi-blasts-wachovia-wells-fargo-merger-plan/?scp=1&sq=citi%20blasts%20wachovia%20wells%20fargo%20merger%20plan&st=cse.

—— 2009. 'The Case for Paying Out Bonuses at A.I.G'. *New York Times*, 17 March 2009. Downloaded at http://dealbook.blogs.nytimes.com/2009/03/17/the-case-for-paying-out-bonuses-at-aig/.

Spence, Michael. 1974. *Market Signaling. Informational Transfer in Hiring and Related Screening Processes*. Cambridge MA: Harvard University Press.

—— 1976. 'Informational Aspects of Market Structure. An Introduction'. *Quarterly Journal of Economics* 90/4: 591–7.

—— 2002. 'Signaling in Retrospect and the Informational Structure of Markets'. *American Economic Review* 92/3: 434–59.

Spinuzzi, Clay. 2008. *Network. Theorizing Knowledge Work in Telecommunications*. Cambridge: Cambridge University Press.

Standage, Tom. 1998. *The Victorian Internet. The Remarkable Story of the Telegraph and the Nineteenth Century's Online Pioneers*. London: Weidenfeld and Nicolson.

Star, Leigh and John Griesemer. 1989. 'Institutional Ecology, "Translations" and Boundary Objects. Amateurs and Professionals in Berkeley's Museum of Vertebrate Zoology, 1907–1939'. *Social Studies of Science* 19/3: 387–420.

Stark, David. 1996. 'Recombinant Property in East European Capitalism'. *American Journal of Sociology* 101: 993–1027.

—— 2001. 'Ambiguous Assets for Uncertain Environments. Heterarchy in Postsocialist Firms'. In Paul DiMaggio (ed.), *The Twenty-First Century Firm. Changing Economic Organization in International Perspective*, pp. 69–104, Princeton NJ: Princeton University Press.

—— and Balazs Vedres. 2006. 'Social Times of Network Spaces. Network Sequences and Foreign Investment in Hungary'. *American Journal of Sociology* 111/5: 1367–412.

Stein, Jeremy. 2001. 'Reflections on Time, Time-Space Compression and Technology in the Nineteenth-Century'. In Jon May and Nigel Thrift (eds.), *Timespace: Geographies of Temporality*, pp. 106–19, London: Routledge.

Stigler, George. 1961. 'The Economics of Information'. *The Journal of Political Economy* LXIX/3: 213–25.

Stinchcombe, Arthur. 1990. *Information and Organization*. Berkeley CA: University of California Press.

—— 2001. *When Formality Works. Authority and Abstraction in Law and Organizations*. Chicago: University of Chicago Press.

Strack, Fritz and Roland Deutsch. 2004. 'Reflective and Impulsive Determinants of Social Behavior'. *Personality and Social Psychology Review* 8/3: 220–47.

Strahler, Frank. 1998. *Economic Games and Strategic Behaviour. Theory and Application*. Cheltenham: Edward Elgar.

Streissler, Eric W. 1994. 'Hayek on Information and Socialism'. In M. Colonna and H. Hagemann (eds.), *The Economics of F. A. Hayek*. Vol. 2, *Capitalism, Socialism and Knowledge*, pp. 47–75, Aldershot: Elgar.

Suchman, Lucy. 1987. *Plans and Situated Actions*. Cambridge: Cambridge University Press.

Suchman, Mark. 1995. 'Managing Legitimacy: Strategic and Institutional Approaches'. *Academy of Management Review* 20/3: 571–610.

Swedberg, Richard. 2003. *Principles of Economic Sociology*. Princeton NJ: Princeton University Press.

—— 2005. 'Conflicts of Interest in the US Brokerage Industry'. In Karin Knorr Cetina and Alex Preda (eds.), *The Sociology of Financial Markets*, pp. 187–206, Oxford: Oxford University Press.

—— 2008. 'The Centrality of Materiality. Economic Theorizing from Xenophon to Home Economics and Beyond'. In Trevor Pinch and Richard Swedberg (eds.), *Living in a Material World. Economic Sociology Meets Science and Technology Studies*, pp. 57–88, Cambridge MA: MIT Press.

Teather, David. 2008. 'J Sainsbury Is "Bang on the Money" as Own-Label Range Defies the Gloom'. *The Guardian*, 13 November 2008: 27.

Thévenot, Laurent. 1993. 'Agir avec d'autres. Conventions et objets dans l'action coordonnée' [Acting With Others. Conventions and Objects in the Coordinated Action]. In Paul Ladrière, Patrick Pharo, and Louis Quéré (eds.), *La Théorie de l'action. Le Sujet pratique en débat*, pp. 275–90, Paris: CNRS Éditions.

Thrift, Nigel. 2001. '"It's the Romance, Not the Finance, That Makes the Business Worth Pursuing": Disclosing a New Market Culture'. *Economy and Society* 30/4: 412–32.

—— 2006. 'Re-Inventing Invention. New Tendencies in Capitalist Commodification'. *Economy and Society* 35/2: 279–306.

—— and Andrew Leyshon. 1994. 'A Phantom State? The De-Traditionalization of Money, the International Financial System and International Financial Centres'. *Political Geography* 13/4: 299–327.

Toennies, Ferdinand. 1971. *On Sociology: Pure, Applied, and Empirical*. Chicago: University of Chicago Press.

Turner, Stephen P. 2003. *Liberal Democracy 3.0. Civil Society in an Age of Experts*. London: Sage.

Underhill, Paco. 2004. *The Call of the Mall*. New York: Simon and Schuster.

Useem, Michael. [1984] 2001. 'The Inner Circle'. In David B. Grusky (ed.), *Social Stratification. Class, Race, and Gender in Sociological Perspective*, 2nd edn, pp. 223–32, Boulder CO: Westview.

—— and Andy Zelleke. 2006. 'Oversight and Delegation in Corporate Governance. Deciding What the Board Should Decide'. *Corporate Governance* 14/1: 2–12.

Uzzi, Brian. 1999. 'Embeddedness in the Making of Financial Capital. How Social Relations and Networks Benefit Firms Seeking Financing'. *American Sociological Review* 64/4: 481–505.

—— and Ryon Lancaster. 2004. 'Embeddedness and Price Formation in the Corporate Law Market'. *American Sociological Review* 69: 319–44.

Vaughan, Diane. 1996. *The Challenger Launch Decision. Risky Technology, Culture, and Deviance at NASA*. Chicago: University of Chicago Press.

—— 2005. 'Organizational Rituals of Risk and Error'. In Bridget Hutter and Michael Power (ed.), *Organizational Encounters with Risk*, pp. 33–66, Cambridge: Cambridge University Press.

Veblen, Thorstein. [1899] 1994. *The Theory of the Leisure Class*. New York: Penguin.

—— 1923. *Absentee Ownership and Business Enterprise in Recent Times*. New York: B.W. Huebsch.

Velthuis, Olav. 2005. *Talking Prices. Symbolic Meanings of Prices on the Market for Contemporary Art*. Princeton NJ: Princeton University Press.

Venkatesh, Sudhir. 2006. *Off the Books. The Underground Economy of the Urban Poor*. Cambridge MA: Harvard University Press.

Vollmer, Hendrik. 2007. 'How to Do More with Numbers. Elementary Stakes, Framing, Keying, and the Three-Dimensional Character of Numerical Signs'. *Accounting, Organizations and Society* 32: 577–600.

Von Neumann, John and Oskar Morgenstern. [1944] 1992. *Theory of Games and Economic Behaviour*. Princeton NJ: Princeton University Press.

Warren, Pete. 2008. 'City Business Races the Games for Power'. *The Guardian*, Technology Guardian, 29 May 2008: 3.

Watson, Rod and Jeff Coulter. 2008. 'The Debate over Cognitivism'. *Theory, Culture & Society* 25/2: 1–17.

Watt, Nicholas and Patrick Wintour. 2008. 'Battle of Corfu. Island Meetings that Left Tory and Millionaire at War'. *The Guardian*, 22 October 2008: 4–5.

Wearden, Graeme and Ashley Seager. 2008. 'Pound Falls to Five-Year Low as Bank Head Admits Recession Is Here'. *The Guardian*, 22 October 2008. Downloaded at http://www.guardian.co.uk/business/2008/oct/22/pound-recession-interest-rates.

Weaver, Matthew. 2008. 'Conwoman Stole £400,000 in Art and Jewellery, Court Told'. *The Guardian*, 26 September 2008: 16.

Weber, Max. [1894] 1924. 'Die Börse'. In *Gesammelte Aufsätze zur Soziologie und Sozialpolitik*, pp. 256–322, Tübingen: J.C.B. Mohr (Paul Siebeck).

—— [1920] 1988. *Gesammelte Aufsätze zur Religionssoziologie*. Tübingen: Mohr Siebeck.

—— [1921] 1972. *Wirtschaft und Gesellschaft* [Economy and Society]. Tübingen: Mohr.

Webster, Frank. 2002. *Theories of the Information Society*. 2nd edn. London: Routledge.

Wherry, Frederick F. 2008. 'The Social Characterization of Price: The Fool, the Faithful, the Frivolous, and the Frugal'. *Sociological Theory* 26/4: 363–79.

White, Harrison. 1981. 'Where Do Markets Come From?' *American Journal of Sociology* 87/3: 517–47.

—— 1992. *Identity and Control. A Structural Theory of Social Action.* Princeton NJ: Princeton University Press.

—— 2000. 'Modeling Discourse In and Around Markets'. *Poetics* 27: 117–33.

—— 2002. *Markets from Networks. Socioeconomic Models of Production.* Princeton NJ: Princeton University Press.

—— 2008. *Identity and Control. How Social Formations Emerge.* 2nd edn. Princeton NJ: Princeton University Press.

—— Frédéric Godart, and Victor Corona. 2007. 'Mobilizing Identities. Uncertainty and Control in Strategy'. *Theory, Culture & Society* 24/7–8: 181–202.

Wilkinson, Nick. 2008. *An Introduction to Behavioral Economics.* Basingstoke: Palgrave.

Wilkinson, Sue and Celia Kitzinger. 2006. 'Surprise as an Interactional Achievement. Reaction Tokens in Conversation'. *Social Psychology Quarterly* 69/2: 150–82.

Williamson, Oliver. 1975. *Markets and Hierarchies: Analysis and Antitrust Implications. A Study in the Economics of Internal Organization.* New York: The Free Press.

—— 1985. *The Economic Institutions of Capitalism. Firms, Markets, Relational Contracting.* New York: The Free Press.

—— 2005. 'Transaction Cost Economics'. In Claude Ménard and Mary M. Shirley (eds.), *Handbook of New Institutional Economics*, pp. 41–65, Berlin: Springer.

Winseck, Dwayne R. and Robert M. Pike. 2007. *Communication and Empire. Media, Markets, and Globalization, 1860–1930.* Durham NC: Duke University Press.

Wintour, Patrick. 2008. 'Treasury Anger at German Savings Move'. *The Guardian,* 6 October 2008: 1.

Yates, JoAnne. 1986. 'The Telegraph's Effect on Nineteenth-Century Markets and Firms'. *Business and Economic History* 15: 149–63.

—— 1989*a*. 'The Emergence of the Memo as a Managerial Genre'. *Management Communication Quarterly* 2/4: 485–510.

—— 1989*b*. *Control through Communication. The Rise of System in American Management.* Baltimore: Johns Hopkins University Press.

—— 1994. 'Evolving Information Use in Firms, 1850–1920. Ideology and Information Techniques and Technologies'. In Lisa Bud-Frierman (ed.), *Information Acumen. The Understanding and Use of Knowledge in Modern Business*, pp. 26–51, London: Routledge.

Yonay, Yuval. 1998. *The Struggle over the Soul of Economics. Institutional and Neoclassical Economists in America between the Wars.* Princeton NJ: Princeton University Press.

—— and Daniel Breslau. 2006. 'Marketing Models. The Culture of Mathematical Economics'. *Sociological Forum* 21/3: 345–86.

Zaloom, Caitlin. 2006. *Out of the Pits. Traders and Technology from Chicago to London.* Chicago: University of Chicago Press.

Zajac, Edward and James Westphal. 1996. 'Director Reputation, CEO Board Power, and the Dynamics of Board Interlocks'. *Administrative Science Quarterly* 41: 507–29.

—— —— 2004. 'The Social Construction of Market Value. The Institutionalization and Learning Perspectives on Stock Market Reactions'. *American Sociological Review* 69: 433–57.

Zbaracki, Mark and Mark Bergen. 2009. 'When Truces Collapse. A Longitudinal Study of Price Adjustment Routines'. Working paper: University of Western Ontario.

Zelizer, Viviana. 1979. *Morals and Markets. The Development of Life Insurance in the United States.* New York: Columbia University Press.

—— 1997. *The Social Meaning of Money. Pin Money, Paychecks, Poor Relief, and Other Currencies.* Princeton NJ: Princeton University Press.

—— 2005a. *The Purchase of Intimacy.* Princeton NJ: Princeton University Press.

—— 2005b. 'Culture and Consumption'. In Neil Smelser and Richard Swedberg (eds.), *Handbook of Economic Sociology*, 2nd edn, pp. 331–54, Princeton NJ and New York: Princeton University Press and the Russell Sage Foundation.

—— 2005c. 'Circuits within Capitalism'. In Victor Nee and Richard Swedberg (eds.), *The Economic Sociology of Capitalism*, pp. 289–322, Princeton NJ: Princeton University Press.

—— 2006. 'Circuits in Economic Life'. *European Economic Sociology Newsletter* 8/1: 30–5.

—— 2007. 'Ethics in the Economy'. *Journal for Business, Economics & Ethics* (Zeitschrift für Wirtschafts- und Unternehmensethik) 8/1: 8–23.

—— 2008. 'Money, Economic Activity, and Social Relations'. Paper presented at the DFG-NSF Conference Contextualizing Economic Behavior, New York City, August 2008.

Zerubavel, Eviatar. 1981. *Hidden Rhythms. Schedules and Calendars in Social Life.* Chicago: University of Chicago Press.

Zey, Mary. 1993. *Banking on Fraud. Drexel, Junk Bonds, and Buyouts.* New York: Aldine de Gruyter.

Zorn, Dirk, Frank Dobbin, Julian Dierkes, and Man-Shan Kwok. 2005. 'Managing Investors: How Financial Markets Reshaped the American Firm'. In Karin Knorr Cetina and Alex Preda (eds.), *The Sociology of Financial Markets*, pp. 269–89, Oxford: Oxford University Press.

Zuckerman, Ezra. 1999. 'The Categorical Imperative: Securities Analysts and the Illegitimacy Discount'. *American Journal of Sociology* 104/5: 1398–438.

—— 2004. 'Structural Incoherence and Stock Market Activity'. *American Sociological Review* 69: 405–32.

—— and Tai-Young Kim. 2003. 'The Critical Trade-Off. Identity Assignment and Box Office Success in the Feature Film Industry'. *Industrial and Corporate Change* 12: 27–66.

—— Tai-Young Kim, Kalinda Ukanwa, and James von Rittman. 2003. 'Robust Identities or Non-Entities? Typecasting in the Feature Film Labor Market'. *American Journal of Sociology* 108: 1018–74.

Zukin, Sharon. 2004. *Point of Purchase. How Shopping Changed American Culture.* New York: Routledge.

—— and Paul DiMaggio. 1990. 'Introduction'. In Sharon Zukin and Paul DiMaggio (eds.), *Structures of Capital*, pp. 1–36, Cambridge: Cambridge University Press.

—— and Jennifer Smith Maguire. 2004. 'Consumers and Consumption'. *Annual Review of Sociology* 30: 173–97.

Zylberberg, André. 1990. *L'économie mathématique en France 1870–1914.* Paris: Economica.

INDEX